MW01625543

# TRACES OF THE REAL

# TRACES OF THE REAL

## The Absent Presence of Photography in South Asian Literature

BIDISHA BANERJEE

LIVERPOOL UNIVERSITY PRESS

First published 2025 by
Liverpool University Press
4 Cambridge Street
Liverpool
L69 7ZU



British Library Cataloguing-in-Publication data
A British Library CIP record is available

ISBN 978-1-83553-729-9 cased

Typeset by Carnegie Book Production, Lancaster

# TRACES OF THE REAL

# TRACES OF THE REAL

## The Absent Presence of Photography in South Asian Literature

BIDISHA BANERJEE

LIVERPOOL UNIVERSITY PRESS

First published 2025 by
Liverpool University Press
4 Cambridge Street
Liverpool
L69 7ZU



British Library Cataloguing-in-Publication data
A British Library CIP record is available

ISBN 978-1-83553-729-9 cased

Typeset by Carnegie Book Production, Lancaster

To my father, my lodestar,
and in memory of my mother,
the absent presence in my life.

"Bringing together photography studies, postcolonial studies, and diaspora studies, this book sheds light on a pervasive trope in contemporary South Asian literature. *Traces of the Real* reveals how photographs evoked by writing may undermine the very texts they appear in, raising urgent questions about observational distance, gendered visibility, diasporic loss, and humanitarian mediation."

—Kartik Nair, Temple University

"This book subtly and convincingly navigates the space between the word and the visual image in South Asian texts. Where many might assume photography offers the picture of reality, Banerjee examines the absent presence of photographs to unearth the complex traces of the real in the intersections between literature and photography. In doing so she provides a new perspective on both of these fields and opens up a new space for literary exploration."

—Professor Bill Ashcroft, UNSW, Australia

"*Traces of the Real* opens up fresh insightful readings by focusing on the postcolonial through the complex lens of absent photographic presences. In this truly original book, Bidisha Banerjee offers us an important and empowering contribution to studies of South Asian fiction."

—Professor Peter Childs, Birmingham Newman University

"*Traces of the Real* is a remarkable contribution to the fields of photography, word and image, and postcolonialism. Through an impressive account of the history of photography and its relationship with both literary criticism and the colonial enterprise, this important book offers a new take on South Asian diasporic literature. Moving away from the 'sclerosis' of photography's 'double indexicality,' as described by Mitchell, as well as from the stalemate reached by the 'visual turn' in South Asian culture, whose focus on the vernacular is still haunted by the hegemony of Western photographic discourse, Bidisha Banerjee posits a 'fourth stage of photography' relying on affect and emotion. Drawing from Azoulay, Rancière, and others, the book offers a new way of looking at South Asian postcolonial literature by discarding the materiality of the visual image to focus on its performative absent presence as metaphor and trace. In so doing, this exciting work presents a subversive form of visual intermediality, or 'countervisuality,' whose 'optics of blindness' purports to 'decolonize trauma studies.'"

—Laurence Petit, Université Paul Valéry-Montpellier 3

# Contents

# List of Illustrations

# Introduction

Why then discuss photography *in the absence of the photograph?*
Ariella Azoulay, *Civil Imagination*, 233

In writing about the origins of painting in *The Natural History*, Pliny tells us about Butades, a potter of Sicyon who was inspired by his daughter to create portraits with the clay he used for his pottery. He thought of this when his daughter traced the profile of her lover's face from a shadow cast on the wall by the light of a lamp, as the lover was to depart on a long journey. Her father filled in the outline with clay, which was then hardened by fire and preserved until the destruction of the city. If Pliny had lived later, instead of connecting the arts of painting and pottery with the legend of Dibutades,[1] he might have credited her with the birth of photography. Her act of tracing over a shadow cast on a wall by a source of light conveys the very essence of photography, as does the desire to capture and preserve the image of an absent loved one. William Henry Fox Talbot, credited with inventing the photographic negative, called his invention "skiagraphy" or "words of light," in other words, the writing of shadow. Jacques Derrida recalls the legend of Dibutades and characterizes her act of tracing, remarking, and retracing as at once both active and passive. He recognizes the simultaneous existence of activity and passivity as "the very moment of the trace: a movement that is apriori photographic" (17). Susan Sontag has also described photography as a trace, a direct stenciling of reality (Sontag 1977: 154) while Rosalind Krauss describes the central fact of photography as follows: "that its operation is that of the imprint, the register, the trace" (Krauss 1978: 34). *Traces of the Real* returns to these key aspects of photography – traces and absent presences – in order to explore the role that the performative absent presence

[1] She is the nameless Maid of Corinth in Pliny's chapter titled "The daughter of Butades," but is called Dibutades elsewhere after her father.

of photography may play in literature, particularly South Asian postcolonial literature.

The book's title plays on the dual meaning of trace – to copy as in a stencil, but also to mean faint remains. While the stenciled copy of something might offer a striking similitude of the original, the alternative meaning of traces suggests only a faint resemblance to the original. Photography is often described in similarly contradictory terms. The frustration with trying to articulate what is "photographic" about a photograph and its relationship to the original object is probably best expressed by Stanley Cavell when he writes:

> We might say that we don't know how to think of the *connection* between a photograph and what it is a photograph of. The image is not a likeness; it is not exactly a replica, or a relic, or a shadow, or an apparition either, though all of these natural candidates share a striking feature with photographs – an aura or history of magic surrounding them. (1971: 17–18, emphasis original)

Cavell's attempts to define the photographic via negation, using terms ranging from the iconicity of "likeness," to the unreliability of "apparition," and finally settling on the rather ambiguous terms "aura" (used here in Walter Benjamin's sense) and "magic," encapsulates the impossibility of this task. However, photography's indexicality suggesting objective truthfulness has proven to be particularly persistent despite ample evidence of its manipulation and ambiguity. In more recent times this has led to calls for photographic erasures or for looking beyond the perceived indexicality of the image. *Traces of the Real* puts these aspects of photography in productive tension in an attempt to study what they have to offer to postcolonial fiction, particularly when photographs exist in an absent (present) form in the fictional text.

Literature and photography are often regarded as sister arts, their cominglings latent in the very etymology of the word "photography" meaning "writing with light." While photography in literature is one of the key areas of word and image research, and many scholars have studied their productive interactions (Adams 2000; Armstrong 1999; Bryant 1996; Creekmur 1996; Garrett-Petts and Lawrence 2000; Horstkotte 2006; 2008; Hughes and Noble 2003; Hunter 1987; Pedri 2005; Rabb 1998), there is scant scholarly work about the use of photography in an absent form in literary texts. Some scholars have propounded the textuality of images by viewing images as texts to be read and deciphered (Mitchell 1995; Petit 2006; Bal and Bryson 1991), while others have considered the inclusion of photographs in fictional works by W.G. Sebald (Horstkotte 2008), Virginia Woolf (Gillespie 1993; Humm 2003; Pedri 2005), and others. Yet other critics have examined the metaphorical evocation of photography in literature and its influence on narrative form (Novak 2008; Armstrong 1999; York 1987), particularly with regard to the Victorian realist novel, while still others have considered the linguistic accompaniments of photography and photography's capacity to "match, complement and even supplant language in narrative enterprises" (Scott 1999: 13). Despite a large amount of scholarly production on the various intersections and interactions between photography and literature, very little work exists on the photograph as an absent presence in literature.

Sandria Freitag (2015) has identified a "visual turn" in studies of South Asian culture, society, and history that can help raise important questions about the changes affecting the region.[2] While the rapid proliferation of media forms and technology heralded a "communicative modernity" (Rajagopal 2011: 11) for South Asia in the two decades after the Gulf War, the period was also dominated first by regimes of visual surveillance in the face of Islamic terror and then by the role of privately owned media in furthering an aggressive Hindu nationalist agenda. Arvind Rajagopal (2011) has demonstrated the ways in which a rapid increase in communication in South Asia has not led to political transparency or a reduction in violence. Postcolonial visual culture in South Asia therefore remains fraught with complexities. I find Gauri Viswanathan's definition of the postcolonial as "an attitude or position from which the decentering of Eurocentrism may ensue" particularly useful to my purposes (in Bahri and Vasudeva 1996: 54). In the context of visual culture, the process of postcoloniality entails reckoning with colonial/Eurocentric forms of representation while also attempting to develop a vernacular visual culture in the postcolonial nation. Despite the large quantity of work on colonialism and photography (Ryan 1997; Maxwell 2000; Hight and Sampson 2004; Behdad and Gartlan 2013), with the exception of scholarship by Christopher Pinney, Zahid Chaudhary, and Sabeena Gadihoke, surprisingly little has been written bringing together the postcolonial and photography in the South Asian context. Only in the last few years, critics like Gayatri Gopinath (2018), Bakirathi Mani (2020), and Allana Rahaab (2022), have begun to address this lacuna.

Bringing together literature and photography studies in the context of postcolonialism, *Traces of the Real* argues that paying close attention to

[2] See for example Karin Zitzewitz's (2008) study of secularist visual culture in India and the threat posed to it by the rise of Hindu nationalism.

what I am calling the performative absent presence of photographs and photography in South Asian postcolonial novels offers alternative modes for looking that are more suited to the postcolonial project. Although no material photographs are included in these novels, photographs are evoked in a variety of ways. These have a performative function that enables us to read these texts in new and different ways. Rather than engaging with the vast and sometimes contradictory history of photography studies, I situate my analyses in the current moment of the discipline. Photography studies has over the past two decades moved away from its emphasis on indexicality and its seemingly permanent and unquestionable connection with the referent to situations where a physical photograph may be absent or to discussions of the affective or even to photography's engagement with senses other than the visual. *Traces of the Real* builds on recent definitions of the photographic as encompassing experiences that do not necessarily contain a material photograph, to argue that the absent presence of photography affords South Asian postcolonial writers opportunities to enhance the themes of their novels in ways that the inclusion of actual photographs may not allow. This practice critiques what may be called photography's "truth-event" (Roberts 2014) and instead considers the power of photographic erasures and absences in engaging the "civil imagination" (Azoulay 2012a) in the postcolonial moment.

## A Very Brief History of Photography

It may be fair to say that no form of representation has experienced the vagaries of acclaim as much as photography. Most scholars agree that photography has been through three stages in the history of its development. It was born out of an impressive technology that brought with it the privilege of indexicality. This indexicality quickly came to be associated, erroneously, with objectivity. Photography was viewed for much of its early history as a passive and objective form of representation that captured the real. This view undertook what has been called "a social turn" in the late nineteenth century. In this phase of its development, photography was used in the service of political reform, bringing to light the desperate conditions of the poor. This marked a shift from the purely objective to the representational. The third phase of photography's history began in the second half of the twentieth century, when photography quickly lost its progressive credentials. Having been misappropriated for various political ends, photography now came to be shrouded with suspicion as a medium that lends itself, through deception and manipulation, to the easy furtherance of ideology and propaganda. Photography, once held in high regard as a symbol of enlightenment, now lay vacated of its truth claims, more than a little tinged by deception and ideological subjectivity.

With the publication of the edited collection *Thinking Photography* (1982), Victor Burgin and his collaborators challenged the transparency, neutrality, and truth-telling power of photography by arguing that the Barthesian notion of the denotative function of photography, which points to its "primitive core of meaning, devoid of all cultural determination" (Sekula 1982: 87), is inseparable from its connotative or culturally determined meaning. The duality of meaning-production inherent in photography, whereby a photograph has an affective meaning as well as an informative meaning, makes it particularly susceptible to misappropriation, as when it was adopted in the service of the colonial enterprise. Mary Price's thesis that "the use of a photograph determines its meaning" (1994: 1), lends further credence to the power of misappropriation in photography. The subsequent digitalization of photography was seen as the final nail in photography's coffin, severing its all-important link with indexicality.

This is where we find ourselves at the turn of the millennium, with photography reduced to "a rotting corpse alongside those of modernism and socialism" (Kelsey and Stimson 2008: xxii). Despite a historical trajectory that seems to suggest a rejection of photography's initial lofty claims, this is hardly a straightforward narrative. Photography is still frequently upheld as an objective reflection of the real and brought to a multiplicity of uses, often contradictory. Anthologies like Richard Bolton's 1989 *The Contest of Meaning*, attempt to unpack the complexity of photography "through a judicious consideration of context" (xi). Writing almost two decades after Bolton, Kelsey and Stimson find photography studies at a crossroad between sheer obsolescence and its meaning "reemerging in a new form" (2008: xxii) that arises from our global concerns and a sense of accountability to them. The confusion at this crossroad is amply suggested by the titles of essays included in their volume *The Meaning of Photography* published in 2005; they range from "Thoughts on the Triumph of Photography" through "Photography in the Post-Photographic Era" to "Photography Is Over if You Want It." William J. Mitchell announced photography's death, arguably somewhat prematurely, in 1992 when he wrote, "From the moment of its sesquicentennial in 1989 photography was dead – or, more precisely, radically and permanently displaced – as was painting 150 years before" (1992: 20). Instead of mourning photography's death, Mitchell welcomes it as an "opportunity to expose the aporias in photography's construction of the visual world, to deconstruct the very ideas of photographic objectivity and closure, and to resist what has become an increasingly sclerotic pictorial tradition" (8). The sclerosis diagnosed by Mitchell in the photographic tradition has to do with its double indexicality or the conflict between the photograph's seemingly objective reproduction of appearance and the photographer's subjective rendition of it. This has led to what Kelsey and Stimson call "the hermeneutics of suspicion" (2008: xxii); their use of this term popularized by Hans-Georg Gadamer in referring to a kind of literary interpretation that involves skepticism on the part of readers in order to unearth the hidden meaning in texts, is well suited to photography's double indexicality. Photography has been unable to shed this suspicion, which has only become further exacerbated by digitalization.

*Traces of the Real* finds photography in a fourth stage of development that elides the thorny questions of indexicality, realism, and truthfulness by moving away from the idea of the materiality, fixity, and visuality of photographs. It locates photography's reemergence in the work of scholars like Ariella Azoulay, Jacques Rancière, Tina Campt, and Shawn Michelle Smith, who have helped focus attention on photography's absences rather than its power to tell a real or manipulated truth. With the publication of titles like *The Civil Contract of Photography* (Azoulay 2008), *At the Edge of Sight* (Smith 2013), *Feeling Photography* (Brown and Phu 2014), *Listening to Images* (Campt 2017), and most recently, *Photography and Its Shadow* (Kenaan 2020), photography has shifted its focus from the visual to the haptic and the affective, from the present to the absent, from the material to the suggested, and, in titles like Zylinska's *Nonhuman Photography* (2017), even from the humanistic to the posthuman.

In what I am calling the fourth stage of photography we find a complication or even a rejection of visuality as it pertains to photography and an attunement to the other senses and the emotive instead. For example, in their 2014 collection *Feeling Photography*, Brown and Phu position themselves in opposition to Burgin et al. and argue for a turn to affect and emotion in photography studies. By challenging the assumed visibility of images in his book *The Future of the Image* (2007), Jacques Rancière argues that images are often dissemblances and are not exclusive to the visible since images may also consist "wholly in words" (7). He concludes that the "commonest regime of the image is one that presents a relation between the sayable and the visible, a relationship which plays on both the analogy and the dissemblance between them" (7). Similarly, Jennifer Bajorek (2020) undermines the fixity of photographic images by revisiting West African archives of the 1940s and '50s and re-viewing them through a decolonial lens. Shawn Michelle Smith's work has gone a long way in drawing attention to the ways in which photography as a visual medium acts paradoxically to make us aware of what we cannot see. Drawing on Walter Benjamin's notion of "the optical unconscious," Smith's work attempts to show the failure of vision and the limitations of photography. Benjamin sees the real potential of photography in providing us access to seeing what lies unacknowledged in our consciousness. Adopting a less psychoanalytic approach, Smith builds on Benjamin's idea in order to apprehend "the sense of the unseen that photography introduces" (2013: 6). In doing so, she takes us to what she calls the "edge of sight." Tina Campt (2017) explores the haptics of images and suggests the rich affordances of "listening" to images; she expands the sensory response to photographs through her notion of image haptics, which not only suggests that photographs are meant to be touched, but also thinks of touch as being affective and emotional. Finally, Ariella Azoulay (2008) undermines the fixity of the material photograph by questioning the oft-held assumption that a photograph is a completed event now firmly in the past. Instead, she calls for spectators of photographs to "watch" (not look at) photographs, thereby creating a space of political relations where we are all participants.

It is worth noting that for these critics the move away from the materiality and visuality of photographs is provoked by the urgent need to call attention to neglected histories of marginalized peoples and may even be read as a reparative gesture to compensate for photography's historical and continuing harms. Investigating photography as modernism's other, Brown and Phu argue that attending to feeling enables us to "account for marginalized subjects such as women, queer subjects and racialized groups who are conspicuously excluded in approaches that focus on thinking" (2014: 7). Campt studies ethnographic images of Black subjects which had previously been used in dehumanizing ways; by listening to them, she now finds in them untold narratives of resistance and subversion. Both Smith and Azoulay compel us to look beyond the limitations of the photographic frame in ways such that viewing a photograph becomes an acutely political act that demands far more than passive forms of empathy, pity, or compassion. Writing about the Israeli occupation of Palestine and the photographs that come out of the region, Azoulay constructs a civil contract of photography which she describes as a covenant between the photographed person and the viewer of the photograph "for the rehabilitation of their citizenship in the political sphere within which we are all ruled, that is, in the state of Israel" (2008: 17).

Following Smith, Rancière, Azoulay, and others, *Traces of the Real* asks what photography studies in its current moment, dominated by absences and erasures, can offer to South Asian postcolonial literature. How have postcolonial writers used the enduring yet deeply problematic legacy of photographic truthfulness and its seeming certainties as icons, metaphors, and traces in their own writing to undermine subversively such certainties? The book avers that reading photography as a continuing event, which can occur even in the absence of a material photograph, rather than a completed event that has already produced a photograph, has powerful implications for the postcolonial moment as well as postcolonial literature. By bringing together literature and photography in its absent form, the book opens up new opportunities for productive interactions between the two that enhance the themes of postcolonial literature while offering ways of rejecting the imperial appropriation of photography and unlearning the dichotomous and indexical modes of representation and ways of seeing that photography perpetuated. Instead, this practice produces new and productive ways of seeing through photographic tropes and the use of absent images making them present *in absentia.*

## Word-Image Studies

Photography's historical journey from objectivity to subjectivity, from truth to manipulation, has had its impact on literature. In tracing the complex history of photography and its relation to the material as well as the cultural, Geoffrey Batchen demonstrates that "photography has never been any one technology" (1994: 140). As photographic technology has developed, photography's meanings have somewhat contradictorily ranged from the reificatory with indexical power to the symbolic with meaning-making capacity. Photography's early claims to representing the real significantly impacted the development of literary realism in the nineteenth century. Critics have engaged with the metaphorical evocation of photography in literature in discussions of realism and the novel in works such as Jennifer Green-Lewis's *Framing the Victorians: Photography and the Culture of Realism* (1996) and Nancy Armstrong's *Fiction in the Age of Photography: The Legacy of British Realism* (1999). Armstrong convincingly argues that photography played an important role in the development of literary realism as early as the Victorian era. She demonstrates how "photography authorized fiction as a truth-telling medium" and vice versa (Armstrong 1999: 27). Lorraine York analyzes the presence of photography in the works of several Canadian writers in *The Other Side of Dailiness: Photography in the Works of Alice Munro, Timothy Findley, Michael Ondaatje and Margaret Laurence* (1988). Playing on Roland Barthes's oft-repeated description of photography as "a message without a code" in *Image Music Text* (1977), York argues that photography is "a message with a code" (York 1988: 9) or a signifying system like language. Emphasizing the textual quality of photography, York explores the links between narrative and photography. York's study is primarily that of the postmodern use of photography and its influence on fictional form. Challenging photography's representation of the real, Daniel Novak's *Realism, Photography and Nineteenth-Century Fiction* (2008) shifts focus from the truth-telling privilege of photography, central to critics like York and Armstrong, to its capacity for manipulation and effacement and its implications for fictional and narrative strategies. Instead of photography's association with objectivity, Novak considers its influence on abstraction and fragmentation in literary form.

If we move away from photography's influence on literary form to consider the inclusion of photographs in literary texts, we find a rich history.[3] We may not routinely expect to find photographs in a fictional text, yet writers began including illustrations and photographs in their works soon after the discovery of photography in 1839 and this has continued well into the present day.[4] The inclusion of photographs in fiction is a complicated matter that raises questions about realism, the normative distinctions between fiction and nonfiction, the use of "fictional" photographs, etc. In the nineteenth century, anxiety among writers about the competing function of photography and literature meant that fictional texts included drawings and illustrations while travelogues or other nonfictional texts included photographs. However, as Timothy Dow Adams points out, "photographic renditions of landscapes, buildings or even crowds of people, grew increasingly common" in the twentieth century, as did the inclusion of "physical photographs which are presented as fictional, despite the presence of actual people, because they represent staged scenes" (2008: 178). The middle of the century witnessed the bringing together of photography and literature in collaborative projects between writers and photographers such as *Let Us Now Praise Famous Men* (James Agee and Walker Evans) and *You Have Seen Their Faces* (Margaret Bourke-White and Erskine Caldwell), and in the works of writer-photographer

3 For a comprehensive history of photography in fiction, see Timothy Dow Adams's "Photographs on the Walls of the House of Fiction" (2008).

4 This has seen something of a resurgence in the first decade of the twenty-first century with the publication of several novels that include photographs. These titles include Dave Eggers's *You Shall Know Our Velocity* in 2003, Jonathan Safran Foer's *Extremely Loud and Incredibly Close* in 2006, Marianne Wiggins's *The Shadow Catcher* in 2008, and Tim Pears's *Landed* in 2011.

Wright Morris.[5] A curious shift occurs in the way postmodern writers incorporate photographs into fictional works. Contrary to earlier writers, these novelists use "photographs as the reverse of representation [...] as another way of providing authenticity for the purpose of having something authentic to undercut" (Adams 2008: 179–180).[6] *Traces of the Real* considers another dimension of this phenomenon where photographic representation is completely erased and replaced instead by a performative absent presence of the visual.

The coupling of photography and literature remains fraught with complexities.[7] Even naming the various hybrid forms arising from the comingling of the two can prove to be challenging, as is suggested by Karen Jacobs's attempt to foreground photography's "often clandestine terminology" in her suggested list: "Iconographics, photoGraphics, phototexts, photo-narratives, photo-fictions, wordscapes, spoken images, intermedial relations, third texts, third spaces, prose pictures, visual fictions, double exposures, word bites ..." (2006: 1, ellipses in original). Silke Hortskotte and Nancy Pedri attempt to take stock of word-image relations in their introduction to the *Poetics Today* special issue titled "Photography

5 Wright Morris endeavored to bring photography and fiction together in his 1948 book *The Home Place*, a first-person narrative that includes many photographs shot and printed by Morris. He calls this a photo-text and comments on the problems the genre created for him, further highlighting its many complexities: "Some people are readers, some are lookers. The reader becomes a more and more refined reader, with less and less tolerance for distractions ... the photograph requires a reading as well as a looking – its details scrutinized in a knowledgeable manner. In my case, this was a crisis. If the photograph overpowered the text, or if the reader treated the text lightly, I had defeated my original purpose. It was also crucial for my publishers who considered me a novelist. *The Home Place* was well received, but pointed up this dilemma. I was losing readers, picking up lookers. Several reviewers asked why this ex-photographer was writing fiction. There was only one way to clear this up. Stop the photo-books. And so I did" (qtd. in Knoll 1977: 148–149, ellipses in original). Morris accurately assessed his failure to achieve equivalence between text and image in *The Home Place*. This is borne out by the fact that Morris's photographs from his "photo-texts" have been exhibited over the years as images unrelated to his writing, most recently in an exhibition titled after his novel, "Wright Morris: The Home Place," that ran from January 24 to March 31, 2020. See https://www.foam.org/museum/programme/wright-morris-the-home-place.

6 Perhaps the most apt representation of the fraught relationship between photographs and literature can be found in Ondaatje's image of a blank frame in his novel *Billy the Kid*.

7 For a fuller discussion see the special issue of *English Language Notes* titled "Photography and Literature" edited by Karen Jacobs (2006).

in Fiction" prompted by the increasing inclusion of photographs in fictional texts. They point out that the "visual turn" in the humanities was less concerned with wanting to give precedence to the study of images over words than focusing on their interdependencies (2008: 2). In exploring these interdependencies, we must contend with the widespread agreement amongst scholars about the hierarchical superiority of word over image and the privilege given to words when they appear in conjunction with images. Even when photographs are given primacy (as they are in genres like photojournalism, portraiture, documentary, etc.) they are often accompanied by words. Max Kozloff plainly states, "However they are conceived, images have to be mediated by words" (1987: 105), while Victor Burgin argues that "the influence of language goes beyond the physical presence of writing as a deliberate addition to the image" (1982: 192), and Mieke Bal argues that images can be read just like texts (2006). This is in part because photographs have long been interpreted semiotically as a system of signs or as visual language. With the decline of structuralism, the semiotic analysis of the visual has also come to be questioned and its claims regarded with great skepticism. James Elkins writes of what he calls "The Antisemiotic" as an attempt to make pictures more difficult. In *On Pictures and the Words That Fail Them* (1998), Elkins tries to resuscitate the opaque, irrational, and incoherent aspects of images. Such a move also takes us away from the materiality of images and Elkins presents a theory of the invisible in his last chapter where he considers the absent forms implied by each image.

Garrett-Petts and Lawrence (2000) account for the privileging of word over image by pointing out the association of deception and the creation of illusions often attributed to the visual, thus making it an untrustworthy medium by definition. They find in this space of photography its revolutionary potential and its ability to disturb, even challenge, mainstream culture. Writing at the turn of the millennium, they locate the rise of disciplines like cultural studies, feminist studies, and postcolonial studies as prompting a need for integrating word and image and their respective literacies. *Traces of the Real* explores the subversive potential of photography and somewhat counterintuitively responds to the privileging of word over image by exploring word-image intermedialities in fictional texts where the visual does not exist in material form. Instead it is communicated using words in a host of ways – as descriptions of photographs, via characters who are photographers, through allusions to real photographs that lie outside the fictional world of the text, etc. Despite such an acute privileging of word over image accompanied by a complete absence of the visual, what is communicated to the reader has a strong visual dimension and is deeply evocative of the visual. This is what I am calling the performative absent presence of photography, which, I argue, offers us new ways of looking.

Although the areas of visual aesthetics, intermediality, and ekphrasis have witnessed a recent resurgence in scholarship, their usefulness to postcolonial studies remains somewhat underexplored. Barring Neumann and Rippl's *Verbal-Visual Configurations in Postcolonial Literature: Intermedial Aesthetics* (2020), scholarship that brings together the ekphrastic with the postcolonial is lacking, although postcolonial writers often use ekphrastic practices in their works. Neumann and Rippl's book considers the representation of visuality and ekphrasis in a range of anglophone postcolonial fiction to argue that the emergent new visual intermedial aesthetics of these narrative texts create the opportunity for hybrid and pluralized modes of being (2020: 4). Focusing on transculturality, Neumann and Rippl counter the well-established practice of "writing back" to Empire by dismantling the center-periphery binary and arguing instead for a plurality of cultural exchanges that are found in today's globalized world.[8] Liliane Louvel has also considered the intermediality of word and image, in particular the photograph. She establishes a "morphological gradient" (2018: 35) by considering the entire range of possibilities from the absence of photographs in literary texts to the visible presence of photography in the text. She posits an intermedial criticism where the process is reversed such that the image is used to read the text rather than the traditional use of linguistic or semiotic devices to read an image (44).

My engagement with the absent presence of photography in South Asian postcolonial texts is not limited to the ekphrastic. Scholars often refer to two definitions of ekphrasis – the original definition to mean the inclusion of any verbal description of the visual (Cluver 2017; Krieger 1992; Wagner 1996) has its origins in its use as a rhetorical device in a literary genre where the word was used to mean "a full or vivid description" (Wagner 1996: 12). These lush descriptions were mostly given to works of art, real or imagined. The word "ekphrasis" is now widely accepted to mean "the verbal representation of graphic representation" (Heffernan 1993: 299) or as Wagner puts it "*all verbal commentary*/writing [...] on images" (1996: 14, emphasis original). I find the slipperiness of the term and its differing meaning based on its purposes somewhat problematic for my purposes and have consequently steered clear of it through much of the book. However, given its recent resurgence, particularly with reference

8 However, Neumann and Rippl's suggestion that through the use of intermedial devices, narrative texts can "stare back" (2020: 13) at readers and thereby counter the colonial gaze, seems to contradictorily suggest a binary model of the gaze.

to the postcolonial, it is important to acknowledge it here. The equally provocative term "iconotexts," defined by Wagner as "the use of (by way of reference or allusion, in an explicit or implicit way) an image in a text or vice versa" (15), may be a more useful term for my purposes. Instead of the entire world of the visual, which currently seems to be the purview of the ekphrastic, I am interested only in the photographic. Also, rather than only considering the descriptions of images in literary texts, I am interested in their absent presence in all forms – ekphrastic descriptions of photographs, metaphoric use of photography, photographic ways of seeing, characters' viewing of absent (narrated) images, and texts that are haunted by iconic images that lie outside the text.

According to Rancière, although words make something visible, they cannot make it present or seen. *Traces of the Real* is concerned with the potential of this absent presence of the visible and what Rancière calls the dual poetics of the visible and the sayable. Other than illustrations or supplements (see Chapter 1), works of literary fiction can only refer to photographs as artifacts that are both present and absent no matter how exhaustively they are described by the narrator or a character; this may be thought of as a form of ekphrastic remediation in which the literary text "frames" the photograph. For the reader, the photograph in literary fiction is always both there and not there, both present and absent. I suggest that the absence of the photograph in the pages of the fictional text is a performative absence that can function in a variety of ways within the text. Though critics like Elkins are skeptical of situations where the descriptions of images substitute for the images themselves, *Traces of the Real* considers such scenarios in literary fiction not to privilege semiotic readings of photographs but, following Elkins, to suggest somewhat differently the evocations of the photographic in these descriptions and absent presences. Occupying one end of Louvel's morphological gradient, *Traces of the Real* explores the intermediality between words on the one hand and images in their absent forms on the other. It suggests that novelists often use absent images to powerfully undercut the apparent messages of the text and allow for new modes of interpretation.

## Photography, Postcolonialism, and Diaspora

Photography's early claim to objectivity and reification led to its ready appropriation by the colonial enterprise. Photography in colonial times often served to justify the project of colonialism by presenting the colonized as fetishized types rather than as real individuals. Such was photography's enormous appeal to the enterprise of colonialism; the evidentiary nature of photography was in keeping with Enlightenment notions of knowledge as something that can be collected, collated, organized, and classified. Hamilton and Hargreaves (2001) write:

> Colonial exploitation opened up vast new populations as much to scientific study as to economic exploitation, and although the need to organize and control was clearly important to the task of classification of racial and other types, the "taxonomic imperative" of Victorian science appears to have been sufficient motivation in itself to promote anthropological photography. (2001: 87)

Colonial photography, a term used to loosely describe photographic depictions of subjects in colonial settings, often served the function of fetishizing the colonized by capturing and freezing the gaze of the colonizer (see Maxwell 2000; Ryan 1997; Hight and Sampson 2004). It was thus used to reinforce Western assumptions, stereotypes, and prejudices of the colonized. These photographs were rarely concerned with representing the "real" and often catered to Orientalist and exotic impulses. Natives were frequently portrayed as types (Hartmann et al. 1998: 13). In the South Asian context, works such as the eight-volume *The People of India* (1868–1875) published in the aftermath of the Sepoy Mutiny of 1857, provide a perfect example of this taxonomic impulse. It attempted to identify and document various groups of people in India who are randomly classified in the volume, sometimes by caste or tribe and sometimes even by sect. Photography in the postcolonial context may then be seen as an attempt at authentic self-representation, an attempt to regain voice and agency. Given the far-reaching influence of photography on the colonial enterprise, the shift in photographic meaning that has taken place over the last two decades, calls for a reassessment of its role in the postcolonial. While critics like Christopher Pinney and Zahid Chaudhary have considered what Pinney calls "photography's other histories," or the rise in vernacular photography particularly in the postcolonial era, *Traces of the Real* considers the relationship between photography and the postcolonial when the very materiality of the photograph is completely erased and all that remains is its symbolic or metaphoric function.

In the postcolonial era, photographic criticism was largely dominated by Saidian and Foucauldian readings that saw the truth of photography as fixed and necessarily reflecting the context and politics of its creators. Christopher Pinney critiques such analyses and calls for a more nuanced reading of the photograph as a "complexly textured artefact" (2003: 5). In *Photography's Other Histories* (2003), Pinney shifts the focus of photography from the disciplinary framework to consider its "postcolonial popular aesthetic" (11) in the rise of vernacular photography in the postcolonial age. For Pinney, the postcolony talks back to the ideologically driven appropriation of photography through a plethora of popular practices and vernacular modernisms, thereby relocating the space of photographic agency in the postcolonial non-metropole. In *Afterimage of Empire*, Zahid Chaudhary provides what he calls "noniconophobic" (2012: 31) readings of colonial photography in order to read them against the grain of mainstream criticism. While neither colonial photography nor vernacular forms of postcolonial photography are the focus of this monograph, my consideration of the erasure or absent presence of the material photograph within the pages of the postcolonial novel responds to Pinney's and Chaudhary's calls to liberate photography from criticisms that see it primarily in the service of fixed, ideologically driven truths.

South Asian diasporic visual culture continues to be haunted by the specter of colonial photographic regimes. In *Unseeing Empire: Photography, Representation, South Asian America* (2020), Bakirathi Mani contends with the diasporic desire for representation that will counter the familiar degrading and dehumanizing representations, and argues that such desire remains "haunted by imperial ways of seeing" (16). The racialized immigrant searches for self-affirmation in photographic representation. Yet, as Mani argues, given that photography as a means of representation is inseparable from its documentary and surveillant mode in the South Asian context, photographic representations of South Asians in the diaspora are often connected to the archives of empire (8). Consequently, authentic forms of photographic representation with restorative power become impossible. Mani rightly attributes the failure of the image to the apparatus of representation and calls for another way of seeing, "a nonmimetic identification with the photographic image" (11) that is not reliant on ethnographic displays of South Asians shaped by colonial regimes of the visual. *Traces of the Real* offers such a nonmimetic mode of representation by foregrounding the absent-present photograph in South Asian diasporic literature.

In her 2019 book, *Potential History: Unlearning Imperialism*, Ariella Azoulay makes an impassioned appeal to unlearn imperialism by refusing "the stories the shutter tells" (7). Azoulay argues that not only did photography legitimize imperialism, it also reconstructed the world on empire's terms. It rewrote histories in such a way as to privilege the propagandist viewpoint. This resulted in the easy labeling of people and objects as one thing or another to fit into a predetermined narrative. Azoulay now calls for the difficult process of unlearning "the conceptual origins of imperial violence" (8) which views people and worlds as resources for imperialism to use for its purposes. Unlearning imperialism involves paying attention to the moment of original violence and adopting strategies of "avoidance, nonaction, stepping back, and losing ground" (8). By doing so, we are able to reject the shutter's divides and reinvent relationships and categories in alternative and often radically different ways. We are also able to question and examine political concepts and institutions such as citizen, archive, art, sovereignty, and human rights (11). Azoulay concludes that to "refuse the shutter is to begin to practice potential history" (10).

Inspired by Azoulay's urgent call to practice potential history and Mani's turn to nonmimetic ways of seeing, *Traces of the Real* asks what happens when the visuality of photography, which endows it with documentary and institutionalizing power, is completely erased in the works of the postcolonial fiction writer – when photography remains only as a trace or metaphor, merely by suggestion as an absent presence. Instead of photographs, we have in these novels words describing images that can no longer provide definitive evidence of the real, or we have texts that are haunted by real images that lie outside the fictive world, or photographers (real or fictive) who attempt to fix their subjects in problematically racialized or gendered ways through their powerful photographic eye. In these novels, the image *in absentia* offers yet another layer of doubt and uncertainty to the already undermined notion of photography's indexicality. Consequently, it becomes an absent presence, a slippage that allows us to probe further the themes of postcolonial literature and to see in new and different ways. Although Neumann and Rippl argue for a move away from binary models of "writing back" to Empire in the context of postcolonial visual intermedial aesthetics, this book argues that, given the enormous power of the colonial visual regime, postcolonial visual aesthetics must attempt to counter the colonial gaze and its disciplining power. Instead of simply countering with a vernacular postcolonial photographic eye (well documented by Christopher Pinney; see also Bajorek 2020), the absent presence of the photographic image in postcolonial literature offers another form of postcolonial visual intermediality that counters the violence of the colonial visual regime.

## Postcolonial Potential of Photographic Absence

The study of photography finds itself in a particular place today. Its focus has shifted in the last few decades from emphasizing its representational quality and its knowledge producing power, to a recognition of its semiotic ambiguities and a consequent attempt to find what lies beyond the frame or what traces a photograph leaves even when it is absent. It has lost much of its humanistic edge as well as its contingent dialectical relations, such as subject-object, photographer- photographed, image-viewer, etc. Instead, it is currently marked by erasure, absence, fluidity, and traces. While critics have repeatedly drawn attention to photography's imperial ideology and suggested that the way to unlearn capitalism (Coleman and James 2021) and imperialism (Azoulay 2012b) is by decolonizing photography, others like Andrew Dewdney have called for us to "reject the frame of reality" prescribed by photography in his provocatively titled book *Forget Photography* (2021). This makes it a particularly opportune moment for literary scholars to see what photographic erasures, absences, and hauntings in literary texts have to offer, particularly in the context of postcolonialism.

Critics have engaged with the interactions between photography and literature in a variety of ways. These have ranged from discussions of image texts in literature and analyses of the inclusion of photographs in fictional texts to the influence of photography on the form of the realist novel. However, scholars have not considered what photography studies today has to offer to literature. While in literature, Empire has written back and has been doing so for several decades, the harnessing of photographic discourses to bolster the truth of dominant ideologies, particularly in the service of colonialism, often remains unacknowledged, as is demonstrated by *National Geographic* magazine's 2018 acknowledgment of and apology for their often racist coverage over more than a century (Goldberg 2018). By delimiting the scope of this book to postcolonial literature in particular, I attempt to draw on the long and troubled history of photography's service to the colonial enterprise. In addition, postcolonial photography itself is plagued by what Christopher Pinney has called "the problem of ex-nomination" (2012) in photography studies. This arises from the predominance of Western photography in the field, which gives it a privileged place of global recognition while photography from the non-Western world is always characterized as having a local rather than a global flavor. Given the vexed history of photography and colonialism as well as the peripheral status of postcolonial photography and the repeated calls to find other ways of seeing, an erasure of the material photograph offers a powerful way to shift the focus from photography's complicitous role as an agent of power. I argue that the current political space opened up in photography studies by critics like Azoulay, Smith, and Mani has much to offer to discussions of postcolonial literature by offering new ways of seeing.

Extending Azoulay's delineation of the ontology of photography, I explore the continuing "event of photography" as it is manifested in the pages of a novel, particularly when the photograph itself is absent. The book analyzes various kinds of photographic "events" as they are performed within literary fiction – from historical photographs that *belatedly* appear in the physical novel (Chapter 1) to atrocity and journalistic photographs (Chapters 2 and 3), mutilated photographs (Chapter 4), family photographs (Chapter 5), disaster photographs (Chapter 6), and staged photographs (Chapter 7). Azoulay's work has created the ground for a new form of politics, which has important implications for postcolonial literature. Moving away from the passivity of Susan Sontag's onlooker, who is "regarding the pain of others" (2004) at a distance, Azoulay instead inserts the spectator of photographs into the drama of the event of photography. My contention is that the absent presence of photographs in these novels invites readers to exercise their civil imagination in analogous ways. In *Traces of the Real*, I argue that the event of photography continues in the allusion to photographs and photography within the pages of the literary text. These postcolonial writers may be read as taking on Azoulay's call and inviting their readers to engage in the practices of civil viewing, through their imagination, of the absent photograph and the tropes of photography. In contending that the absent image functions as an icon, metaphor, and trace, through the photographic "events" discussed in the chapters, I move the focus away from photography's colonial disciplining gaze to postcolonial civic engagements via new materialist understandings and attend to the intermedial aspects of language, particularly as it is mediated by photography.

This book begins by arguing that in using photography as an absent presence in their writing, South Asian postcolonial writers question the indexicality of photography, thereby challenging the hegemony of Western photographic discourse. Instead, they suggest new ways of seeing more suited to the postcolonial project. The book goes on to demonstrate that the absent presence of photography affords postcolonial writers metaphors of loss in representing diasporic identities. Finally, the book concludes with two examples of the ways in which the event of photography originating with a single or iconic image haunts the postcolonial novel, either through photographic spectatorship or in posthuman ways by suggesting assemblages between what lies within the text and the absent images that haunt the text from the outside.

The book is divided into the three following parts.

## Part I: The Absent Image as Icon

Part I deals with the ways in which postcolonial literature may respond to the objectifying, imperial gaze of photography. By focusing on the figure of the photographer (both real and fictional), I argue that the absent presence (or the belated presence in the first case) of photography in these texts raises difficult questions about photographic witnessing and representation in the context of postcolonial trauma and the way in which such photographs often fail to provide restorative justice to victims of postcolonial violence and upheaval. While the appending of Margaret Bourke-White's images of the Partition of India to the fiftieth anniversary edition of Khushwant Singh's 1956 novel *Train to Pakistan*, assumes documentary photography's ability to witness and accurately represent postcolonial trauma by problematically relying on its indexicality for affective impact, Michael Ondaatje's novel *Anil's Ghost* and Mahasweta Devi's short story "Behind the Bodice: Choli ke Pichhe" question the witnessing and representational power of Western photographic praxis in the context of postcolonial trauma. I propose instead an optics of blindness or an alternative mode of witnessing based on absence and intuition as opposed to documentary evidence. The analysis of texts in Part I together suggest the pitfalls of an overreliance on the iconicity or indexicality of images, even when those images are absent from the text.

*Traces of the Real* begins at the cusp of South Asian postcoloniality with Khushwant Singh's novel *Train to Pakistan*, written nine brief years after Indian independence. Contrary to my claims so far, the opening chapter of the book, titled "The False Promise of Affective Intentionality: The Violence of Documentary Photography in Khushwant Singh's *Train to Pakistan*," engages with a special edition of Singh's novel that includes real photographs taken by the American photographer Margaret Bourke-White. However, these photographs were added fifty years after the first publication of the novel; so by dint of their belatedness, these photographs are also an absent presence in the novel, I argue. I situate Bourke-White's Partition photographs within the context of documentary photography while also attempting to understand what she wanted her images to convey. Citing critics like John Tagg who have called into question documentary photography's capacity to bear witness, I argue that despite being politically progressive, Margaret Bourke-White's photographs of Partition convey an ideological naiveté and evidence of what Tagg calls "the pleasures of the paternalistic gaze" (Tagg 2009: xxxiii). I suggest that Bourke-White's obsessive documentation of death in all its horror and disgust runs counter to Singh's treatment of death in the novel, as something heroic and unexpected. In conclusion, this chapter considers the affective consequences of the coupling of Singh's text with Bourke-White's images. The always already present discourse of colonial photography, coupled with Bourke-White's often staged and artificial documenting of the great migration of India's Partition and the trauma it brought to millions, ensures that such a naive coupling of text and image can never be straightforward.

Continuing with the themes of witnessing and representation, Chapter 2 – "Optics of Blindness: Countervisuality in Michael Ondaatje's *Anil's Ghost*" – questions the suitability of Western photographic praxis in the postcolonial context. *Anil's Ghost* (2000), Michael Ondaatje's novel about the Sri Lankan civil war, is the story of Anil Tissera, a Sri Lankan-born, Western-educated forensic expert who returns to her homeland to investigate possible atrocities committed by the government. Through a discussion of the photographer protagonist Anil's efforts to unearth truths about the civil war, I consider whether she enables the characters in the novel to access the truth about violence and trauma or whether her efforts only painfully heighten the impossibility of this endeavor. I argue that Ondaatje proposes alternative modes of seeing, grounded in situated knowledges and therefore more suitable to postcolonial witnessing than the Western photographic eye.

Chapter 3, "Photography's Sonic Recall: Decolonizing Trauma Studies in Mahasweta Devi's 'Behind the Bodice,'" looks at Mahasweta Devi's short story as an attempt to decolonize Western trauma theory and its privileging of aporia and unspeakability, through its use of absent images and the photographer figure Upin Puri. "Behind the Bodice: Choli ke Pichhe" tells the story of Gangor, a Dalit woman and a migrant laborer who is photographed by Upin, a freelance photojournalist. These essentialized images, ironically taken by Upin in order to "save" Gangor and other brutalized tribal women like her, lead directly to Gangor's gang rape by the police. The absent photographs take on a sonic connotation in the refrain "choli ke picche" as they become the recurrent images that come to represent the traumatic instant. Devi's story decolonizes established discourses of trauma by positing an alternative category of affect and response – one of resilience, fierce rage, and defiance – in the post-rape depiction of the brutalized Gangor.

Together, the three fictional texts analyzed in Part I, argue for a retreat from the reliance on photography's iconicity from which arises its problematic indexicality. My critique of the flawed photographic eye of the real and fictional photographers in these texts underscores the need to look differently in the postcolonial context.

## Part II: The Absent Image as Metaphor

In the second part, the focus of the book shifts to diasporic literature, where photography becomes a metaphor of loss. Diasporic literature with its attendant themes of loss, longing, mourning, and trauma, has obvious resonances with photography as the immigrant protagonists of the diasporic novel are haunted by their separation from the homeland. The photograph is often described in terms suggesting "the idealization of absence," to use Vijay Mishra's term for the way in which mourning works (2007: 8). Jhumpa Lahiri's novel *The Lowland* and her novella "Hema and Kaushik" both deal with characters who are haunted by memories of the past and are unable to shape their identities in diaspora. Again, the absent presence of photography in these novels offers valuable ways of analyzing migrant identities enabling us to see the protagonists more empathetically.

In "Diaspora's Darkroom: Photography and the Vision of Loss in Jhumpa Lahiri's "Hema and Kaushik" (Chapter 4), I analyze the recurrent metaphor of photographs and photography in Lahiri's novella. I argue that photography allows Kaushik to counter the unrootedness of his diasporic condition by providing him a sense of presence. However, given photography's double edge – its ability to capture a moment and preserve it for posterity and, conversely, its inalienable connection with absence, loss, and even death – it ultimately renders his efforts false and exacerbates his sense of phantom loss and diasporic mourning.[9] The contradictions within photography provide Lahiri with the means to reflect the ambivalent nature of home, belonging, and diaspora for characters like Hema and Kaushik.

In the second chapter of Part II, "Finding Gauri: *Allo*-Portraits of a Mother in Jhumpa Lahiri's *The Lowland*" (Chapter 5), I argue that several absent images or imagetexts in Lahiri's novel offer us valuable insights into the "stunningly selfish" character Gauri (Kakutani 2013: n.pag.), a mother who abandons her husband and daughter; these absent images offer us the possibility of viewing Gauri more sympathetically. Using photographic theory in general and Marianne Hirsch's work on family photographs, the familial gaze, and the connection between photography and motherhood, I argue that Gauri is a more sympathetic character who fails to fulfill the hegemonic familial ideology imposed upon her. The trope of photography also enables Lahiri to suggest an inextricable "twinning" of the two

9 Delphine Munos writes about the second generation's attachment to a "lost and yet 'un-dead' world, long after their parents have themselves managed to disengage from it" in her eloquent article on Jhumpa Lahiri's "Once in a Lifetime" (Munos 2010).

brothers Subhash and Udayan, such that Gauri remains haunted by the past and her memories of her first husband, Udayan, even after she moves to America following his death, as Subhash's wife. I further contend that the trope of photography allows us glimpses into Gauri's inner life and provides a more nuanced portrayal of motherhood in diaspora, of a woman who fails to mother because she is in perpetual mourning, haunted by the past, rather than the monstrous mother that Gauri is often simplistically assumed to be.

## Part III: The Absent Image as Trace

Based on the duality of subject and object, model and copy, photography emerges from an acutely humanistic, Enlightenment tradition. These dualisms and photography's human-centric perspectives have not received adequate scrutiny as we enter the age of the Anthropocene where the privileged anthropocentrism of humanism has come to be questioned and replaced by an egalitarianism of species. By dismantling the humanistic construct of photography with its subject-object, photographer-photographed divide, in Part III I posit a more posthuman reading of photography based on doublings and entanglements between the (textual) spectator and the (imagined) photograph or between the text and images that lie outside it.

By considering the absent presence of an iconic photograph, Indian photographer Raghu Rai's image of a fetus in a bottle, taken in the aftermath of the Bhopal tragedy, in Indra Sinha's novel *Animal's People* (2007), Chapter 6, "Imagistic Haunting: Posthuman Photography and Photographic Traces in Indra Sinha's *Animal's People*," brings together photography and the posthuman in the context of postcoloniality. Adopting Daniel Rubinstein's rhizomatic approach to photography (2018), I contend that Sinha uses the absent presence of photography to present a posthuman postcoloniality made up of assemblages of the human, the animal, the nonhuman, and the digital, animated by the haunting of real images, which never appear within the work. Instead, the evocation of these images creates a nexus of sensations and new assemblages, which enable Sinha to critique neoliberal slow violence (see Nixon 2011) and offer posthuman, postcolonial alternatives.

In the final chapter of the book, "A 'fresh way of looking at the photograph': Citizenship and Photographic Spectatorship in Siddhartha Deb's *Surface*," I consider a single absent image, the discovery of which marks the point in the novel from which all events will flow and elucidate the mystery behind the image. By giving this disturbing image iconic status, the novel ostensibly seems to be about the power of photographic indexicality as evidence. However, moving from index to trace, and reading Deb's novel as a manifestation of Ariella Azoulay's "event of photography," allows me to undermine the importance of the photograph and to read Amrit, the novel's protagonist charged with solving the mystery of the woman in the photograph, as the spectator of the photograph who continues the event of photography. I argue that Amrit's spectatorship of the photograph becomes an act of civic duty that acknowledges the citizenship of the photograph's subject through what Azoulay has termed the "civil contract of photography."

Through these readings of the absent image as icon, metaphor, and trace, I suggest that the absent presence of photography in these postcolonial texts offers a literary counternarrative to the primacy of the visual image and hints at the potency of the postcolonial moment, which invites civic engagement. In its examination of a photographic point of view in narrative theory with reference to several South Asian postcolonial, diasporic texts, *Traces of the Real* makes a valuable contribution to the field of postcolonial literature, which is in need of interdisciplinary analyses (see Huggan 2008). It is hoped that this study will open up other fictive archives, which can be subjected to similar analyses.

The title of the book, "Traces of the Real," is a phrase borrowed from Roland Barthes's analysis of the photograph as providing a material trace of the real. The duality of meaning encapsulated in "traces" serves my purpose well – to analyze the indexical, metaphoric, or haunting use of something that purports to be a true copy but which ultimately doesn't exist and can at best only offer an absent presence of what it records. The absence and inaccessibility of the assumed real in the narrated image offers us productive ways of analyzing common themes of postcolonial and diasporic literature such as memory, loss, trauma, agency, identity, mourning, longing, etc.

In concluding *Traces of the Real*, I return to Azoulay's compelling theorization of a civil imagination and her question, "Why then discuss photography *in the absence of the photograph*?" (2012a: 233, emphasis original) with which I began this book. Azoulay argues that in order to understand the complete circumstances surrounding a photo and the relation between the event of photography and the photographed event, we need to exercise our civil imagination and reconstruct what happened at the moment the photo was taken. She describes the civil imagination as "a tool for reading the possible within the concrete" and calls for the extending of this practice to photographs that were not taken or are unavailable for scrutiny. Such a practice allows us to "gather all the participants in the event of photography on a single plane without allowing the perspective of any single participant to be privileged" (234).

Such an approach does a number of things – it eliminates questions of indexicality and its attendant privileges, it democratizes and even erases the binaries that have long dominated photography studies, and it dramatizes the spectatorial role, which can no longer remain passive. In *Traces of the Real,* in concert with critics who have shifted the focus of photography away from the material, I argue that such an understanding of photography has much to offer to postcolonial literature. The absent presence of images in these texts compels us to exercise our civil imagination in compassionate ways. Whether it be Devi's brutalized protagonist Gangor; Lahiri's Gauri, haunted by her past, or Kaushik, trying to find his; Sinha's dehumanized Animal; or Deb's silenced Leela – in each case the writer's use of the absent presence of photography allows us to understand these characters in more sympathetic and compassionate ways. *Traces of the Real* thus offers a model of postcolonial engagement, which moves beyond talking back to the West's scopophilic visual regime. Instead, through photographic traces and absences, it suggests the power and promise of the postcolonial moment.

Versions of Chapters 3 and 4 have been previously published as:

Banerjee, Bidisha. 2022. "Defiance and the Speakability of Rape: Decolonizing Trauma Studies in Mahasweta Devi's Short Fiction." *The Journal of Commonwealth Literature,* 57.3, 673–690, https://doi.org/10.1177/0021989420911435.

Banerjee, Bidisha. 2010. "Diaspora's 'Dark Room': Photography and the Vision of Loss in Jhumpa Lahiri's 'Hema and Kaushik'." *The Journal of Commonwealth Literature,* 45.3, 443–456, https://doi.org/10.1177/0021989410377393.

# PART I

# The Absent Image as Icon

In 1867, Cardinal Pecci, who was to become Pope Leo XIII, wrote the Latin poem *Ars photographica*, extolling the virtues of the medium that was then only a few decades old:

> Drawn by the sun's bright pencil,
> How well, oh glistening stencil,
> You express the brow's fine grace,
> Eyes' sparkle, and beauty of face.
> O marvelous might of mind,
> New prodigy! A design
> Beyond the contrived
> Of Apelles, Nature's rival. (trans. by Robert M. Adams, qtd. in Hannavy 2008: 74)

A decade later, as pope, he commissioned a fresco for the Vatican's Galleria dei Candelabri, celebrating the arts. The painting depicts personifications of Sculpture, Architecture, and Painting paying their respects to Ecclesia. Photography, represented by the camera, is depicted in a lower realm alongside Weaving. While Pecci's poem depicts photography as a mechanical process acted upon by Nature representing divine agency, photography's fall in the hierarchy of the arts, suggested by the position of the camera in the mural, exemplifies the ambiguous position it has occupied since its very inception. A combination of the mechanical, operated by the human, yet somehow touched by divinity, the response to photography has also always been paradoxical, ranging from strong faith in its evidentiary nature to a deep questioning of its manipulation.

Photography's veracity is often associated with the role of the image as icon in early Christianity. An icon is considered to be the original likeness of the divine. Icons are images of the divine but also venerated as the divine. Images were thought to be of supernatural origin and imbued with miraculous powers. Similarly, "photographs continue to serve the manifest function that was facilitated in earlier time periods by a wide succession of types of images (icons, funeral portraits, death masks)" (Freeland 2008: 51). Thus, the image as icon in the religious context makes visible the divine or that which is invisible and unrepresentable. Though in medieval Europe the images that were worshiped as icons were paintings rather than photographs, as suggested by Pope Leo's faith in photography as "A design / Beyond the contrived / Of Apelles," photography quickly took on a similar stature in religious iconography soon after its inception, which it continues to hold to this day. Hans Belting wrote about the canonization of the doctor Giuseppe Moscati in Naples in 1987, sixty years after his death. A larger-than-life-size photograph of Moscati was placed at the altar,[10] its size differentiating it from ordinary photographs: "The authenticity inherent in a photo supports the claim of authentic appearance always raised by icons; the image was to give an impression of the person and to provide the experience of a personal encounter" (1994: 11).

The truth claims of photography may be traced back to its function as religious icon. The image as icon is not a manifestation of the divine in any real sense but only thought to be so. What Belting calls the "claim of authentic appearance" is constantly undermined by the awareness that the photograph makes present what is absent and consequently otherwise unrepresentable. I argue that the photograph as icon is attributed the problematic burden of veracity. In their reading, Frances Guerin and Roger Hallas extend photography's power to make visible the invisible to its ramifications for representing traumatic events. Given photography's power to remarkably reproduce the likeness of lived experience, photographs are thought to re-present or to make present again the historical event. However, just as the likeness of God in the image is not a real resemblance but a spiritual one, so also the material image is ultimately inauthentic. "The truth exists in its likeness" (Guerin and Hallas 2007: 9).

Part I of *Traces of the Real* considers the burden of authenticity granted to the photograph and its related power to witness. It includes discussion of three texts – two novels and a short story – all of which include characters who are photojournalists. In Chapter 1, the photojournalist in question is a real, historical one while those in chapters 2 and 3 are fictional. The three texts also deal with traumatic events – the Partition of India, the Sri Lankan civil war, and the rape and abuse of Santal women by the ruling elite in

10 At the Chiesa del Gesu Nuova or New Church of Jesus in Naples, Italy.

postcolonial India. The first chapter begins with the presence rather than the absence of images that have achieved an iconic status. The American photographer Margaret Bourke-White's images of the Partition of India, taken for *Life* magazine, attempted to document the vast migration of people that took place in its wake. I analyze the belated inclusion of these images in the fiftieth anniversary edition of Khushwant Singh's fictional text on the Partition, *Train to Pakistan,* in order to undermine the power and agency granted to images, particularly in the context of witnessing trauma. Despite the supposed authenticity of the images, Bourke-White's cold objectivity fails to capture the real trauma of the event. In contrast, Singh's characters, I argue, are far more grievable.

My analysis of the conjoining of text and image in Singh's novel, brings to the fore the difficulties of treating the image as icon while bringing together narrative and photography in postcolonial literature, particularly in the case of trauma narratives. In Chapter 2, I move toward absenting the image in the depiction of trauma in South Asian literature, by critiquing the photographic eye of Anil, the protagonist of Michael Ondaatje's novel *Anil's Ghost.* Anil tries to capture the "truth" of the Sri Lankan civil war through her forensic photography and ultimately fails. In Chapter 3, Upin, the photographer in Mahasweta Devi's short story "Choli ke Pichhe" endeavors to record the trauma and suffering of the dispossessed tribal women in West Bengal and Bihar. He obsessively photographs Gangor in an attempt to save her and others like her through his photography. Again, this false belief in the iconicity of the photograph and its attendant power is severely critiqued by Devi, as Upin unwittingly becomes the very agent of Gangor's degradation.

Part I makes the claim that the photograph as icon carries with it the dual connotation of an evidentiary force as well as suspicion about its authenticity. This makes it unsuited to representations of trauma in South Asian literature. Erasing the image and making it only an absent presence in these texts is to critique their iconicity while also reducing their iconic import. Doing so allows us to consider alternative ways of looking more suited to the postcolonial project.

1

# The False Promise of Affective Intentionality: The Violence of Documentary Photography in Khushwant Singh's *Train to Pakistan*

> The celebration of abstract humanity becomes, in any given political situation, the celebration of the dignity of the passive victim. This is the final outcome of the appropriation of the photographic image for liberal political ends; the oppressed are granted a bogus Subjecthood when such status can be secured only from within, on their own terms.
>
> Victor Burgin, *Thinking Photography*, 109

## Introduction

Photography has struggled with questions of representation since its very inception. These issues become especially complicated when it comes to representing people of other classes, nationalities, genders, and races from those of the photographer. The history of photography during colonial times in many parts of the world is replete with troubling representations of the colonized. Such representations often reinforce racist stereotypes thereby justifying the colonial enterprise. The 2018 move by *National Geographic* magazine to reckon with its colonialist past and the blunt admission by editor Susan Goldberg, in the editorial titled "For Decades, Our Coverage Was Racist. To Rise Above Our Past, We Must Acknowledge It," bears testimony to this issue. The magazine asked the preeminent historian of race and photography, University of Virginia professor John Edwin Mason, to delve into their archives. He found damning evidence that unlike *Life* magazine, *National Geographic* did little to make their readers question their racist assumptions. On the contrary, coming into existence at the height of colonialism, the photographs published in the magazine often reinforced stereotypical, racist views that had currency at the time by depicting "natives" as "exotics, famously and frequently unclothed, happy hunters, noble savages – every type of cliché" (Goldberg 2018). Documentary photography attempts to deal with some of the problems of photographic representation, with its claim to journalistic realism and non-intrusion. It is often assumed that documentary photographs have the ability to bear witness since they show real people in real situations. However, these assumptions have come under suspicion and have been debated by critics like Susan Sontag, Martha Rosler, and Allan Sekula since as far back as the 1970s (Sontag 1977; Rosler 1981; Sekula 1984) and by Juanita Brown (2024) more recently. These critics argue that documentary photography calls into question the moral integrity of the photographer who often does nothing to ameliorate his subjects' suffering and may even manipulate the situation in the service of a powerful photograph. Questions of the circulation and reception of such photographs as well as their aesthetic value versus their truth-telling capacity further obfuscate the issue.

On the fiftieth anniversary of the publication of Khushwant Singh's 1956 novel *Train to Pakistan,* Roli Books launched a special illustrated edition of the novel. Edited by Pramod Kapoor, this edition of Singh's novel is supplemented by sixty-five hitherto unpublished photographs taken by the celebrated American photographer Margaret Bourke-White for *Life* magazine during her stay in India in 1946 and 1947. Almost all commentators seem to agree that this is a creative and novel idea on Kapoor's part. The editor himself believes that Singh's novel and Bourke-White's Partition images "were made for each other. Through their own mediums, both were conveying the same truth, she through her photograph and he through his prose" (Singh, xvi). Anita Joshua contends that it seemed as if Singh himself "had commissioned [...] Margaret Bourke-White to freeze frame the Partition for his book" (Joshua 2006). However, this sort of forced and belated coupling of text and photograph results in the creation of a third text, which is anything but simple and ultimately, I argue, does injustice to the literary text.

Pramod Kapoor's intention seems to have been to heighten the novel's realism as well as introduce an additional affective dimension to it by appending Margaret Bourke-White's photographs to the novel resulting in the creation of what he calls an "almost unbearably heart-rending subtext" (*Train to Pakistan,* initial pages). The brief introductions to the novel, one written by Kapoor and the other by Singh, provide insights into their respective attitudes toward this edition of the novel. Kapoor devotes considerable space in his introduction extolling Margaret Bourke-White's professionalism and her unflinching commitment to recording the real, no matter how horrific. He writes: "Her hands did not shake even when photographing a stray dog biting into a dead man lying across a railway track" (xv). He also writes at length about the elements of the novel that, by Singh's own admission, have their "own share of reality. All the characters, major or minor, had lived a real life and passed through Khushwant's as one or the other" (xvi). He goes on to enumerate who the characters in the novel, Hukum Chand, Jugga, Nooran, and others, were based on and how Singh knew them. Kapoor concludes his introduction with a reiteration of the work's realism by suggesting that the novel was much more than a painful experience; rather it was one Singh had endured himself. In Singh's own introduction, the emphasis is not on how the novel represents real people or events, nor his own experience of the Partition (though he has written about that elsewhere in discussions of this novel), but rather on individual stories of suffering across community divides, "heart-rending tales from the survivors of the holocaust on either side" (xxiii). The novel, for him, is another cautionary tale that attempts to "promote closer integration of people of different races, religions and castes living in the sub-continent" (xxv). Most notably, there is no mention of Margaret Bourke-White or her Partition photos in Singh's introduction. Although Kapoor informs us that he approached Singh with the idea of illustrating the fiftieth edition of his novel with her photos, there is no clear indication of Singh's views on the matter, except that he thought this would grant the novel "a new lease of life" – a welcome thought for any writer.

I do not wish to argue about the intended realism of Singh's novel but to suggest that, unlike for Kapoor, the realism of the novel was secondary to Singh. While categorizing *Train to Pakistan* as historical fiction, critics have also referred to it as "a blend of fact and fiction" (Parthiban and Dhanaraj 2019: 369). Kapoor's purpose in adding the photos seems to have been twofold – to increase the realism of the novel and to add to its affective import. These aims are interrelated in that Kapoor expects the iconicity of Margaret Bourke-White's photographs to add to the realism of Singh's depiction of the same traumatic event of Partition. This impulse is not difficult to understand. Nancy Armstrong (1999) has demonstrated the way in which the pictorial turn in Victorian realist fiction coincided with the rise of photography in the nineteenth century. Photography and the novel form so influenced each other, Armstrong argues, that Victorian novelists used the same visual conventions of photography to represent the real. Consequently, the realism of a fictional text was considerably bolstered when it invoked a photograph. In a similar fashion, Kapoor hoped the evidentiary power of the images would arouse strong emotions in the reader. However, given that Bourke-White's photographs are very much in the tradition of what Christopher Pinney has called "camera indica" – the production of the Indian subject through the apparatus of the camera and colonial discourse – the effect of conjoining Bourke-White's photos with Singh's novel is far more complex and layered than Kapoor might have intended and even, I argue, works at cross-purposes to Singh's primary storytelling impulse.

In her reading of the illustrated edition of *Train to Pakistan*, Ira Sarma agrees that the text and the photographs do not provide "mutually supporting narratives, but rather a complex blending of deviating viewpoints" (2015: 270). She reads this edition as a Hirschean postmemory project offering second-generation survivors of Partition (like Kapoor himself) ways to process this historical trauma. While I agree that this may be one way of reading Kapoor's edition, my own reading of it is more critical. Rather than add affective dimensionality to Singh's powerful novel, I suggest that the photographs compel us to take on the role of passive spectator "regarding the pain of others," to use Sontag's phrase. While the other chapters of this book will consider the absence of real photographs in a literary text, my reading of the *belated* insertion of photographs to Singh's novel in this chapter, creating an absent (formerly) presence (currently) of a different kind, sees this as an act of violence and violation. The always already present discourse of *camera indica*, coupled with Bourke-White's sometimes staged[1] and artificial documenting of the Great Migration and the trauma it brought to millions, in the service of consumer realism of the Western world, ensures that such a naive coupling of text and image can never be straightforward. The chapter begins by situating Bourke-White's Partition photographs in their particular context while also attempting to understand what she wanted her images to convey. I then argue that instead of Kapoor's affective intentionality being borne out in the addition of the images to Singh's novel, this strategy runs counter to Singh's own purposes of celebrating the untold sacrifices of common people in the face of shallow communalism, which quickly descended into the horrific violence the nation witnessed during the Partition. I conclude with the assertion that the heroic and grievable lives of Singh's novel are somehow erased by Bourke-White's images that depict the dead of Partition as faceless masses. Thus, Kapoor's dependence on the

1 Pramod Kapoor writes admiringly of Bourke-White's strategy of staging her photos in his introduction to *Train to Pakistan*: "She was a committed professional, who would sometimes go to such extremes as asking her subject to enact their miseries for the camera so that she could put the most extraordinary images on the first flight to the US to catch her magazine's deadline" (Singh xv).

iconicity of Bourke-White's images to heighten the emotional impact of the novel is in my opinion a failed endeavor.

Theorists of photography like Susan Sontag and John Tagg have established the essential violence of the photographic act. They have asserted that the perpetrator of the violence in these dialectical schemata is always the photographer while the one acted upon is the photographed person. This is replicated in the semantic language of the medium where the photographer is "armed" with his camera and other equipment with which he "shoots" his subjects. This becomes especially ideological and problematic in the colonial context as it comes to serve the purposes of colonialism quite handily. Christopher Pinney's influential texts like *Camera Indica* and his edited collection *Photography's Other Histories* have gone a long way to restoring the lopsidedness of the above relationship. Pinney has demonstrated that postcolonial visual economies often found ways of self-representation despite the prevalence of a colonial photographic schema. Though Pinney's work is interesting and valuable, my interest here is in analyzing Margaret Bourke-White's Partition photographs in the terms laid out by the former group of critics. By doing so, I will suggest that despite not necessarily intending to replicate colonial stereotypes of representation in her photographs, Bourke-White's work on the Partition ultimately fails to transcend the existing schemata. Consequently, the appending of her photographs to Singh's text creates problems for the articulation of Singh's message in his novel.

## Margaret Bourke-White's Complicated Photographic Gaze

Acclaimed American photographer Margaret Bourke-White begins the preface to her book *Halfway to Freedom* with an anecdote about the women of Swat, a remote principality in undivided India. Bourke-White visited Swat in the fall of 1947 as a photographer for *Life* magazine, sent to document the Partition of India:

> Until my visit, Swatis had never seen a woman photographer, and my interpreter informed me that they were thoroughly puzzled by my "costume" – well-worn slacks and jacket literally dripping with camera trappings. "It wears clothes like a man," they reasoned, "but it has hair like a woman." The interpreter, a scholarly man and tutor to the young Prince of Swat, had settled the sex question, but he was unable to answer the next query: Was I a movie actress or a circus performer? (1949: ix)

Bourke-White's decision to begin a book that chronicles her journey through India taking photographs as the new nation is born with this particular anecdote indicates what a novelty she must have seemed to her photographic subjects. This seemingly androgynous woman, with a combination of glamor and wizardry, must have seemed like an apparition to the women of Swat who, almost three quarters of a century later, remain trapped by strong patriarchal beliefs. The mere act of resisting such beliefs and seeking an education, even today, has the potential to produce icons like Malala Yousafzai, Swat Valley's native daughter.

The above anecdote tells us about the gaze of the natives toward Bourke-White, while her pictures provide us with startling images that capture her counter-gaze. Bourke-White had recently spent time in Germany documenting the liberation of Jews from concentration camps in the aftermath of World War II. She captures the Partition which she calls "a massive exercise in human misery" (5) at a moment in India's history which is contradictorily also a moment when India "stood eager and shining with hope on the threshold of a new life" (5). In the absence of other photographs, Bourke-White's images are a valuable visual documentation of the Partition. Most of the reviews and analyses of her Partition photographs seem to be almost as much in awe of her prowess as a female photographer as the women of Swat. She and her *Life* magazine reporter Lee Eitington, are described as "notoriously resourceful" (French 2016) as they bravely courted danger amidst the chaos of the large-scale human migration. Bourke-White herself tells us that they were warned of abductions and told that this was not a woman's job (7). She even describes their jeep coming under fire on one occasion (8). However, with the help of reliable drivers and translators, they were able to complete the assignment.

Although Bourke-White's assignment is usually discussed in laudatory terms, little attention is paid to certain disturbing aspects of her approach. There is ample evidence that she staged some of her photographs. Referring to a striking image of a Sikh man carrying his ailing wife on his shoulder as they made their way to safety, Eitington recalled, "We were there for hours. She told them to go back again and again and again. They were too frightened to say no. They were dying" (qtd. in Foote 1986: n.pag.). This suggests that Bourke-White was very clear about the exact picture she wanted, even if she had to stage it. In her article on Bourke-White's photographic essay on the Partition, Dilpreet Bhullar writes that *Life* magazine was established in 1936 by Henry Luce, "with carefully crafted strategies of representation: catering to the strategies of the upper and middle classes; redefining national consciousness; and hinting at the growth of consumer realism" (2013: 301).

This concept of consumer realism as the avowed aesthetic of *Life* magazine has come under scrutiny by Wendy Kozol (1994) and Chris Vials (2006). Kozol concludes that *Life* is unequivocally realist; however, Vials parses Luce's concept of "partisan objectivity,' in which blatantly partial claims are anchored in the seemingly un-authored, 'real' nature of the photographs [...] a mode of reading amenable to consumerism, based on simultaneity, titillation and what Raymond Williams calls 'total flow'" (2006: 80–81).

Margaret Bourke-White's essay on the Partition, "The Great Migration: Five Million Indians Flee for Their Lives," was published in the November 3, 1947 issue of *Life* magazine, accompanied by twelve photographs, many of which are included in Kapoor's edition. The piece is sandwiched between essays on Roosevelt and Philadelphia lawyer Richardson Dilworth's run for mayor. It is immediately preceded by advertisements for "Simplicity Printed Patterns" and Pan-American Airlines. Bourke-White's Partition photographs sit nestled between various representations of all things American – leaders who take on larger-than-life dimensions after their death, images of travel and leisure. The faces of the traumatized, displaced Indians as they travel across the country, their lives forever altered, look out of the pages of the magazine at the typical *Life* magazine readers, middle- or upper-class, predominantly white Americans. The opening image of Bourke-White's essay emblematizes many of the tropes of Partition. It is the aforementioned image of a Sikh man carrying his "ailing wife" on his shoulders as he marches across the landscape (Figure 1). Also within the frame are three other figures – a man and two young women, one of whom carries a bundled infant in her arms. The man and older of the woman carry their meager belongings on their heads. These three additional figures are probably relatives of the couple who make up the centerpiece of the image. Shot from a low angle, all four figures caught in mid-stride with their legs almost equally apart, the photograph conveys, above all, purposeful movement, weary but determined. The captured swing of the arm, the billowing garments, the dust beneath their feet, all suggest motion. The bundled belongings, one of which is a baby, tell a story of the precious little that has been salvaged. Most of the figures are barefoot, though the elderly patriarch wears shoes as well as socks. Although we are told in Bourke-White's caption that the man's wife on his shoulder is "ailing," she is upright and even proud and defiant as she looks down directly at the camera. The identifiable tropes of Partition – movement, weariness, domestic upheaval, determination, and uncertainty – are all powerfully captured in a single image.

This stands in some contrast to a similar image a few pages later, called a "strange litter," showing an aged Muslim woman being carried by her son

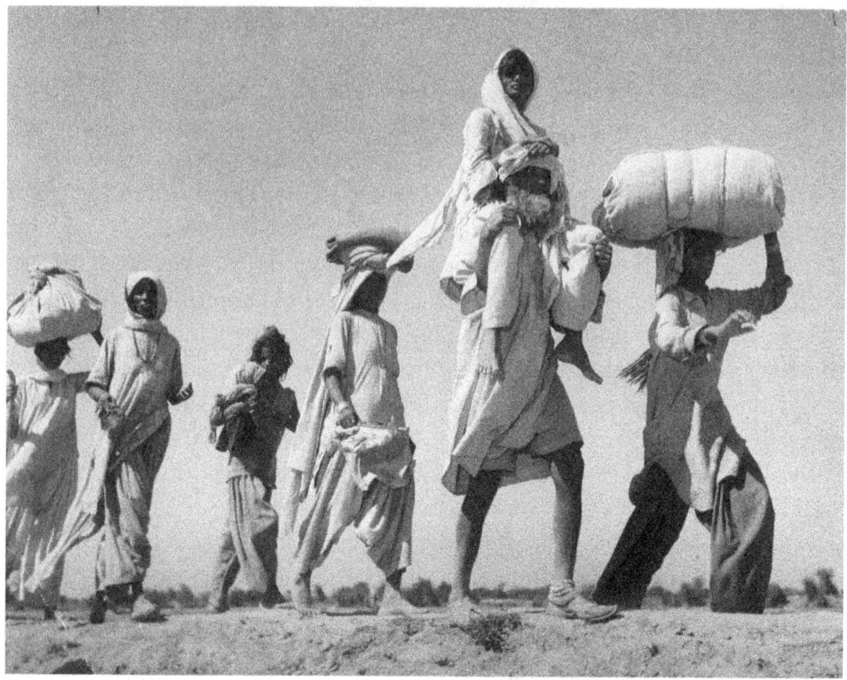

Figure 1. Margaret Bourke-White/Shutterstock.com

and brother-in-law in a makeshift cloth sling suspended from a bamboo pole; clearly she is the titular "litter" (Figure 2).

Unlike the earlier image, which was taken in mid-stride, this photo captures a still moment; the men have paused for the photo to be taken, as is evident from the direct look into the camera of two of the three figures in the frame. The woman is so frail that there is no danger whatsoever of the pole snapping under her weight. We learn that "When this photograph was made, the family had been four days without food, but [the] men were managing to keep up with [the] convoy" ("Punjab 1947" 2020: n.pag.). This photograph was taken from the same low angle as the other image, but though the woman in this image looks directly at the camera, she seems far more frail than the earlier "ailing" wife. Her body seems almost stunted as it disappears into the sheet that encloses her. She, too, holds a tiny bundle of possessions that seems as weightless as she does. This image is reproduced on the back cover of Kapoor's edition of *Train to Pakistan* with the deeply problematic caption, "A burden borne by two countries." Other images included in the *Life* magazine piece are far more disturbing in their

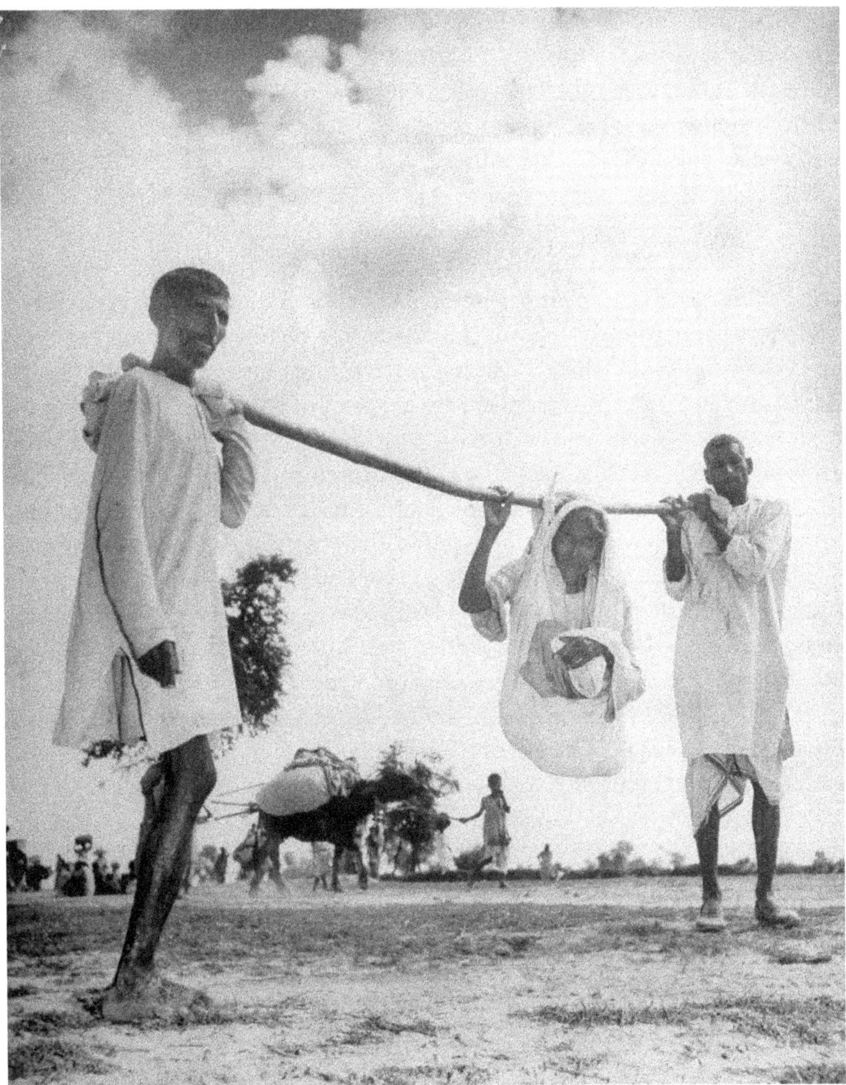

Figure 2. Margaret Bourke-White/Shutterstock.com

depiction of the dead and dying. In the first half of the article, most of the photos present images of migration creating a sense of the sheer scale of displacement, processions of families on ox-drawn carts, dwarfed by the giant trees and the unforgiving landscape. However, the later images are replete with putrefying and decayed bodies, the stillness of death emblematic of the cost of failure to keep moving.

By all accounts, Margaret Bourke-White was politically progressive and she made it her life's work to document oppression and discrimination through her photographs. She garnered fame for capturing images of the historic upheavals of her time, be they struggles for decolonization, the Holocaust, or apartheid in South Africa. However, as has been argued by John Edwin Mason, her essays could sometimes be politically naïve, as was the case with her story on the dedication of the Voortrekker Monument, entitled "South Africa Enshrines Pioneer Heroes," published a few short years after her piece on the Partition of India. Though a powerful piece, her photos "uncritically reproduced the heroic myths of colonial conquest and Afrikaner nationalism" (Mason 2012: 157). A later essay called "South Africa and Its Problem" is another moving piece of writing foregrounding the exploitation of Blacks in South Africa. However, even in this essay, Mason argues through his analysis of a single iconic image, Bourke-White fails to chronicle an accurate image of South African society under apartheid in 1950. Instead, Mason demonstrates that her words and photographs depict Africans as "essentially rural, pre-modern people, trapped between a collapsing 'tribal' culture and a modern industrial society with which they could not fully cope" (164). Despite her best intentions, then, Bourke-White places the blame for the Africans' condition squarely on their own inability to progress. Mason seems not to want to be too critical of Bourke-White, often excusing her political naiveté by attributing it to her being new to the country and therefore probably "seduced by the occasion" or suggesting that "she saw more than she understood" (162). Despite this, Mason repeatedly demonstrates that Bourke-White was in the final analysis catering to the tastes and predilections of *Life* magazine's typical reader, the middle- to upper-class, white American. When she was working for *Life* magazine, a particular aesthetic mode of producing images of colonized peoples was already well established; it was common to represent the colonized in Orientalized terms that depicted them as the Other in contrast with the rational colonizer figure, thereby justifying the colonial enterprise. Margaret Bourke-White's images of the Partition often represent the migrating masses in similarly fixed, stereotypical ways.

## Documentary Photography's Realism and Affect

John Tagg's work on capturing photographic truths has firmly established the association between photography and state disciplinary apparatus. In *The Burden of Representation* (1988), he reads photography as the function of a particular apparatus or machine in the Foucauldian sense. Documentary photography is founded on the inherent properties of the camera, based on what Barthes called the "evidential force" of the photograph. In his subsequent books, *Grounds of Dispute: Art History, Cultural Politics and the Discursive Field* (1992) and *The Disciplinary Frame: Photographic Truths and the Capture of Meaning* (2009), Tagg demonstrates the ways in which the power effects of photography are produced via the articulation of the apparatus of discipline and that of photography. In the latter book, Tagg offers a definition of documentary as a sociopolitical rhetoric in the 1930s which established and maintained a particular politics of capture. Dismantling the evidential value of photography arising from its supposed indexicality, Tagg posits that "the institutions whose dissemination constituted the disciplinary regime could only operate, insofar as they did, when certain technologies, techniques, practices, and codes of representation had been pulled into place" (2009: xxxi). In this way, photography came to function as an instrument of surveillance, record, evidence, and truth. Tagg identifies documentary as a particular practice of representation which he describes as "a hybrid of discipline and spectacle, of documentation and publicity" (xxxii). Documentary photography's capacity to bear witness had been questioned by critics long before Tagg's theorizing of its disciplinary aspects. While debating documentary photography in the 1970s, Susan Sontag, Martha Rosler, and Allan Sekula argued that documentary photographers often augmented the misery and victimization of their subjects in the service of their own ambitions. They questioned whether such photography really drew public attention to the plight of those photographed. Juanita Brown's recent work (2024) showing the *fungibility* (to use Saidiya Hartman's term) of Black lives as represented in documentary photography suggests that work remains to be done in accurately representing marginalized people through a photographic lens.

In light of the work done on documentary photography, it is easy to see the ways in which it feeds into the overdetermining practices of photography's use under colonialism. Capturing the great migration brought about by the Partition of India in 1947, Margaret Bourke-White's images carry with them all of the burden and violence of representation already associated with documentary photography. The practice of documentary photography was still quite new in Bourke-White's day and she quickly made a name for herself as one of the foremost photographers of her time. The subsequent critiques of documentary practices urge us to revisit her photographs in their light and compel us to question a decision like Kapoor's to use them to illustrate a fictional narrative of Partition. Matthias Christen suggests that although the critique of documentary photography that first arose in the 1970s never managed to reform the practice, it served to set standards by which we still judge documentary photography. He goes on to argue that according to these standards, "staging scenes" (as Bourke-White often did for her images of the Partition) "undoubtedly qualifies as an ultimate threat to the images' testimonial value, as well as the photographer's moral credibility" (2007: 58). Given these critiques of documentary photography, we can say that at best the realism of such photos is tainted by suspicion and representational bias.

An overwhelming number of Bourke-White's images are of the dead and the dying. Although only a small proportion of these images finally made it into the issue of *Life*, analyzed as a complete set, the images are unrelenting in their depiction of death. We see human bodies in all stages of decomposition and putrefaction. The entire landscape, whether it be fields or rivers, is littered with bodies. There are images of mass graves and funeral pyres, vultures feeding on carcasses and hideously bloated bodies floating in the waters. The images of the emaciated and dying are no less horrifying. In a particularly haunting set of parallel images, we see a man's body on a cart alongside another photo, taken minutes later we are told, of his child's body thrown onto his. The first is a close-up of the man, the spokes of the cart's wheel framing his head. He almost looks alive with his open eyes and his arm thrown over his head. He looks out with a fixed, blank stare. It is only in the next image, taken from greater distance, that we realize that this is in fact a pile of bodies, the most recent addition to which is that of the man in the photograph.

I would argue that while the ostensible purpose of Bourke-White's images is documentation, there is evidence of what John Tagg calls "investment in pictures of misery, the power of horrors, and the pleasures of the paternalistic gaze" (2009: xxxiii). The perversity of a pile of dead bodies on a cart juxtaposes the possibility of movement with the fixity and stasis of death. In the hitherto unpublished images chosen by Pramod Kapoor to include as illustrations of Singh's novel, there is also a distinct preoccupation with death. At least half the images depict the dead or the dying. The images of the dead, like the one discussed above, are often confrontational and horrifying. Even on the rare occasion when they are suggestive rather than direct, such as several images of vultures on rooftops waiting to feed on the dead, the images evoke horror and disgust. In stark contrast to the earlier photos where we see powerful portraits of individuals or families, the sheer profusion of bodies depicted in the later photographs serves to erase all individuality of the victims.

When it comes to the question of affect, photography studies took an affective turn with the publication of Brown and Phu's collection *Feeling*

*Photography* in 2014. The editors draw attention to the oversights of the "thinking" approach (propounded by Victor Burgin [1982]) and argue that the "affective turn" (Clough 2007) has powerful implications for photography studies because it "solicits [re-engagement] with the politics of viewing" (Brown and Phu 2014: 7). They argue that focusing on the affective elements of photographs serves to bring to the forefront "abject subjects" (9) who have largely been overlooked in the thinking framework. However, for Allan Sekula, whether a photograph has an affective impact or not depends on where it fits within the "binary folklore" of symbolist versus realist folk myth that he proposes (1982: 108). He maps this on to the popular but misleading opposition between art and documentary photography, determining two polar ways of seeing: expression vs. reportage, imagination vs. empirical truth, affective value vs. informative value, and metaphoric vs. metonymic signification (108).

Brown and Phu's "abject subjects" are Sekula's "passive victims" evoked in the epigraph to this chapter. While art photography (to use Sekula's term) can arouse affect in the viewer for marginal subjects, documentary photography fails to do so and instead grants the oppressed a "bogus Subjecthood" (Burgin 1982: 109) used to serve liberal political ends. The inclusion of Margaret Bourke-White's photographs in Singh's novel is intended to arouse an affective response to the "abject subjects" of Partition while also bolstering the novel's realism. I do not agree with Sekula's binary formulation of art versus documentary photography or his resulting claim that the latter can only have informative value and not affective import. However, given that Bourke-White's images are strongly rooted in the tradition of documentary photography, they lack affective import in the context of Singh's novel. Her distancing gaze, coupled with the violent capture of the camera, makes for photos that fail to humanize her subjects, portraying them instead as the always already precarious and suffering "wretched millions" (Bourke-White, qtd. in Singh 2009: xiv). In contrast, the powerful characters delineated by Singh in his novel convey the trauma of Partition far more effectively with stronger affective import than Bourke-White's largely clinical images.

## Grievable Lives

Having established the complexities of the documentary mode of photography, its relationship with affect, as well as the avowedly dispassionate yet often colonialist tone of Margaret Bourke-White's photography, I now turn to the coupling of her Partition images with the first work of fiction on the cataclysmic events of 1947 on the subcontinent, Khushwant Singh's 1956 novel *Train to Pakistan*. I argue in the rest of this chapter that Bourke-White's images and Singh's text are not complementary to each other and rather than enhancing the affective import or the realism of the novel, the images and text violently clash in their avowed purposes. Judith Butler again poses her now-famous question, "What makes for a grievable life?" (2004: 20) in her book *Frames of War: When Is Life Grievable* (2009), this time in the context of photography and media representations of precarious lives. In doing so, she repeats some of the earlier criticisms of documentary photography in order to show that our response to the suffering of others "depends upon a certain field of perceptible reality having already been established" (64). In the essay "Torture and the Ethics of Photography" Butler includes an extended discussion of Susan Sontag's differentiation between narrative and photography. Sontag argues that while the former enables us to understand, the latter simply haunts us and consequently it remains a lesser medium in the evocation of pathos when compared with writing. Furthermore, the affective import of photographs, according to Sontag, inhibits cognition such that "when sentiment crystallizes, it forestalls thinking" (Butler 2009: 70). However, Sontag's preference for writing about atrocity over photographing it is compromised by her admission that the evidentiary force of photography is necessary to prove that an atrocity has been committed. Butler extends this to conclude, "there can be no truth without photography" (70). She then evokes the oft-made critique of documentary photography – that all documentary images are framed and deliberately so – to argue that this framing means that the photograph interprets the reality it documents. Therefore, for Butler, the photograph does more than simply refer to acts of atrocity.

Sontag's views and Butler's subsequent engagement with them offer a useful framework for reading Khushwant Singh's illustrated edition of *The Train to Pakistan*. The horror of Margaret Bourke-White's Partition images included in the novel is unquestionable and no doubt what compelled the editor to couple them with Singh's novel, providing what he calls an "almost unbearably heart-rending subtext" (front matter). However, because of the ways in which writing about traumatic and violent events differ from photographs of them, the coupling does not cause an arousal of affect or pathos for the characters, but instead is a strategy that interferes with our interpretation and understanding of Singh's novel in detrimental ways. I will demonstrate this through an analysis of the theme of death and heroism in the novel; I will conclude with the assertion that in the final analysis the inclusion of Bourke-White's images in the novel reduces the grievability of Singh's characters.

The two epigraphs to the illustrated edition of the novel, one a quotation from Khushwant Singh and the other from Margaret Bourke-White, capture their differentiated aims in their respective texts which have been yoked together in this edition – one a fictional novel and the other a commissioned portfolio of photographs, both on the Partition of India. Here I quote them in their entirety:

> Then life in Mano Majra is stilled, save for the dogs barking at the trains that pass in the night. It had always been so, until the summer of 1947. (Khushwant Singh)

> With the coming of Independence to India the world had the chance to watch a most rare event in the history of nations: the birth of twins – India and Pakistan. It was a birth accompanied by strife and suffering. (Margaret Bourke-White)

Singh's words gesture toward a brief moment in the summer of 1947 that shattered the stillness of a tiny village known more than anything else for the trains that passed through it. In its brevity and astute use of the word "stilled" on which the entire phrase turns, Singh powerfully conveys a watershed moment in Mano Majra's otherwise inconsequential history when the stillness of village life was transformed into the stillness of death and desolation. Bourke-White's words, in contrast, stand witness to a pivotal moment in the history of modern India and its violently conceived twin, Pakistan. Her tone is far more optimistic than Singh's, framing the moment as a rare birth, a new dawn for not one but two nations, the acknowledgment of "strife and suffering" almost an afterthought. Ironically, the strife and suffering is caused by the very event that Bourke-White sees as rare and celebratory, the birth of twins, not merely the independence of India. Perhaps it is this contrast in the aims of the two artists that makes the yoking of their work, the one in the purported service of the other, so problematic.

Pramod Kapoor's selection, arrangement, and captions for Margaret Bourke-White's photographs in the anniversary edition merit some discussion. Kapoor's selected images seem to fall into a few broad categories – images of trains that evoke Singh's title in rather obvious ways, images that might remind us of characters in the novel, and finally (and these are the most numerous) images of death. The photographs are interspersed throughout the text with no clear logic or purpose. The cover image is a predictable choice designed to visualize the title of Singh's novel – it is an image of two

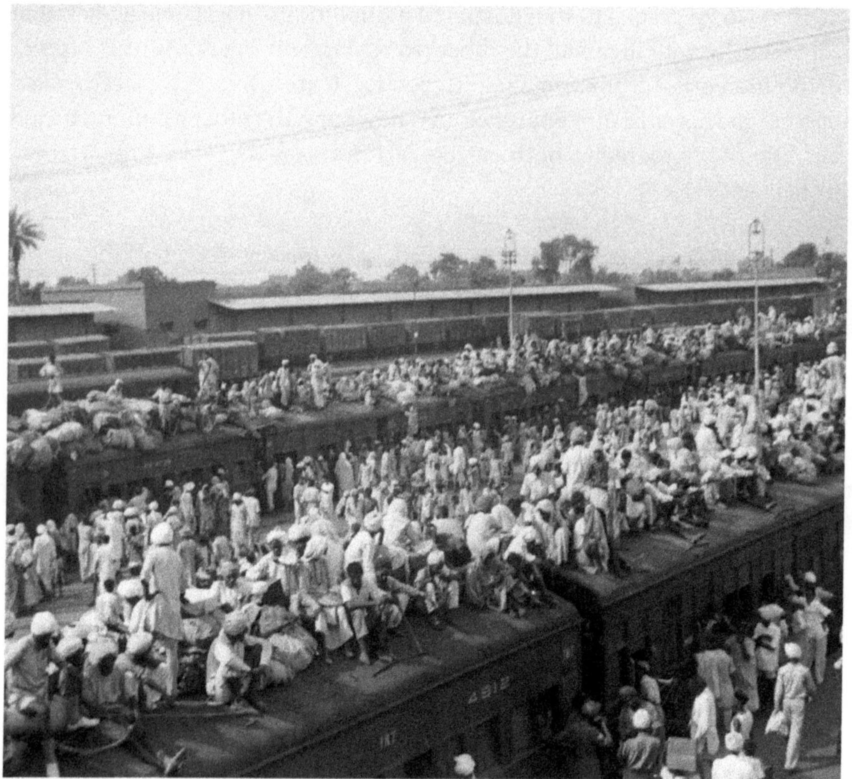

Figure 3. Margaret Bourke-White/Getty Images

trains packed to the rafters carrying people, as the caption announces, "to their new homeland balanced precariously on the roofs of trains" (Figure 3).

This seeming desire to "match" text and image governs much of the edition and appears driven by Kapoor's desire to underscore the novel's realism. However, somewhat contradictorily, Kapoor adopts a rather fluid approach to providing captions for the images he has chosen. Some of the captions are quotations from Singh's novel, others are quotations from Bourke-White's book *Halfway to Freedom*, and still others are remarks made by Vicki Goldberg, Bourke-White's biographer, or editorial commentary by Kapoor himself. A few of the captions remain unattributed to a source, mainly those included alongside the introductions by Kapoor and Singh before the novel begins. There is no clear indication as to what determines the source of a particular caption. However, Kapoor seems driven by the instinct to establish some recognition of Singh's novel in Bourke-White's photographs and vice versa, an instinct propelled by his belief that the novel and images "were made for each other" (2006: xvi). For example, one of the early images is that of a town called Miya Mir. It is a double-page image of the village landscape.

Miya Mir is cut through by railway tracks and a mosque is visible in the distance. A couple of engines sit on the tracks; on either side, we can see a barren and desolate landscape. The caption begins with a quotation from the novel introducing Singh's locale, Mano Majra: "All of northern India was in arms, in terror, or in hiding. The only remaining oases of peace were a scatter of little villages lost in the remote reaches of the frontier. One of these villages was Mano Majra." The quotation ends but the caption includes another sentence, presumably Kapoor's own: "Miya Mir is not very different from the fictional village Mano Majra" (4). This forced suturing of Miya Mir's verisimilitude captured in Bourke-White's photo of the village with the fictionality of Mano Majra does not withstand simple scrutiny. The image fails to show the river Sutlej which, we are told on the next page, runs half a mile from Mano Majra. Nor can we see the magnificent railroad bridge, "its eighteen enormous spans sweep like waves from one pier to another" (4) that lies a mile north of Mano Majra. Also absent is the "colony of shopkeepers and hawkers" that has grown up alongside the station selling various consumables to travelers. The "appearance of constant activity" emphasized in Singh's description of the station is completely lacking in the photograph, which does not include any people at all in a rather desolate-looking Miya Mir. Kapoor's attempt to give Singh's novel a veneer of realism by using Bourke-White's images becomes even more egregious a few pages later, when the portrait of a young Sikh man carrying a shovel on his shoulder is captioned using Singh's words from the novel: "You must remember Juggut Singh. He is like a stud bull" (17). This particular coupling of text and image invites us to suspend our disbelief and believe that the man we are seeing on the left is in fact Juggut Singh from the novel.

The adducing of photographic evidence to bolster the "realism" of Singh's novel by combining the images with quotations from the latter is completely abandoned at other points, when Kapoor uses captions acquired from Bourke-White's writings. Quoting one of the most eminent chroniclers of India's Partition in this way firmly reorients us in the real world outside of Singh's novel and often at some distance from it, as in the inclusion of Bourke-White's image of a young man sitting "on the walls of Purana Qila transformed into a vast refugee camp in Delhi" (253). Kapoor often includes captions in which Bourke-White refers to herself in the first person and speaks of her experience documenting the Partition, though not necessarily the particular image in question. Even these attempts often seem like an inauthentic tethering, as in the image of an overcrowded refugee camp whose caption quotes Bourke-White recalling her encounter with a rich Muslim woman who had hurriedly thrown her jewelry into a well in her former home in Amritsar when forced to flee and later tried desperately to cross the border to retrieve them. The inclusion of images depicting scenes and locales completely unconnected to Singh's novel, along with the strong authorial presence of Bourke-White over these images, has the jarring effect of drawing us away from the narrative and even underscoring its fictionality rather than heightening its realism. Susan Sontag asserts that the "caption of a photograph is traditionally neutral, informative: a date, a place, names." Anything more than that she considers unnecessary because "unless there's been some tampering or misrepresenting, it is the truth" (2004: 41). Although she concedes that all photographs, including documentary ones, are framed, she still finds photography's assertion of truth compelling. Pramod Kapoor's rather free appropriation of Bourke-White's images within the pages of Singh's novel and his use of lengthy narrative captions articulated in a variety of voices confuses genres, resulting in a tendentious effect that confounds sentiment and cognition.

The text and images work most at cross-purposes in their depiction of death. In his novel Singh deftly used one of the most iconic symbols of Partition literature, also echoed in its title – the train. During the Partition, the largest single displacement of people in history, trains carried well over a million Hindus and Sikhs to India from Pakistan within a span of four months. There was a complementary journey of similar magnitude in the other direction, carrying Muslim refugees to Pakistan. Contrary to all that trains might represent – progress, modernity, convenience – many of the Partition trains quickly turned into death trains. Members of one community attacked the passengers of the other and butchered them in large numbers. Marian Aguiar reads the migration trains of Partition as symbolic nation spaces, "a national, secular space that could transcend the religious difference that now manifested itself in violence" (2008: 75). However, she quickly adds that these trains were far from safe spaces; they lacked protection and the guards on board had their own communal allegiances, often standing by as silent spectators when violence erupted. Singh uses references to trains throughout the novel to suggest the gradual degeneration from a unified and harmonious society to one torn apart by communal violence of the worst kind. Although the train in Singh's title refers specifically to the final train in the novel headed for Pakistan carrying Mano Majra's Muslims, trains play an important role from the beginning. Mano Majra is a tiny village and even though most trains do not even stop there, it "has always been known for its railway station" (6). A single stationmaster, who sells and collects tickets, and his attendant, operate the entire station. As if mimicking the journeys of the death trains that will haunt Mano Majra's landscape later in the novel, we are told early that the only two trains to stop for a few minutes in the village are "one from Delhi to Lahore in the mornings and the other from Lahore to Delhi in the evenings" (7). The trains shape Mano Majra's daily routine. The village awakens before dawn as the mail train passes through on its way to Lahore; the 10.30 a.m. train goes through when people are busy with their work; the midday express reminds them of their lunch and siesta break. With the evening train, everyone returns to work and finally when the goods train passes, "It is like saying Goodnight" (9). In the brief prelude to the novel, Singh introduces to us the way in which the trains that pass through the village every day shape Mano Majra's identity and daily routine. The village identity articulated in terms of the railway is an idealized one. Singh is sure to mention the mullah making his call to prayer when the early morning mail train passes, followed by the Sikh priest, and the day ends in similar fashion with the last call to prayer by the mullah and the priest timed according to the last goods train. The village represents Muslim-Sikh unity and harmony until later in the novel, when interested parties stoke communal hatred. This tragic turning point in Mano Majra's history is subtly foretold at the end of this prelude with a line that is also used as one of the illustrated edition's epigraphs: "Then life in Mano Majra is stilled, save for the dogs barking at the trains that pass in the night. It had always been so, until the summer of 1947" (9).

As the novel progresses, the schedule of the trains begins to change, throwing off the temporal sequence of life in Mano Majra. We are told that after Partition, the trains run four or five hours late "and sometimes as many as twenty" (51). "People stayed in bed late" and "Children did not know when to be hungry" (120). The trains were now packed with refugees crossing the border from one country into the other. The trains that reminded the villagers of their daily routine suddenly became spectral: "There was something uneasy about it. It had a ghostly quality" (120). The first ghost train came from Pakistan laden with bodies and was set alight in Mano Majra, filling the air with "a faint acrid smell of searing flesh" (127).

There are no direct descriptions of death scenes in Singh's novel. Minor characters like the sub-inspector report the death trains without providing great detail: "There wasn't very much left – just a big heap of ashes and bones" (141). The horror of the trains is implied but never articulated. There seems to be no need for such articulation since, "They all knew. They had known it all the time. The answer was implicit in the fact that the train had come from Pakistan" (127–128). The nightmare of magistrate and deputy commissioner of Mano Majra, Hukum Chand, conveys the most vivid description of the horror of these trains. He has always been obsessed with death; his helplessness and inability to prevent the violence haunt him. Although a staunch believer in the inevitability of death and even a fatalist by nature, Hukum Chand finds death by massacre difficult to stomach. On the day that Mano Majra receives its second death train, Hukum Chand returns home exhausted and falls asleep only to have the worst nightmares torment him. He sees "a man holding his intestines," "lavatories jammed with corpses of young men" amid "the nauseating smell of putrefying flesh, faeces and urine" (129). He finally wakes up when he imagines an old man stretching out a cold hand grotesquely to grab his foot. Though Singh provides very detailed descriptions of the train massacres in these pages, in a sense they do not seem "real" since they are filtered through the magistrate's consciousness. We hear about the increase in deaths and the death trains being set alight; with the advent of the monsoons, Hukum Chand imagines "a thousand charred corpses sizzling and smoking while the rain put out the fire" (139).

Toward the end of the novel, the frequency and number of death trains arriving in Mano Majra seem to increase. As if these were not enough, the stretch of the Sutlej flowing through the village becomes filled with bloated corpses from a massacre somewhere upstream. The villagers see bodies of the murdered victims in various forms of decay. In these pages, we witness by far the most horrific scenes of the novel. A child with a hole at the back of his head, women with slashed breasts and torn bellies, limbless bodies floating down the river (202). The section ends with yet another death train from Pakistan. By now, the villagers know what to expect but after setting alight a number of these corpse-filled trains, they are left with no more oil and the remaining wood is wet from the rain. This time they dig a fifty-yard-long trench and bury the bodies in it, transporting them from the train in canvas stretchers all day long. As if trying to restore some semblance of dignity in death, two "soldiers were left to guard the grave from the depredations of jackals and badgers" (203).

Fourteen pages of Margaret Bourke-White's images follow this section; the darkest in the novel, all of them capturing the death of Partition's countless refugees. In these images, we see evidence of bloated bodies floating in shallow waters in various states of decay, corpses with their eyes wide open as if they might sit up at any moment, detached limbs and piles of bodies being set alight. Again, Kapoor mixes the captions of these images, sometimes using Bourke-White's words and at other times Singh's words from the novel. In a series of six images that conclude this section, Kapoor uses Singh's words from various parts of the novel as captions to recreate the various death scenes visually. These are scenes of mass cremation with "red tongues of flame" leaping into the sky and the "acrid smell of searing flesh" or the digging of a fifty-yard-long trench to be filled with bodies and covered in earth. Undeniably, Singh's words accurately "match" Bourke-White's images, but to see it simply as a matching exercise would be to misread Singh's novel and naively yoke together text and images with starkly conflicting purposes. Bourke-White's aim in these photographs is to capture the anonymity and indignity of the mass deaths. Singh's aim in the novel is quite different. He uses the anonymous, meaningless deaths to lead up to a single heroic, purposeful one: that of Juggut Singh, who sacrifices his life to save the last train to Pakistan in the novel's melodramatic climax. The climactic moment of the novel delineates a death that is heroic and sacrificial. The death of a single, unexpectedly heroic figure then becomes emblematic of the strength of interethnic bonds even in the face of almost-genocidal communal violence. In Bourke-White's images, on the contrary, death is very real in all its horror and putrefaction. It is inescapable and unrelenting in scale.

The concluding pages of Singh's novel bring to the forefront the single moral question that dominated the tit-for-tat journeys of the countless death trains in both directions: was a massacre ever justified? Hukum Chand, the Hindu magistrate, and Jugga Singh, the village "badmash" (scoundrel), both are romantically involved with Muslim women. While Hukum Chand's interest in an underage prostitute is exploitative and somewhat disturbing, Jugga is in love with Nooran, the daughter of the village mullah, Imam Baksh, an even-tempered, wise, and generous man. Nooran, we know, is carrying Jugga's child but she is forced to leave Mano Majra with the other Muslim villagers because of the danger to their lives. Malli[2] and his gang have plotted to intercept the train and massacre all the passengers. Aware of this plan, Hukum Chand has masterminded Jugga's release from prison, hoping that he might do something to prevent the carnage moved by his love for Nooran. Hukum Chand's risky wager pays off when Jugga climbs the bridge to cut the rope that has been tied there to derail the train as it passes through. He is shot at as he attempts to slash the rope but is successful in the very last minute as the "rope snapped in the centre as he fell" but the "train went over him, and went on to Pakistan" (263). In the pages leading up to this climax, Hukum Chand

[2] Leader of a local band of young men who frequently rob the villagers and turn to violence in the wake of the Partition.

begins to doubt the effectiveness of his plan. In his moment of doubt, he recalls the stories of two of his acquaintances, Sundari the daughter of his orderly and Sunder Singh who had worked for Hukum Chand before being recruited by the army. Both were brutally massacred on trains – Sundari traveling with her husband, Mansa Ram, four days after their wedding, and Sunder stranded on a death train with his family in 115-degree heat. He fed his children his own urine to keep them alive and when that dried up, he shot his wife and two infant children only for the train to begin moving. Hukum Chand's recollection of these terrifying and heartbreaking stories function only to somewhat assuage his rising anxiety that the train to Pakistan may not be saved. If that turned out to be the case, he could tell himself that Malli and his gang were justified in their massacre, that it was simply an act of retaliation for the deaths of Sundari and Sunder Singh (both names interestingly mean "beautiful") and hundreds more like them. The false morality of this is immediately apparent to him and, wracked by guilt and longing for the child prostitute, Hukum Chand "raised his face to the sky and began to pray" (261).

There are no obvious heroes in *Train to Pakistan.* With the brave act of ultimate sacrifice, Juggut Singh is catapulted to heroic status on the penultimate page, but Singh depicts him as hotheaded and lacking in intelligence throughout the novel. Similarly, Hukum Chand, who arranges for the release of Jugga and Iqbal Singh in the hope that either one of them will take action to prevent the massacre, is a tormented man whose lecherous desire for the child prostitute evokes disgust in the reader. Yet we see him in moments of vulnerability and deep self-awareness, we learn about the death of his young children and, despite what we may think of him, we are told that he is neither corrupt nor immoral (131). Meet Singh and Imam Baksh, the village's Sikh priest and mullah of the village mosque, respectively, are honorable and simple men who cannot stem the tide of violence despite their position of authority.

This lack of heroism in the novel is a deliberate choice on Singh's part – it serves to both underscore the ordinariness of the lives depicted and to throw into relief Jugga's unexpected heroism. Though these characters are not heroic in any way, Singh portrays them in fine detail and they remain etched in the reader's memory. In contrast, little from Margaret Bourke-White's photos appended to the novel is memorable in any comparable way. The overriding impression they leave is that of the horror and the grotesque nature of the violence of Partition. Death in her images is putrid and repulsive, while in Singh's novel, death is what makes Jugga Singh heroic and memorable.

Returning to Judith Butler's assertion that narrative enables us to understand while photographs simply haunt us and fail to evoke pathos in the way narrative does, I conclude that the bringing together of both forms in the fiftieth anniversary edition of Khushwant Singh's *Train to Pakistan* fails to deliver the hoped-for affective import. Not only that, the evidentiary force of Margaret Bourke-White's photographs serves to contradict the fictionality of the novel while her gruesome depiction of death works at cross-purposes to Singh's elevation of the ordinary to heroic proportions via death. Bourke-White leaves us with images of decaying corporeality while Singh's novel leaves us with memories of ordinary characters who become heroes through tragic destiny. In the final analysis, Singh's characters seem far more grievable than Bourke-White's subjects.

2

# Optics of Blindness: Countervisuality in Michael Ondaatje's *Anil's Ghost*

## Introduction

In his book *The Right to Look* (2011), Nicholas Mirzoeff somewhat contradictorily urges us to think with and against visuality. He explains this contradiction by suggesting that visuality preceded the authority that comes with looking. Visuality, or what Mirzoeff calls the right to look, claims autonomy. However, this autonomy runs counter to the authority that comes with looking, an authority that Mirzoeff reminds us is falsely rendered natural. We might think of Margaret Bourke-White's documentary gaze, which I have critiqued in Chapter 1, as this kind of visuality with an almost preordained sense of authority. Visuality, as a discursive practice with material effects, Mirzoeff argues, functions by classifying, segregating, and organizing; the refusal to be classified and segregated in this manner is crucial to claiming autonomy and ultimately to democratic politics. Countervisuality in Mirzoeff's sense is therefore an act of countering existing realisms with alternative ones and "democratizing democracy" (2011: 5). For him, these countervisualities are not necessarily visual and particularly are not "a simple or mimetic depiction of lived experience" – a phrase that might be used to define photography. In this chapter, I argue that Michael Ondaatje's novel *Anil's Ghost* (2000) uses the absent presence of photography to suggest a powerful politics of countervisuality in order to propose alternative ways of seeing in the postcolonial era. The novel's historical context of the Sri Lankan civil war and its unspeakable traumas provides the perfect opportunity to propose alternative visualities that are not necessarily based on the visual but on a powerful interfacing of the visual and the intuitive or even the spiritual. Ondaatje's protagonist, the forensic scientist Anil Tissera, represents the authority of visuality, overly reliant on her technological devices and confident in her ability to excavate and represent the truth; however, Ondaatje powerfully suggests that alternative visualities are necessary in order to record postcolonial truths. These visualities must be grounded in situated knowledges and not in the simple, evidentiary bases of Anil's visuality.

The inherently paradoxical nature of photography has probably been most effectively conveyed in recent times by Shawn Michelle Smith, who takes us to "the edge of sight" (2013) by suggesting the revelations as well as the limitations of the medium. While photography significantly enlarged our vision by enabling us to see more, in doing so it also heightened our awareness of how much went unseen. It gestured toward the vast realms that would forever remain invisible to us despite the revelations of photography. Smith describes this as "the sense of the unseen that photography introduces" (2013: 6). Photography not only reduced our confidence in our own vision but also attributed the blind spots of human vision to those of the mind, both the physical and the cultural or what Kracauer describes as things that "habit and prejudice prevent us from noticing" (1997: 53). Other scholars have also emphasized photography's ability to expose what our cultural biases and the blind spots of our mind prevent us from seeing. James Elkins argues that "photography also always shows us things we would have preferred not to see, or don't want to see, don't know how to see or don't know how to acknowledge seeing" (2011: 98). Elizabeth Abel concurs, claiming that photography allows for a more "democratic signifying field" because it shows us what "the mind's eye chooses not to see" (2010: 79). While I have no argument with these viewpoints privileging the perspective of the spectator of photographs, they arise from the belief that the camera eye works independently of the human eye behind the camera. Once we acknowledge that this is not necessarily always the case, we must also immediately acknowledge the influence that "habit and prejudice" may have on ways of looking through the camera. Therefore, I do not entirely agree with Smith's claim that the "camera sees beyond the physical and cultural limitations of sight" (2013: 7). With its superior technical accuracy, it may be able to see beyond the physical limitations of the human eye, but the cultural limitations as well as advantages of the latter create other ways of seeing that may or may not be limiting. In fact, I would go so far as to say that the cultural limitations of sight may in some cases influence what the camera sees, as was the case under colonialism when it was used as a disciplinary apparatus in the service of the colonial enterprise. As recent postcolonial and feminist scholars engaging with photography have demonstrated in response to its use as a technology of surveillance or oppression, photography also allows for resistance to such categories of domination through slippages and disruption. In this chapter, I wish to move beyond Smith's edge of sight to the place where, instead of "habit and prejudice," we have situated knowledge that allows for localized ways of seeing. In the face of this kind of sight, photography that clinically sees beyond the "cultural limitations" of sight becomes inadequate and of limited use. The Mirzoeffian countervisuality necessary to record postcolonial truths must, I argue, abandon clinical, technologically advanced, and purportedly neutral but culturally uninformed ways of seeing. Through his use of the absent presence of photography in *Anil's Ghost*, Ondaatje pits these two ways of looking against each other with his eponymous protagonist representing the clinical, photographic eye unencumbered by culture or history while Sarath Diyasena represents a way of looking imbued deeply with cultural and historical knowledge.

*Anil's Ghost* is the story of Anil Tissera, a Sri Lankan-born, Western-educated forensic expert who returns to her homeland to investigate possible atrocities committed by the government. In Ondaatje's novel, as a Westernized, diasporic individual, Anil replicates the Eurocentric view of historical trauma. By making his protagonist something of an outsider and by further aligning her gaze to the Western gaze and the supposedly "objective" camera eye, Ondaatje complicates the notions of witnessing, historical/political truth, testimonial, and representation. This chapter seeks to explore the ways in which photography and the visual complicate Ondaatje's themes of trauma, truth, and testimony. I argue that Ondaatje proposes several modes of seeing in this novel. He aligns the photographic eye with a Western notion of documentation and truth-telling that, he argues, fails in the context of postcolonial trauma which calls for a more localized, grounded, intuitive, and even spiritual way of seeing. Following Walter Benjamin and Shawn Michelle Smith, I call this alternate visuality the "optics of blindness," contradictorily a blind seeing, or a way of intuitively apprehending the truth.

One of the first sentences spoken by Anil is, "I just want to look" (9), thereby underscoring the importance of visuality in the novel. We are told a couple of pages later that Anil "had now lived abroad long enough to interpret Sri Lanka with a long-distance gaze" (11), the repetition of "long" suggesting her remoteness, both physical and emotional, from her native country. Ondaatje's emphasis on the vocabulary of sight while referring to Anil suggests the dominating power of her gaze. Hers is a qualified gaze, one that holds back, without comment or emotional investment. Albeit fictional, Anil Tissera, the photographer in this chapter, like Margaret Bourke-White in Chapter 1, is also rendered ineffectual in bearing witness to historical atrocities. Anil, armed with her forensic tools and her camera, is the only character in this novel unaffected by the civil war in Sri Lanka and therefore a seemingly neutral observer. Writing about the rendering of international justice to victims of postcolonial trauma such as the war in Sri Lanka, Suvendrini Perera questions the "structures and identities that enable their entry into global perceptibility" (2015: 5). She argues that seemingly neutral humanitarian organizations representing the international community, such as the United Nations, are often invested in the maintenance of a "necro-geopolitical order" (20) that continues to determine the visibility or invisibility of bodies. Using Eyal Weizman's focus on the "technological continuum" (qtd. in Perera 2015: 17) between military violence and the technologies used to assess that violence, she reminds us that such processes are rarely neutral. Employed by the Centre for Human Rights in Geneva as a forensic anthropologist, Anil is already considered an outsider. She is allowed to work in Sri Lanka by the local government only if she teams up with local officials. She is assigned to work with Sarath Diyasena, an archaeologist in Colombo. In terms of their respective professions, this is an "odd pairing" (17) that makes sense only in the context of Sri Lanka's extrajudicial executions, where hundreds of people disappeared daily before their bodies were found buried or burned beyond recognition. Sarath and Anil work together to try to identify a suspected victim of torture from a skeleton that has been found in an ancient excavation site but clearly does not belong with the other bodies buried there. Through Sarath, Anil meets several people, all touched by the war. These include the blind and wizened Palipana, who has retreated to live an ascetic life in the forest; Sarath's brother Gamini, a doctor who has treated innumerable victims of the war working in the most appalling conditions; and Ananda, an alcoholic sculptor who is forever changed by the disappearance and presumed death of his wife Sirissa in the war. All these characters are connected with visuality in different ways. Though blind, Sarath's former teacher, the erudite Palipana, continues to write, imparting his wisdom; Gamini ascribes the cause of death to unidentified bodies by first looking at photographs of the bodies and then examining them; and Ananda is an artificer tasked with reconstructing the head of the skeleton they have named "Sailor." Establishing Sailor's identity becomes crucial to Anil's mission in Sri Lanka. Sarath's strategy of having Sailor's head reconstructed from his skull by the temperamental artificer frustrates Anil. The novel gradually develops a tension between Anil's and Sarath's different approaches to their task; this tension, I argue, is based on different notions of visuality. In the novel's conclusion, Sarath pays the ultimate price and in doing so proves the efficacy of his approach. Despite Anil's scientific knowledge and astute sense of forensic science, her approach proves to be inadequate given the complex realities of postcolonial Sri Lanka.

Photography is a recurring motif in much of Ondaatje's work. At least two of his novels have chapters with the word "Photograph" or "Photography" in the title – the one-and-a-half-page chapter in his 2007 novel *Divisadero* called "The Photographs" (187–188) and the chapter called "Photograph" in *Running in the Family* accompanied by the ironic picture of his parents enacting "What we think of married life" (1982: 161–163). Elsewhere he has commented that the starting points of his books have often been images. There is the blank picture of Billy the Kid in his verse novel of the same name or that of the patient with his "burnt out body" in *The English Patient.* Therefore, whether it is a real photograph reproduced within the pages of his novel, a blank photograph, or a narrated image, photographs occupy an important place in Ondaatje's repertoire. Although photographs do not feature in a significant way in *Anil's Ghost,* I would argue that in a novel so preoccupied with trauma, witnessing, and truth in the postcolonial context, the passing references to photographs and photography are rich with meaning.

## Anil Tissera's "long-distance gaze"

The postcolonial civil war depicted in Michael Ondaatje's *Anil's Ghost* raged in Sri Lanka from the mid-1980s to the early 1990s; the war arose from a complicated history of inter-ethnic tension and violence that both predated colonialism and was exacerbated by it. Despite Ondaatje's own insistence that "the book isn't just about Sri Lanka; it could be Guatemala or Bosnia or Ireland" (in Jaggi 2004: 253) and his assertion that he did "backflips" to avoid having it "taken as representative" (251), several geographical, linguistic, and cultural details locate the reader specifically in a postcolonial Sri Lanka grappling with ethnic violence and its traumatic aftermaths. Into this scene, Ondaatje inserts his protagonist Anil Tissera, a forensic scientist and a returnee to Sri Lanka after a period of fifteen years and an advocate for a United Nations human rights organization in Geneva. She teams up with Sarath, a local archaeologist assigned by the government to work with her. Together they unearth the remains of a recent killing in a government-protected burial site in Bandarawela. Anil's quest to establish the identity of the skeleton they name "Sailor" drives the story. Contrasted with Sarath's gaze, as a Westernized outsider with little emotional connection to Sri Lanka, Anil replicates a Western gaze in the novel. Sarath is skeptical of Anil's Western training and worries that she will be as useless as "one of those journalists who file reports about flies and scabs while staying at the Galle Face Hotel" (44). When Sarath insists that she have a look at some bones recently excavated from a sixth-century monastic site, Anil is annoyed at their irrelevance – "she hadn't come here to deal with the Middle Ages" (20). Yet she realizes very quickly that one of the bone fragments is in fact contemporary, suggesting that someone is using the ancient site to conceal the remains of recent victims and since this is a site constantly surveilled by the police, the government's responsibility is indisputable. Anil herself strongly identifies with the West. When her Western lover Cullis asks her whether her background is Sinhalese, she says, "I live here ... in the West" (36, ellipses in original). Her Western education and her love of Western literature shape her outlook on life. Trained as a scientist, she thinks in classificatory terms – for her, truth is real and certifiable in bodies and bones.

Not only is Anil's gaze aligned or identified with that of the Western gaze, Ondaatje also likens her gaze to that of the camera. As the Westernized outsider, she has the power to document, but also to stop that documentation. Sarath's brother Gamini remarks dismissively:

> American movies, English books – remember how they all end? [...] the American or the Englishman gets on a plane and leaves. That's it. The camera leaves with him [...] He's going home. So the war, to all purposes, is over. That's enough reality for the West. It's probably the history of the last two hundred years of Western, political writing. Go home. Write a book, hit the circuit. (285–286)

In this scathing criticism of the Western perspective, Gamini alludes to the limitations as well as the power of the Western viewpoint in narrating non-Western histories. In these few lines, he utterly dismisses all that shapes Anil's intellectual universe – American movies, English books, Western political writing. As Margaret Scanlan has argued, "Her story, then, has the potential limits of one of those films shot from the perspective of an English or American visitor to a violent Third World country" (2004: 305).

Early in the novel, Anil is introduced to us when she arrives in Colombo and a local UN worker receives her. Her otherness is immediately evident as she excuses herself from conversing with the man during the ride into town by saying, "*Look*, do you mind if I don't talk in the car on the way into Colombo – I'm jet-lagged. I just want to *look*. Maybe drink some toddy before it gets too late" (9, emphasis added). The man laughs at her use of the word "toddy" and comments, "First thing after fifteen years. Return of the prodigal," to which Anil curtly replies, "I'm not a prodigal" (10). Her extravagant tastes and the power of her "look" immediately mark her as the outsider with the privileged but remote gaze.

The first reference to a photograph comes on the very same page when Anil, a champion swimmer, recalls a photograph of her at the age of sixteen that was published in *The Observer* after she had won a two-mile swimming race. "The photographer had caught Anil's tired smile in the photograph, her right arm bent up to tear off her rubber swimming cap, some out-of-focus stragglers (she had once known who they were). The black-and-white picture had remained an icon in the family for too long" (11). Everything about the photo is outdated and irrelevant to Anil's current life – its black-and-white agedness, the stragglers she has long forgotten, and its false iconic status in her family. Similar to the irrelevance and nonexistence of the photo, which she only recalls in her memory, Sri Lanka too has become irrelevant to Anil. Although it is a photo from her adolescence and might evoke some sense of nostalgia in her for a childhood spent in Sri Lanka, she feels no connection to it. Surprisingly though, a few pages later, when she first meets Sarath, he identifies her as "the swimmer," aligning her with the girl from the photo. Anil is determined to put a distance between the self portrayed in the photo and her current self. She clashes with Sarath in this, their very first meeting: "The swimming was a long time ago" (16). When Sarath persists in establishing a connection from the past by saying that they went to the same school, she says, "Mr. Diyasena ... let's not mention swimming again, okay? A lot of blood under the bridge since then" (16, ellipses in original), her slight alteration of the idiomatic expression no doubt intended to underscore the significance of her mission. The indexicality of the absent photograph serves to freeze an image of Anil from a time shortly before her departure from Sri Lanka, a country she left at the age of eighteen. The memory of the photograph establishes her connection with Sri Lanka and her past, a connection she has mostly severed and is not keen to re-establish: "The island no longer held her by the past" (11). So while establishing her ties with Sri Lanka, the photo also simultaneously fixes her as being out of touch, far removed from the events, like the Anil captured in the photo. She feels no emotional connection to the island and positions herself as someone who had "now lived abroad long enough to interpret Sri Lanka with a long-distance gaze" (11). Her vision, likened to the photographic eye, is then contrasted throughout the novel with an alternative vision, complex and more sincere, that relies on local, situated knowledges, on absences and suggestions, rather than the fixity and assuredness of Anil's photographic vision, which proves to be utterly inadequate in documenting Sri Lanka's postcolonial trauma.

Albeit inadequate, Anil's gaze is a privileged one with the power to document. This is obvious in a scene early in the novel, set not in Sri Lanka but instead in Miami. This is from the time when Anil, working with a forensic team in Guatemala, flew to visit her boyfriend Cullis in Miami. She wakes up naked in the hotel room next to the sleeping Cullis, instinctively pulls out from her travel bag a "secondhand television camera that the forensic team used"; she inserts a cassette and begins to film. This is a playful scene as Anil moves around the room, naked and wet from the shower, filming various objects, the sleeping Cullis, and even her own reflection in the bathroom mirror:

> She began with the room, then returned to the bathroom [...] A close-up of the texture of the towels [...] She stood on the bed and shot down at Cullis's sleeping head, his left arm out to where she had been all night beside him [...] his mouth, his lovely ribs [...] down to his ankles. Walked backwards to take in their clothes on the floor, and then to the table to his notebook. Close-up on his writing. She then removed the cassette from the machine and buried it under some clothes in his suitcase. (35)

Seemingly, this is a playful and romantic scene depicting Anil creating for Cullis a snapshot of their relationship. Presumably, he will be surprised to find this cassette in his suitcase but then delighted to see the film on it. It will make him fondly recall the brief romantic interlude he shared with Anil in the Miami hotel room. Anil's action is reminiscent of Susan Sontag quoting Diane Arbus, who said, "I always thought of photography as a naughty thing to do – that was one of my favorite things about it" (Sontag 1977: 12). Sontag agrees, suggesting that the naughtiness of the act arises from the "disreputable, taboo, marginal" nature of the subject. Sontag goes on to claim that

> using a camera is not a very good way of getting at someone sexually [...] The camera doesn't rape, or even possess, though it may presume, intrude, trespass, distort, exploit, and, at the farthest reach of metaphor, assassinate – all activities that, unlike the sexual push and shove, can be conducted from a distance, and with some detachment. (13)

This brings me to what I see as deeply disturbing and intrusive about this scene. The naked, camera-toting Anil conveys a hybrid image of vulnerability and authority, the latter coming solely from the oversized camera on her shoulders and her power to wield this while the unsuspecting Cullis sleeps. It is no mere coincidence that a forensic team uses the camera in question. With it, Anil is documenting her relationship with Cullis, collecting indisputable evidence of this rendezvous.

Through this early scene, Ondaatje subtly establishes the power of photography to document and provide evidence. The detached and exploitative nature of Anil's act undermines any suggested sexual playfulness of this scene. It is hardly surprising therefore that her and Cullis's relationship ends in another hotel room like this one on the opposite coast (in Borrega Springs, California) when Anil stabs him in the arm and leaves him bleeding while she calmly packs her belongings and waits for the taxi that will take her away from him. Ondaatje writes, "Their romance had been a long intimacy that had existed mostly in secrecy, the good-bye was quick and fatal" (101). This scene is strangely reminiscent of another in Ondaatje's earlier novel *The English Patient* where the spy Caravaggio enters a woman's room to steal her camera. The woman had taken pictures of German officers at a party, capturing Caravaggio in one. Wanting to remove evidence of his presence, he enters her room completely naked so as not to leave any print and in order to be completely quiet. In both scenes, photography's evidentiary power is foregrounded. In *Anil's Ghost,* Anil's outsider status, her diasporic location, her Westernized outlook, her privileged gaze, and the power of photography to document create a complex concatenation which brings to the fore the limitations and contradictions of bearing witness to historical trauma.

## The Truth

Ondaatje's novel takes up the greater philosophical question of what constitutes truth in the recording of a conflict. The professions of both main characters of the novel, Sarath the archaeologist and Anil the forensic expert, are endeavors that enable us to arrive at the truth. However, an atmosphere of deep distrust pervades the novel. Anil is distrusting of Sarath until the very end, when she realizes that he has saved her life and paid for it with his own. She feels that there is a slipperiness and unreliability to truth in Sri Lanka: "A paranoid is someone with all the facts, the joke went. Maybe this was the only truth here" (54). This destabilizes her, knocking her confidence, and ironically she feels more "completed abroad" (54) than she does returning to her own country. In her discussion of *Anil's Ghost* Teresa Derrickson has argued that it "troubles the idea that the 'truth' of human rights violations is both, on the one hand, *discoverable,* and, on the other hand, *desirable*" (2004: 132, emphasis added). Minoli Salgado detects in the novel a tension between "exploring *truth as a register of conformity to fact*s (or truth as a register of objective veracity) and *truth as a marker of allegiance to faith* (or truth as a register of subjective interpretation)" (Salgado 2013: 212, emphasis original). Extending this idea, I argue that the avowed objectivity of photography, undercut by its uncertain truth-value, allows Ondaatje to use it effectively to communicate the particular quality of truth in the context of the Sri Lankan conflict and to suggest that we need alternative visions to decipher and record this truth. Anil's Western training, which has stood her in good stead on her travels elsewhere, is useless in Sri Lanka, where "she realized she was moving with only one arm of language among uncertain laws and a fear that was everywhere [...] Truth bounced between gossip and vengeance. Rumor slipped into every car and barbershop" (54). Contrasted with Anil's notion of "permanent truths, same for Colombo as for Troy," we get Sarath's assertion that "it's different here. Dangerous. Sometimes law is on the side of power, not truth" (44) and Palipana's "We have never had the truth [...] Most of the time in our world, truth is just opinion" (102). Both men emphasize the connection between locationality and truth, and consequently locational knowledge is imperative in unearthing these truths. Although a skilled forensic scientist, Anil lacks such knowledge. For example, we learn that Palipana deciphered ancient runes "not with a historical text but with the pragmatic awareness of *locally inherited* skills" (82, emphasis added). Ondaatje further underscores Palipana's skillful visuality: "His eyes recognized how a fault line in a rock wall might have insisted on the composure of a painted shoulder" (82). This kind of visuality is essentially different from the photographic eye that can only report what it captures, not what subtle implications lie behind the capture. The power of Palipana's blindness is described as a "potent sightlessness" (97) or a seeing blindness.

Photography in general, and colonial photography in particular, has a fraught relationship with truth. Established analyses of colonial photographs have demonstrated the Orientalist and othering nature of much of colonial photography. The ideological impulses of colonialism produce such discourses and seek to establish a binary worldview where the West is in a privileged and powerful position. Writing about the massive, eight-volume ethnographic book *The People of India*, which contains almost 500 photographs, Zahid Chaudhary argues, "Colonial photography produces a visibility that legitimates and records the 'value' of the colonial effort in the same frame as it measures the colonial subject" (2012: 8). He goes on to analyze a number of photographs that fix their subjects as the othered native, thereby justifying the colonial project. This kind of discursive production relies overly on the implied truth-value of photography. Chaudhary dismantles this claim and even inverts it by demonstrating that the notion of the "primitive" is often imposed on the subjects of these photographs. He argues, "this intervention, in turn, secures the photographer in the certainty of his own foreignness to this scene, distinguishing himself from the undifferentiated primitiveness surrounding him in India" (7–8). Ondaatje uses photography in *Anil's Ghost* to represent a similar Western perspective that is overly reliant on the power of photographs to document and fix in particular ways. With this, he contrasts alternative ways of looking in the novel. He undermines the notion of a fixed truth that works in the service of the production of a particular discourse. Truth in the context of the Sri Lankan conflict is a far more elusive concept, constantly changing and redefined.

In the novel, Sailor embodies the notion of *corpus delicti* – the legal principle that evidence must prove that a crime has been committed before someone can be charged with committing that crime. This principle is the cornerstone of Anil's approach: "the central truism of her work was that you could not find a suspect until you found a victim" (176). The victim, in this case Sailor, is evidence that a crime has been committed. Yet, because of Anil's overreliance on the evidentiary, she is unable to solve the mystery of Sailor's death. The evidentiary reliability of photography is often used in criminal cases to establish the existence of evidence, thereby proving that a crime was committed. However, in the novel, this established form of visuality in solving crimes is pitted against an older and far more intuitive form of visuality, based on situated knowledge and intuition rather than the indexicality of photography. Anil's own lack of situated knowledge in the context of postcolonial Sri Lanka causes her to be deeply suspicious of Sarath, who she can never fully trust. This leads to her missteps toward the end of the novel when Sarath leaves to find Sailor's name (Ruwan Kumara) in a list of those wanted by the government. When he fails to return, convinced that he has betrayed her, Anil discloses their location to the authorities; she returns to Colombo without her evidence, Sailor's skeleton. Finally, Sarath saves the day by smuggling Sailor's skeleton out and leaving instructions for Anil to leave the country with the evidence. The scene in which the now-dead Sarath's voice emanates from the cavity of Sailor's skeleton telling Anil what to do is a powerful scene that underscores the limitations of *corpus delicti*. Anil is unable to use Sailor's corpse to solve the mystery of his death. The skeleton transforms into a witness only when coupled with Sarath's voice; it is almost as if Sailor comes back to life momentarily to tell his story. The transformation of the *corpus delicti* (evidence of crime) into a witness is possible only because of Sarath's way of looking and his deeper understanding of the conflict. It proves the complete failure of Anil's approach and underscores the need for alternate visualities like Sarath's in dealing with the traumas of postcoloniality.

## Witnessing Trauma at the Edge of (Photographic) Sight

The iconicity of photographs is closely connected with Anil's notion of truth as being fixed and universal. Guerin and Hallas draw an analogy between the Christian belief that images of God represent not only his likeness but contain within them the presence of God and the power of photography, "not simply to evoke the violence and trauma of the event, but to represent it, to make it present again" (2007: 9). It is widely believed that photographs can bring an event to life far more effectively than words. However, much like the prohibitions against false images and idolatry in Christianity, a contradictory impulse governs photography where faith in its capacity for mimicry is coupled with a suspicion about its claims of authenticity. This is particularly evident in images of traumatic events. The critiques of documentary photography laid out in Chapter 1 underscore the skepticism about the authenticity of such images despite the evidentiary force of the medium. From photographs of the liberation of Nazi concentration camps in 1945 to images of tortured Iraqi prisoners in Abu Ghraib prison in 2004, questions are always raised about the limitations of these images or their excesses, their avowed purpose versus their real intent. Notwithstanding their indexicality, a popular skepticism often surrounds questions of their production, dissemination, and interpretation. Guerin and Hallas suggest that the shared assumptions of visual studies and trauma studies and the iconoclastic impulses of both, work in a way to dismantle the very representations they so urgently seek. They credit this to the fact that "both formations developed partially in response to the poststructuralist critique of representation that understood the categories of truth and the real as effects of discourse, and therefore, as historical constructs" (2007: 3).

Ondaatje uses this contradictory impulse and the absent presence of atrocity photographs in *Anil's Ghost* to convey a complex understanding of truth and witnessing in the context of postcolonial trauma. Photographs of the victims of political killings are sent to Gamini once a week. These are the photographs of torture victims. While most of these bodies disappeared without a trace, "some came back as evidence into the arms of the country" (212), the word "evidence" underscoring the importance of documenting the marks of torture found on these bodies in the hope of providing justice at a later date. The bodies of these victims arrive in the hospital for identification. The interns list the wounds and photograph the bodies. It falls to Gamini to confirm these reports by studying the photographs and to comment on the injuries and the scars, interpreting them one way or the other and recording his observations into a tape recorder. While he performs his task, he feels compelled to cover "the faces with his left hand, the pulse in his wrist jumping" (213). He appreciates the anonymity of the victims afforded by this act: "there was no danger of his recognizing the dead" (213). Here we see several layers of distancing. First, he distances himself by choosing "not to deal with the bodies" (212). The anonymity of the photographs offers him another layer of distance. Contrary to the visceral response and ethical imperative associated with viewing atrocity photographs (see Prosser 2012: 9–10), there is a certain clinicality to Gamini's weekly task, a distancing and a homogenizing of the dead, each one reduced to an identificatory number on his file. A further erasure of their identities is suggested when the newly arrived bodies are likened to thousands of fish caught in fishermen's nets: "The doors opened and a thousand bodies slid in [...] as if they had been mauled. A thousand bodies of sharks and skates in the corridors, some of the dark-skinned fish thrashing" (213), the word "thrashing" creating an illusion of life.

Given that the photographs arriving on Gamini's desk are of men who are already dead, they are beyond his help or healing skills. However, with his medical gaze, he has the power to give voice to these bodies, to speak for them and testify to their wounds and suffering. Tasked with writing the narrative of their death, Gamini documents the "scars caused by acid or sharp metal" (213) which may be used later as evidence of atrocities committed. His task of narrativizing the deaths of these victims by studying the reports and photographs is therefore of utmost importance and casts him in the role of witness to these acts of unspeakable violence. In the words of Guerin and Hallas, visualizing the consequences of horrific violence often perpetrated on the body in times of conflict "has become a principal and necessary component of witnessing practices," but it is also "fraught with the risk of dehumanization" (2007: 13–14). In recording the victims' fatal injuries, although from a distanced perspective, Gamini is bearing witness to historical trauma, enacting it as a performative speech act and providing testimonial. There is an absent, implied listener to his recordings and the performative act of bearing witness affirms the reality of the event (of torture and death) evidenced in each photograph he studies closely. Guerrin and Hallas write, "In the moment of testimony, the witness bears witness to the event by re-presenting it – in the sense of bringing it into presence – before his addressee" (12). This is also essentially what a photograph does – it re-presents and brings into presence an event from the past. This scene establishes two ways of looking – one documented by the camera eye and recorded in the photographs and the other by Gamini's gaze as the witness, recorded in his testimony.

This scene is only a foreshadowing of a far more gut-wrenching scene mirrored later in the novel. In another similar "darkest hour of the week," Gamini is going through a pile of photographs, speaking into the tape recorder describing the wounds he sees and documenting their probable cause, when he suddenly "recognized the wounds, the *innocent ones*" (285, emphasis added) in one of the photographs. The bodies of the victims are in a ward just down the corridor from him and Gamini rushes there to confirm what the photograph has already revealed to him – that one of the seven bodies photographed that day and sent for Gamini's expert perusal is that of his brother Sarath. What follows is one of the most moving scenes of the novel – Gamini begins to dress Sarath's wounds as if he were alive and to speak quietly to his dead brother in a poignant yet belated attempt to heal the fractured relationship he had with him. Despite the truth-telling power of photographs, it is ironic that Gamini feels compelled to rush down the corridor and verify the truth of the photograph. Although Gamini routinely worked by covering the faces on the photographs, thereby avoiding the danger of recognizing any of the dead, when a photograph of his brother's corpse appears on his desk, he recognizes him instantly. Ironically, this recognition comes from what Ondaatje calls "the innocent" wounds on Sarath's body – the gash of a scar he got on the side of his elbow "crashing a bike on the Kandy Hill" (287). This suggests a scope of knowledge beyond what the frames of the photograph can provide. Gamini immediately recognizes his brother from the photograph, not from the information or documentary evidence provided by the photograph – his face (which is covered) or the marks of torture on Sarath's body – that is the avowed purpose of the photograph. This powerfully suggests the limitations of photography. The purpose of photographing the bodies of the torture victims is to document the truth of their deaths, to record the atrocities committed on their bodies, and presumably to bring the responsible parties to justice later. Yet what Gamini notices in the photos is not the evidence of torture but the innocent scars of childhood accidents. This particular photo fails in its avowed purpose. All it does is precisely what it is not supposed to do – give proof of the person's identity. Once Gamini recognizes the body as that of his brother, the photo is of no interest or use to him and he rushes to see the actual body in the morgue down the corridor.

In this scene, Ondaatje dismantles all that he had established in the earlier scene of Gamini as witness, recorder, and testimonial provider of the atrocities of the civil war. He delineates the difference between the photograph of Sarath's body and his actual corpse in stark terms. Though his face in the photograph is covered to prevent recognition, we are told that the face is often the site of the greatest infliction of torture: Gamini "had seen cases where every tooth had been removed, the nose cut apart, the eyes humiliated with liquids, the ears entered [...] It was the face they went for in some cases" (289–290). Although Sarath's face is untouched, Gamini's anxiety about seeing his brother's face so that he may verify this highlights what the photo has not captured. Similarly, the giant sleeves of Sarath's shirt conceal the fact that "below the elbows the hands had been broken in several places" (290). This is revealed only when Gamini rips the sleeves down to the cuffs. This latter scene, which mirrors the earlier one of Gamini studying the photos of bodies left on his desk once a week, brings into deep doubt the veracity of photographic images and their power to record and document atrocities by way of providing proof. Gamini's intimate knowledge of Sarath's childhood scars and his understanding of torture wounds from years of being a doctor on the front lines provides him with far more knowledge about Sarath's identity and death than the photograph of Sarath's body. Here we arrive beyond the edge of photographic sight.

Gamini's attempt to speak for the dead by using photographs to "re-present" the traumatic incident is again severely undermined in the scene where Anil must examine Sailor's skeleton, which has been confiscated by the government so that her truths are now rendered useless. Unbeknownst to her, Sarath had tracked down Sailor's body just before his own torture and death. Anil discovers a tape recorder secreted in Sailor's rib cavity. She presses the button and a disembodied voice begins to speak – it is the voice of the now-dead Sarath speaking through the body of Sailor, his voice "very clear and focused. He must have held the recorder close to his mouth as he whispered" (284). This immediately evokes a parallel image of Gamini speaking into a tape recorder as he examines photos of the bodies of tortured victims. In the former scene, Gamini's role is rendered superfluous, as Sailor's body seems to speak for itself from beyond the grave. As Burrows argues in her reading of this scene, "Sarath's dead voice, speaking from the cavity of another who had also died a death of trauma, lives on as Anil's whispering ghost" (174).

## Photography and the Pain of Disappearance

The specter of disappearance haunts *Anil's Ghost.* Gabriel Schwab has suggested that by focusing on the civil war in Sri Lanka, the novel explores "the politics of disappearances as a global phenomenon" (2014: 645). We know that photography played a major role in this conflict (as it always does in conflicts of this kind) in trying to bring back, remember, or memorialize the dead and disappeared. In her description of the ethnic conflicts in Sri Lanka, Malathi de Alwis writes about the notion of the "disappearance" of victims where their erasure is the ultimate goal. She describes the family members of such victims who are left behind as "chronic mourners" since they have no sense of closure and many continue to believe that their missing relatives will return. Furthermore, these chronic mourners must deal with the anxiety that at any moment their efforts at locating their loved one and thereby ending their temporary absence may contradictorily result in making that absence permanent by confirming their death (2009: 379). She further argues that in such situations, objects like photographs play a particularly important role in making the disappeared metonymically present. In the Sri Lankan context, she finds especially relevant photography's "unique ability to simultaneously encompass both presence and absence, by signifying absence but simultaneously keeping absence at bay by producing a simulacrum of presence" (380). Ondaatje uses this quality of photography to make the absent present or to heighten the absence through a form of photographic presence, in order to further comment on his theme of disappearance in the novel. He does so ironically by using the absent presence of photography itself.

The scenes delineating the assassination of President Katugala, blown to bits by a suicide bomber, convey the absent presence of photography in the starkest terms. Ondaatje outlines the final moments of the man's life – journalists take a few photos of him and the police from a tall building, minutes before he is caught between two processions of his supporters and of the public celebrating National Heroes' Day. This is where the suicide bomber approaches the president and detonates the bomb strapped to his body. Ondaatje writes, "the cutting action of the explosion shredded Katugala to pieces. The central question after the bombing concerned whether the President had been spirited away, and if so, whether by the police and army forces or by terrorists. *Because the President could not be found*" (294, emphasis added). The president disappears without a trace, like so many of his fellow citizens. The photographs taken of him minutes before the assassination tell a number of stories – they show him as old and frail, a reality that his party members conscientiously avoided acknowledging. However, in the photo can also be seen "a giant cardboard cutout, where he looks vibrant, with thick white hair. And behind him you can also see the armored vehicle that he has left for the last time" (293). These photographs ominously capture both a real and a doctored image of the president while also documenting the moments immediately prior to his disappearance. This scene raises the question of absence/presence and alludes to the novel's engagement with what constitutes truth. While the later photographs of Katugala tell the "truth" of his aging and frail body, the image on the cardboard cutout dissembles, portraying him as vigorous and larger than life. Finally, the president's literal and very real "disappearance" when he is erased by the suicide bomber is heightened by the repetition of the italicized phrase "*Where was the President?*" (294, original emphasis), the ambiguity in the past tense painfully underscoring his absent presence. Once the news had spread that the president was in the crowd when the bomb went off, "each hospital waited for the possibility that his wounded body would be brought in. But it never arrived. The body, what remained of it, was not found for a long time" (295). The hospitals waiting for the injured president cruelly mirror the waiting relatives whom de Alwis evokes. Ondaatje is aware of the vast numbers of people who disappeared in the ethnic conflict in Sri Lanka. He evokes this powerfully in the list of names of the missing (41), providing bare details like their age, the place they disappeared from, the date, and the time marking the "hour of disappearance" (41). The prologue to the novel captures the painful search for the missing and the eternal fear of confirmation of their death, in a scene far from Sri Lanka – a forensic archaeological site in Guatemala where the families of the missing provide a vigil for the dead: "There was always the fear, double-edged, that it was their son in the pit, or it was not their son – which meant there would be further searching [...] The possibility of their lost son was everywhere" (5).

Ondaatje uses the trope of photography and its absent presence to suggest the trauma of the survivors and family members of the disappeared. Here, too, he contrasts Anil's approach with those of others like Sarath and Ananda. Anil's approach is marked by what Schwab characterizes as her "professional ethos of scientific control" (2014: 649) driven by the quest for evidence and incontrovertible proof. Ananda, on the other hand, deals with the disappearance of his wife Sirissa by affectively making her visible again through his sculptural rendering of her face. His visuality allows him to transform his art into a mourning ritual, a powerful exercise in healing.

## Optics of Blindness: An Alternative Way of Looking

Although photography is credited with contributing to the restoration of justice by providing legal evidence of crimes and atrocities by the ruling classes in Europe and elsewhere in the postwar period, photographic evidence has not always been successful in bringing justice. Writing about the Latin American context, Jose Luis Falconi demonstrates the utter failure of photographic evidence to provide proof of crimes and thereby help bring the offenders to justice. Falconi argues that the repeated and constant dismissal of photographic evidence as representing the truth has irreparably damaged its reputation as the always-reliable provider of evidence. This failure has brought home "the extent to which evidence (i.e. reason) is predetermined by ideology" (2008: 136). Falconi goes on to powerfully analyze photographs from an exhibition showcasing the work of contemporary artists in Latin America that constantly "short circuit the spectator's expectations" (131) as if to draw attention to the fragility and unreliability of photographic evidence. By questioning the spectator's premature reaction caused by the assumption of the photograph's evidentiary force, and not the indexicality of the photograph itself, these artists, Falconi suggests, call for us to abandon our faith in photography's ability to provide evidence and learn to look in different ways.

It may be argued that Palipana and Ananda offer such alternative ways of looking, an optical blindness, in Ondaatje's novel. In Anil's case, Ondaatje seems to posit that despite its claims to veracity and authenticity, photography ultimately fails to represent postcolonial trauma since it subscribes to a Western logic of universal, fixed truths, and incontrovertible evidence. Instead, Ondaatje suggests, the response to trauma must be processed in localized ways through situated knowledges and the resources of the psychological self. This is brought home most starkly in the outcome of Anil and Sarath's endeavor to establish Sailor's identity. They seek Palipana's advice on how they might be able to do so from his skull and the old man suggests they pay Ananda, an arrack-drinking artisan who paints eyes on holy images, "to rebuild the head" (108). Anil and Sarath have starkly contrasting attitudes toward this suggestion. She admits she has never done reconstruction and openly expresses scorn for such an approach: "They look like historical cartoons to us. Dioramas, that sort of thing" (161). She is deeply distrustful of Ananda, reluctant to hand over Sailor's skull to him, and very dismissive of his talent: "Well, let's find the guy first and see if he can even hold a paint brush without shaking" (161). When Ananda studied the skull, "Anil felt there was little he could learn from such a viewing" (162). Continuing to see the project as "Sarath's folly" (168), Anil becomes convinced that Ananda will only create "a five-and-dime monster" (168). Sarath, on the other hand, understands and believes in Ananda's methods. He also understands that Anil's pursuit of truth prevents her from appreciating these methods. His own skepticism of Anil's methods, as well as his distrust of photography, is revealed in the following lines: "Sarath knew that for her the journey was getting to the truth. But what would truth bring them into? [...] [He] had seen truth broken into suitable pieces and used by the foreign press alongside irrelevant photographs" (156). The reference to photographs again and their use to distort the truth suggests the failure of photographs to document the truth and record trauma. Not only is this approach unsatisfactory in Sarath's view, it carries with it the potential to cause significant harm, "a flippant gesture towards Asia that might lead, as a result of this information, to new vengeance and slaughter" (156–157).

In sharp contrast with Anil's notions of truth, Ananda's handiwork shows a perfect example of Sarath's variety of truth. When Ananda unveils the newly chiseled face of Sailor, it looks nothing like what Anil had imagined from her forensic work on Sailor's skeleton. She is astonished by the "serenity in the face she did not see too often these days. There was no tension" (184). Sarath explains to her that this is what Ananda "wants of the dead" (184). Ananda is tormented by the trauma of his young wife Sirissa's sudden disappearance three years earlier. She had disappeared at a time when victims' heads began to appear on poles. "The head he had made is therefore peaceful," Sarath explains, "a calm Ananda had known in his wife, a peacefulness he wanted for any victim" (187). It is important to note that Ananda has not been delinquent in his duties and simply produced a sculpted head of his wife, ignoring the task assigned to him. He has carefully researched aspects of Sailor's identity and physical features by spending time observing and chatting with the people in the village: "He wanted to discover what the people drank here, whether there was a specific diet that would puff up their cheeks more than usual, whether lips would be fuller than in Batticaloa. Also the varieties of hairstyle, the qualities of eyesight. Did they walk or cycle? Was coconut oil used in food and hair?" (166–167). His is a well-researched and carefully executed artistic reconstruction of the head, but it is also a powerful act of resilience and of mourning.

Although Ananda's artistry seemingly thwarts Anil's pursuit of truth – "Anil knew it was unlikely that identification would occur" (205) – it helps the latter to process the trauma of Sirissa's death and bring about some kind of closure for his trauma through a physical sculpting of her face. From Anil's perspective, Ananda's work is a failure since it is not a reconstruction of Sailor's face; in fact, by giving the purportedly male Sailor a female face, Ananda takes the search for Sailor's identity farther from the truth. However, this gender-altering transformation is a revelation despite being a false truth that brings comfort and allows Ananda to memorialize his wife. He is exercising his artistic agency in altering the traumatic course of Sirissa's journey. Instead of remembering her as one of the many who were lost in the Sri Lankan civil war and were probably tortured in unspeakable ways before being killed, Ananda chooses to bestow upon her a peacefulness that he demands for all victims of the war. This is another way of looking, a visuality very different from what might be demanded by the indexicality of a photograph of Sirissa's body/head (were it ever to be found). Its truth is not indexical but rather lies "in character and nuance and mood" (259), as Sarath would say.

Anil Tissera disappears from the pages of the novel much like the slain President Katugala soon after she discovers Sailor's skeleton with Sarath's instructions for her playing from a tape recorder deep within the skeleton's ribcage. In a brief concluding section, she reminisces about the Diyasena brothers, Sarath and Gamini, as she contemplates her return to the West. She remembers Gamini's words about how all Western texts end: "The American or the Englishman gets on a plane and leaves. That's it. The camera leaves with him" (285). These words could well be describing Anil, the reference to the camera implying photography's complicity in this charade. Having entirely discredited Anil's gaze and her strategy for finding the truth of the Sri Lankan civil war, Ondaatje moves to the novel's conclusion. The last chapter, titled "Distance," offers a metaphor for what he wishes to propose as a model for dealing with trauma in the postcolony. Instead of closing with Anil's return to the West, Ondaatje chooses to devote the concluding pages of his novel to the artificer Ananda Udugama and his masterful and creative gaze. The chapter begins with thieves detonating a 120-foot statue of the Buddha and Ondaatje is quick to point out that "This was, for once, not a political act" but simply a solution for hunger (300). Ananda, the artist, is assigned the task of overseeing the reconstruction of this statue. The statue is built on the same earth that had been a killing field and burial ground for a while; thus out of death and destruction rises the Buddha.

Ondaatje devotes the last three pages to depicting the scene of the "netra mangala" or eye painting, exactly as Palipana had described it to Sarath and Anil much earlier in the novel. The significance of *netra mangala* is the granting of vision to a statue, thereby imbuing it with a life force through which it is transformed into a god. As Palipana says, "Without the eyes there is not just blindness, there is nothing. There is no existence. The artificer brings to life *sight and truth and presence*" (99, emphasis added). Since no mortal can look upon the god, Ananda paints the eye by holding his brush over his shoulder and looking at a reflection of the statue in a mirror – that is, he paints it blind. The complex layering of visuality in this scene – Ananda's human eyes are cast upon the reflected image of the statue's "eyes unformed, unable to see" (306) as he draws them into life without looking at them – grants a position of privilege to Ananda. The statue is only a piece of stone until the eyes are drawn and then it becomes the Buddha. Ananda is the privileged artist who grants holiness to the statue. He is also in a privileged position of proximity to the Buddha, the recipient of the "first and last look given to someone so close" (306). Ananda's vision aligns with that of the divine for one brief moment, as they both look north from the same vantage point high above the city and the "eyes he had cut and focused with his father's chisel showed him" (307) the landscape below; through this act, Ananda becomes the witness to his nation's painful history. Joanne Freed interprets this in terms of a universal aesthetic as a means of overcoming postcolonial violence. She reads Ananda's renditions as "a putatively apolitical appreciation of beauty that transcends the particularities of nation, culture and politics" (28). I would argue on the contrary that Ananda's artistic vision is firmly grounded in the localized, situated ethos of Sri Lanka and its history of conflict. This is illustrated in Ondaatje's use of the language of natural history and meteorology as he describes what Ananda's almost divine vision enables him to see: the storms coming down from the mountains to the plains, "the great rainstorms of May and June," the weather of "the temperate forests and seas," and the birds flying "through the shelves of heat currents" (307).

Ondaatje evokes an exquisite beauty imbued with a healing quality in the closing pages of the novel. This suggests a complete rejection of and opposition to the implied accuracy of the photographic eye. The reflected image of the eyes that Ananda sees in the mirror is far more inexact than Anil's camera eye; there is in it a humility, and a deference to the holiness of the statue. Ironically, it is Ananda, the artificer, who will grant holiness to the statue by painting the eyes. Until then, there is only "the blank stare of the statue. The eyes unformed, unable to see. And until he had eyes [...] he was not the Buddha" (306). Through this act, Ondaatje provocatively asks what it means for a god to see through eyes chiseled and focused by an "artificer." I would argue that it is deeply suggestive of an alternative way of looking, one that is not simply about looking and gazes – like the photographic eye – but instead, one that is imbued with situated knowledges, with ancient practices, with the holy and the human, and the rhythms of the natural world. In the final paragraphs of the novel, we see the conjunction of Sri Lanka's natural beauty – her "deciduous hills [...] coast of mangroves, lagoons and river deltas" (307) – along with the value of art in processes of healing. Ondaatje invokes a sense of generational continuity as Ananda uses his father's chisel to cut and focus the eyes. As he does this, he feels his nephew's concerned hand on his, "this sweet touch from the world" (307), and he feels Sirissa's presence in the natural world around him, "a small brave heart" (307). These are the things that will ultimately restore peace and stability and bring about healing, not Anil and her documents and photographs, valuable as these may be in garnering the attention of the West.

## Conclusion

As I have attempted to argue, in *Anil's Ghost* Ondaatje considers the value of photography and the photographic eye and the role that it can play in documenting historical trauma or excavating the truth that lies behind acts of postcolonial violence. However, he finds it severely limited and places the responsibility of recording and responding to historical trauma not in photography but rather in art and in an alternative aesthetic vision or a countervisuality imbued with indigenous knowledge, radically different from the vision of photography. In the introduction to *Picturing Atrocity*, Jay Prosser lays out the contradictory nature of atrocity photographs. He argues that while the iconic function of photography is tremendously powerful and atrocity photographs can be used by news media and judicial systems in the service of human rights and can even underwrite democracy, "photography's powers of representation can quickly harden into stereotypes" (2012: 8). In doing so, it can exacerbate global North-South inequalities, since the audience of these photographs is often located in the global North. He even likens the act of viewing atrocity photographs to "looking at some kinds of pornography or other modes of domination through acts of representation" (9). This problematic of the power differential between the photographer and the photographed, as well as the far-reaching influence of the former to shape the narrative of the latter and package it for consumption in the international community, is subtly implied in the comments the brothers make about Anil's role in Sri Lanka. She is the quintessential outsider, well intentioned but surprisingly unaware of her privilege and power.

Critics of *Anil's Ghost* have suggested that it pathologizes violence and stereotypes the postcolonial as a space of violence. In so doing, it is argued that Ondaatje caters only to a Western (in this case, Canadian) audience whose own civilizational superiority and stability is reinforced by such stereotypes. For example, Mrinalini Chakravorty writes:

> The risk is that Ondaatje's Sri Lanka [...] will remain only a foil for the West's self-assurance and self-complacency, a vision of "impermanence" against which to measure Western stability [...] In *Anil's Ghost*, Sailor's murder in the midst of a tumultuous civil war and the murkiness of

> seeking redress for it suggests that the novel endorses a stereotype of civilizational difference where the generic fictionalization of mass deaths leads readers to affirm the meaninglessness of individual life in the postcolony. (2014: 120)

However, I would argue that rather than writing from a Western positionality that reinforces a problematic stereotype, Ondaatje in fact critiques Western notions of visuality that are often employed inappropriately and imposed upon the postcolony. He uses the absent presence of photography to do so and to suggest that the understanding and processing of violence and trauma in the postcolony demands an alternative strategy, a radically different vision – an "optics of blindness" that is embodied by characters like Sarath, Ananda, and Palipana.

# 3

# Photography's Sonic Recall: Decolonizing Trauma Studies in Mahasweta Devi's "Behind the Bodice"

## Introduction

Lisa Saltzman and Eric Rosenberg (2006) have argued that the "metaphors of visuality" (2006: xi) are often used to convey the unrepresentable in the discourse of trauma and consequently the language of trauma is "emphatically, if not exclusively, visual" (xii). Despite this, much of trauma literature focuses on the domain of language, in particular the failure of language in the face of trauma, instead of the visual domain. Objecting to the privileging of language over the visual, Saltzman and Rosenberg instead locate the space of trauma in the domain between the visual and the verbal. In this chapter, via a reading of Mahasweta Devi's short story "Behind the Bodice: Choli ke Pichhe" (henceforth "Behind the Bodice"), I explore the intersections of the visual and the verbal in the context of postcolonial trauma. If Ondaatje's Anil Tissera is distanced from and distrusting of vernacular modes of seeing, Mahasweta Devi's Upin Puri is naively idealistic about the photographer's power to document and bring about change in the context of postcolonial trauma. "Behind the Bodice" tells the story of Upin, a photographer who becomes obsessed with saving a tribal woman named Gangor and others like her from the atrocities perpetrated on the tribals by the postcolonial ruling elite. Ironically, though, his photographs of her set in motion a series of actions that lead to her rape and brutalization. I suggest that Devi's story explores the visual and the verbal in representing trauma by sharply contrasting Upin Puri's absent images of Gangor naively intended to "save" her, with Gangor's own unashamedly resilient voice even in the face of her denigration. If we recall Jacques Rancière's assertion that visibility does not always necessarily reside in images and that words can "deploy a visibility that can be blinding" (2009: 7), the impotence of Upin's absent photographs in Devi's story stands in sharp contrast to the power of Gangor's words in registering her trauma. My reading of the story and of Devi's use of the absent presence of photography allows me to suggest that "Behind the Bodice" offers us an opportunity to decolonize trauma theory. On the one hand, through the portrayal of the photographer Upin and his misguided but well-intentioned efforts to seek justice for tribal women, Devi's story suggests a failure in visually representing trauma. On the other hand, through her portrayal of a defiant and articulate Gangor in the face of utter abjection, Devi rejects Western trauma theory's privileging of aporia and unspeakability.

In "Behind the Bodice," Devi connects visuality and trauma through the figure of Upin Puri, whose photographic gaze is transformed into a scopophilic one and works to objectify Gangor's body, albeit unwittingly. It has been argued that due to the failure and even destruction of language in the face of physical pain, contemporary trauma has been conceived through the compulsive repetition of "the recurrent image, the unbidden flashback that abolishes time and reimmerses you in the visual field of the inaugurating traumatic instant" (Lockhurst 2008: 147). In Devi's story, Gangor's absent photograph becomes the recurrent image that comes to represent the traumatic instant, ironically not because it recorded that instant but because it led directly to the traumatic act itself. Therefore, in the story's climax, we have a strange but powerful reversal: instead of the image standing in and speaking for the unspeakable traumatic act, the victim Gangor remains articulate and resilient, while Upin, the author of the image, is traumatized, and haunted by his work of art and his own unwitting role in causing the traumatic act. As a photojournalist in a postcolonial state, Upin's role is important in documenting the abuse and resulting trauma of the underprivileged. Instead, he unwittingly becomes the agent of that abuse and comes to be traumatized himself by Gangor's rape.

Ariella Azoulay has discussed the complete erasure of rape from photographic representation. This is unsurprising since rape almost always occurs away from the gaze of witnesses. However, as Azoulay points out, this has not prevented the development of large repositories of images documenting other acts of violence. Whatever rape images do exist are never made available to the public gaze. The usual reason provided for this is twofold: that any photographic representation of rape will cause distress to the victim or the victim's family, and that such images may result in a problematic sexualization of the woman and may appear pornographic. Azoulay points out that images of rape are crucially different from other images of violence and there is a "comprehensive abstention" from distributing such images; consequently, she questions the feminist movement's assertion that rape is only an act of violence, not unlike other acts of violence (Azoulay 2008: 253). She asserts that rape "'itself' cannot be photographed except in part and in such a way that an active gaze is required to reconstruct the event and acknowledge it as rape" (251). She concludes that the prohibition on images of rape also affects the ways in which we talk about rape. It places the burden of proof on the victim, who must then "confess" to being raped. Azoulay critiques the "problematic framework of the confessional" (255) in which any discussion of rape in the first person remains trapped and which always assumes besmirchment. She laments the absence of rape photographs, arguing that the prohibition on such images further silences the victims of rape. It obscures women's testimonies. Consequently, she urges us to look for photographs of rape in images that already exist and carry within them traces of rape that have not been seen for what they are. I will argue that by making Upin the unwitting agent of Gangor's rape through his act of photography and by refusing to cast Gangor in the role of confessor to her own brutalization, Devi simultaneously critiques the failure of photography to document trauma while also foregrounding the female voice refusing shame and demanding justice. The absent images that triggered Gangor's rape take on a sonic connotation as we are made to repeatedly "listen" to the image (using Tina Campt's counterintuitive concept) in the titular refrain "choli ke pichhe"; this also becomes the endless repetition of the originary moment of trauma. Devi's story decolonizes established discourses of trauma by positing an alternative category of affect and response – one of resilience, fierce rage, and defiance.

## Decolonizing Trauma Theory

The spring/summer 2008 issue of *Studies in the Novel* was a special issue on the postcolonial trauma novel in which the editors, Stef Craps and Gert Buelens, called for "theorizing colonization in terms of the infliction of a collective trauma and reconceptualizing post-colonialism as a post traumatic cultural formation" (1) as a corrective to the Eurocentric bias of much of trauma studies (such as the work done by Cathy Caruth, Shoshana Felman, Geoffrey Hartman, and Dominick LaCapra, among others). The special issue's purpose was to critique the central tenets of trauma theory, which are exclusively based on discourses originating in an Euro-American context, and to question its application to the postcolonial condition. Craps and Buelens begin their introduction by questioning the apolitical and ahistorical textuality of trauma studies; they argue that, contrary to the stated purpose of trauma studies, which is to promote cross-cultural ethical engagement, "by ignoring or marginalizing non-Western traumatic events and histories and non-Western theoretical work, trauma studies may actually assist in the perpetuation of Eurocentric views and structures that maintain or widen the gap between the West and the rest of the world" (2). The special issue therefore attempts a "rapprochement" between trauma theory and postcolonial criticism, yet, as Rothberg argues in his response to the issue, the contributors question whether trauma in its current form "provides the best framework for thinking about the legacies of violence in the colonized/postcolonial world" (Rothberg 2008: 226). Irene Visser further studies the relationship between trauma theory and postcolonial studies and calls for a radical rethinking of several concepts of trauma theory, such as its lack of historical particularity, its transmissibility, and its understanding of collective trauma, if it is to be "postcolonized" (2011: 279). In *Postcolonial Witnessing: Trauma out of Bounds* (2013), Stef Craps critiques the Eurocentric bias and modernist aesthetic of mainstream trauma theory. Ananya Kabir has also called for "'provincializing' the 'Europe' [...] within the heart of trauma theory" by proposing an affect-mediated approach to postcolonial trauma studies. Similarly, in their edited collection *The Future of Trauma Theory: Contemporary Literary and Cultural Criticism* (2013) Buelens, Durrant, and Eaglestone attempt to chart the future of trauma studies, characterizing its interdisciplinarity as a 'knot' or assemblage of "representation, the past, the self, the political and suffering" (4). Abigail Ward's 2015 collection *Postcolonial Traumas: Memory, Narrative, Resistance* attempts to explore new ways of understanding postcolonial traumas. Emphasizing the plurality and heterogeneity of postcolonial *traumas*, the key concerns of the essays therein, as suggested by the subtitle, include dealing with memories of trauma, the difficulties of narrating traumatic events, and forms of resistance to trauma. Many of the essays in the collection engage with the continuity of historical traumas, which is of particular relevance to the postcolonial context, where decolonization is often replaced by forms of neocolonialism.

Inspired by these interventions into trauma theory and postcolonial studies, this chapter considers the ways in which the photographic image intended to speak for the subaltern ironically becomes the cause of traumatic violence enacted upon the body of the female subaltern in a short story written by the Bengali writer Mahasweta Devi. The story depicts forms of traumatic expression that do not readily fit into the mainstream discourses of trauma studies, which emphasize the aporia and unspeakability of trauma. These are key terms in Western trauma theory. Cathy Caruth's *Unclaimed Experience* (1996) hinges on the notion of aporia or an unresolvable paradox where the traumatic event is seared into the psyche, yet paradoxically does not appear in conscious memory. This leads to a failure of language to articulate the traumatic experience. Consequently, Western trauma theorists privilege the high modernist aesthetic of fragmentation, nonlinearity, and anti-narrative as the only mode for trauma narratives. In Devi's story, the figure of the photographer represents the well-intentioned postcolonial elite who want to raise awareness about the exploitation of the marginalized by the ruling classes and seek redress for the injustices and traumatic violence they encounter. However, in this case the (absent) images produced by the photographer Upin, of the tribal woman Gangor, instigate Gangor's violent rape by the police, compelling the young mother to turn to prostitution. Determined to make amends, Upin revisits Gangor and becomes a witness to her brutalized body. Despite his power as "Camera Sir," this time he is unable to document Gangor's trauma and seek justice on her behalf. Instead, his encounter with Gangor traumatizes him and he is forced to acknowledge the utter failure of photography to capture the subaltern's trauma. The climax of the story, the scene of encounter between Upin and Gangor, dramatizes the stark contrast between the (failure to make) visible and the sayable.

Rape as a particular form of traumatizing experience struggles with its own questions of representation and articulation. Visualizing rape may invite the scopophilic or even pornographic gaze while speaking about it may call into question the victim's lack of agency and thereby her victimhood. Seeking to dismantle established binaries in rape narratives such as passivity and agency, master and victim, articulation of truth and powerlessness, the editors of *Feminism, Literature and Rape Narratives: Violence and Violation* sought to subvert such narratives and "begin to position the rape 'victim' outside of a hierarchical structure in which they are inevitably disenfranchised" (Gunne and Thompson 2009: 11). Mahasweta Devi's story, with its acutely graphic depiction of the violated protagonist who remains fiercely articulate in the face of her degradation, offers an example of a subverted rape narrative. Instead of the aporetic aesthetic so valued by mainstream trauma theory, we find in Devi's story a woman who gestures toward defiance and agency in the face of acute trauma, thereby calling for retributive justice and social change. Photography, often valued in the context of historical trauma for its evidential force, ironically becomes the cause of the traumatic event in Devi's story. The multiple connotations of the absent image within the story allow Devi to complicate questions of the visual representation of trauma and the role of the postcolonial artist/intellectual in representing the subaltern or documenting their trauma as a consequence of state violence. Such a portrayal, I argue, highlights some of the postcolonial critiques of literary and cultural trauma theory and offers us opportunities to decolonize cultural trauma theory by focusing on agency and empowerment instead of the unspeakability or visual representability of trauma.

In his essay "Colonial Trauma/Postcolonial Recovery?" David Lloyd writes, "Trauma entails violent intrusion and a sense of utter objectification that annihilates the person as subject or agent" (2000: 214). In Western trauma theory, trauma, whether it be caused by colonialism, war, or sexual violence, always leads to the utter annihilation of subjectivity, a pathological fragmentation of the self. Critiquing the primacy given to the neurobiological features of trauma in mainstream trauma theory, Michelle Balaev has argued that the unspeakability of trauma can be understood "less as an epistemological conundrum and neurobiological fact, but more as an outcome of cultural values and ideologies" (2012: 19). Devi's protagonist Gangor shows no evidence of neurobiological fragmentation as a consequence of rape, nor does she have any concern for cultural injunctions against speaking about her violation. In boldly challenging the neocolonial agents of her torture and violation, Gangor provides yet another alternative model that runs counter to and cannot be addressed by the existing categories of mainstream trauma theory. In the post-rape depiction of women in Devi's fiction, we find neither unspeakability nor an imperative silence surrounding the trauma; instead, Devi presents a bold articulation of the traumatizing violation along with a powerful accusation and condemnation of the structures of patriarchy, caste, and class that enable such violations in decolonized India. This is not the kind of testimonial and self-therapeutic "speaking up" proposed by Felman and Laub (1992), but rather a fierce critique, sharpened by rage and resilience, against the pervasiveness and depravity of the violence wrought by the decolonizing elite upon marginalized populations in India. The female subaltern in the fiction of Mahasweta Devi is a complex figure of femininity. Her body is the site of exploitation and torture, yet she is transformed into a figure of resistance.

## Rape and the Female Subaltern in Mahasweta Devi's Fiction

Much of Devi's fiction focuses on the plight of the dispossessed in a decolonized nation. The delineation of subaltern life and resistance also becomes for Devi the site for her severe critique of the processes of decolonization. Decolonization in India, having been led by a nationalist bourgeoisie, becomes a continuation of colonization for populations such as the tribals, who have neither been included in the elite historiography of nationalist resistance nor benefited from the fruits of decolonization. Instead, they have been further marginalized and pauperized by the government while their land has been illegally usurped in the name of industrial development. Rape is not a surprising subject in Devi's fiction given that tribals are the protagonists of her stories. In an interview with Spivak, Devi said of the tribals of India, "Among the tribals insulting or raping a woman is the greatest crime. Rape is unknown to them. Women have a place of honour in tribal society" (Devi 1995: xviii). One of the causes of the great Santal revolt of 1855–1856 was the raping of tribal women by European railway officers (Guha 1983: 4). Though the rebellion was brutally quashed, it proved to be a precursor to the Sepoy Mutiny of 1857, which many have called the first war of independence in colonial India.

The female protagonists of several of Devi's stories are brutally raped and tortured; however, they emerge ultimately as proud and resilient, challenging the very agent of their degradation, or they die in extreme deprivation, offering a fierce indictment of the structures that exploited them. Mahasweta Devi's fiction radically destabilizes the basic premise of female vulnerability and the violent objectification of women in the context of rape as well as the expected traumatic aftermath. Time and again in her fiction, sexual violence is exposed as the signifier of the impotence of masculinist social power rather than as the "reality" of that power. In her short story "Draupadi" (*Breast Stories*, 1998), the protagonist Dopdi Mejhen is a tribal revolutionary who is arrested and gang-raped in custody. The protagonist of "The Hunt" (*Imaginary Maps*, 1995), Mary Oraon, is not raped but anticipates it and murders the would-be rapist. In "Behind the Bodice: Choli ke Pichhe" (*Breast Stories*, 1998), Gangor, a Dalit woman, is gang-raped by policemen. Finally, in "Douloti, the Bountiful" (*Imaginary Maps*, 1995), Douloti is a mere child when she is sold into prostitution to repay the debt of her father, who is a bonded slave. Rape, therefore, functions on two levels in Devi's fiction. On one level, it functions as a critique of the stark reality and extent of the violence perpetrated daily on the bodies of women. On another, it works as a trope or concept metaphor where the violation of the woman's body becomes symptomatic of the violation of the land and its oppressed people by the ruling elite under decolonization. On this level, rape in Devi's fiction can be read allegorically as a critique from within of nationalism and the failure of decolonization to reach the marginalized tribal populations of India. However, it is important to note that even while functioning as national allegory, rape in her fiction does not become reductive but rather remains an unflinching assertion of resistance and defiance.[1]

Devi's use of rape as a concept metaphor and national allegory does not prevent her from representing rape in all its horror and reality, unlike in the phallocentric discourses of nationalism, where rape is used as a metaphor of exploitation and the violence and reality of the rape of real women are elided (Suleri 1992: 16–17). In Devi's stories, the very graphic descriptions of the woman's body after a rape and the complete absence of any "shame and humiliation" on the part of the women portrayed, forbids the subsuming of women's exploitation and violence under issues of decolonization, such as the marginalization of tribal populations, even while the resonance of rape calls attention to the trauma of state oppression. By refusing shame, the rebellious women in Devi's stories render the state and its agents culpable. Shame and humiliation are powerful concepts in the South Asian context and rape has a long history of being used as a punitive measure in ethnic and caste conflicts with the explicit intention to induce shame and humiliation and thereby assert power and superiority, not only over the victims of sexual violence, but by extension over the community as a whole. In her depiction of women who feel no shame or humiliation as a consequence of rape, Devi is thus able to foreground and critique, simultaneously and with equal power, both types of violence: the violence perpetrated on women's bodies in the name of patriarchal power, and the violence perpetrated upon marginalized communities. Rape is no longer merely a concept metaphor or symbol for Devi's purposes. It becomes instead a means for her to critique processes of exploitation along caste and class lines in the period of decolonization, and to discuss how these are practiced on the bodies of women as well as on the land.

Devi's protagonists offer us models of individual female agency in the face of traumatic experiences. Thus her stories can be interpreted as answering Irene Visser's call for the need for agency and empowerment to be incorporated into trauma's aftermath if cultural trauma theory is to be decolonized (2011: 279). The representation of the female figure in these stories reiterates the politics of resistance. In "Life after Rape: Narrative, Theory and Feminism," Rajeshwari Sunder Rajan attempted an exploration of the "different ways in which rape and the raped woman enter representation as the subject of narrative, as well as the different politics they engender within feminism" (1994: 61). She concluded that feminist texts of rape counter

[1] I will discuss rape, defined for the purposes of this chapter as the threat or perpetration of sexual violence on a woman's body, in Mahasweta Devi's short story "Behind the Bodice."

narrative determinism by structuring a *post-rape* narrative of survival, by literalizing rather than mystifying the representation of rape, and finally by implying that the cost of rape is higher than the loss of female selfhood. Rajan suggests that in this way narratives can develop a feminist "thematics of liberation" (77). Instead of aporia and unspeakability in the face of traumatic brutalization, this resistance and liberation is enacted in the figure of the female subaltern of Devi's fiction. None of her stories reifies female victimhood and there is no mystification of the concept of rape, which is acknowledged in stark, brutal terms as the very premise on which the narrative is built. The women in these stories are never objectified by the act of rape and neither is their suffering spectacularized. Instead, they retain their subjectivity even after the rape. In this way, male desire is decentered and Rajan's "thematics of liberation" is structured around the figure of the female protagonist. Devi does not stop at the decentering of male desire; her stories destabilize and radically revise the basic assumption of male power and female vulnerability by often portraying the raped woman as proud and defiant. Women like Gangor have a certain strength and magnetism of personality, which are reflected in their physicality even when that physicality has been violated. By contrast, the figure of the photographer Upin Puri, representing the well-intentioned postcolonial elite, is portrayed by Devi as obsessive, irrational, and ultimately ineffectual. As though to underscore his ineffectuality, his first appearance in the story is in the form of a reference to his death being reported in "only an inch-and-a-half of space in the newspaper" as "a nameless person's corpse crushed by the wheels of a railway train" (140).

## "Choli ke Pichhe"

Mahasweta Devi alludes to a song from a popular Hindi film in the title of her story "Behind the Bodice: Choli ke Pichhe", whose lyrics run:

> Choli ke pichhe kya hai? Choli ke pichhe ...
> Chunri ke nichhe kya hai? Chunri ke nichhe ...
> Choli me dil hai mera,
> Chunri me dil hai mera
> Yeh dil mein doongi yaar ko. (ellipses in original)
>
> (What lies behind the bodice? Behind the bodice ...
> What lies behind the scarf? Behind the scarf ...
> My heart lies behind the bodice

My heart lies behind the scarf
This heart I'll give to my friend.) (my translation)

The words of the popular song "Choli ke pichhe"[2] from the film *Khal Nayak* ("Villain," 1993), elide and therefore erase the physicality and sexuality of the female body and draw attention instead to the woman's beating heart – the site of a desexualized love. This song is forever inextricably linked in the minds of Hindi audiences with the visualization of arguably Bollywood's most beautiful and sexiest heroine, Madhuri Dixit, gyrating to the rhythm of the song. The titillation aroused in the male viewer by the image of Dixit asking, wide-eyed and querulous, "Choli ke pichhe kya hai?" ("What lies behind the bodice?") is undercut in the very next line of the song, "Choli me dil hai mera …" ("My heart lies behind the bodice …"). The absent presence of the breasts implied in the lyrics of the song comes to be visualized in the film's dance sequence where, contrary to the lyrics, little is left to the imagination regarding what really lies behind the bodice. The two actresses leading the dance – Madhuri Dixit and Neena Gupta – as well as the accompanying female dancers, are all dressed in figure enhancing *cholis*. The dance moves, with repetitive pelvic and chest thrusts, and the way in which the camera moves, panning and fragmenting Dixit's torso, visually contradict the song's lyrics, leaving no doubt about the answer to the question posed by the song. This song generated great furore and many heated debates about the "corruption" of Indian culture. Several social groups, consisting primarily of self-declared moral defenders of Indian culture, sought a legal stay order banning the song.[3] In her article on the debates surrounding the song, Monika Mehta quotes from a legal petition filed by R.P. Chugh, an advocate and Bharatiya Janata Party (BJP) supporter, alleging that the song "is obscene, defamatory to women community [*sic*] and is likely to incite the commission of offence. The song is grossly indecent and is being sung through cassettes at public places, annoying the people at large, the undersigned specially" (Mehta 2001: para. 8). In an ironic reenactment of the song itself, the debate provoked by the song also disallowed any discussion of the female body. In the debate, the covert reference to a woman's breasts suggested in the line "Choli ke pichhe kya hai" becomes the subject of attack by those seeking to preserve Indian tradition and culture. The exposure of the breast or even an allusion to its very existence will result in cultural degradation. Devi's evocation of this song and the controversy it generated in

[2] https://www.youtube.com/watch?v=3OXiqmUhB7o&ab_channel=TipsOfficial.

[3] For a detailed discussion of the censorship history of the song see Monika Mehta (2001).

the title of her short story, serves to highlight her critique of the indexicality of visual forms of representation (as in the Bollywood dance number as well as in Upin's absent images) and their problematic powers of provocation.

Devi appropriates this song and its filmic visualization in various ways in her short story. By using the song's refrain – "choli ke picche" – as her title, Devi evokes multiple connotations – that of the breast (the part of the female anatomy that the *choli* covers), but also images of Madhuri Dixit's dance number which would have been very familiar to her readers at the time. She transfers the visual association we have with this phrase to Upin's (absent) photographs in the story. She opens the story with the song's questioning refrain – "choli ke pichhe kya hai? – sarcastically calling it "the national problem" (138) that year. Referring to the furore the song aroused with scathing irony, she points out how this ridiculous question became a "national issue" (138) while other matters pertaining to egregious acts of caste and gender violence, police torture, and the silencing of social activists "remained non-issues" (138). In a scathing attack on the false modesty of those guarding against what they see as cultural invasion, Devi calls "choli ke pichhe" "an elixir for the times" (140). She reminds us that ideas of female modesty in rural areas of India differ drastically from what the self-proclaimed moral guardians would have us believe: "Shaili's mother wraps her huge and ever-enlarging corpus in just one piece of cloth and goes on to say, 'Never dragged on a *belouse* [blouse] in my life, how to put on a choli now!'" (140).

In her groundbreaking 2017 book *Listening to Images*, Tina Campt urges us to think counterintuitively when considering photographs; instead of privileging the visual, she argues that we think of photographs as haptic objects that touch us in various affective ways as we encounter them in particularly embodied ways. She calls for us to engage the "sonic frequencies of photographs" (8). She thus juxtaposes the haptic, sonic, historical, and affective aspects through which we view photographs. I argue that Devi's story achieves a similar affective and inter-sensorial quality through the refrain "choli ke pichhe." For Devi's readers, this refrain emphasized repeatedly in the story's opening section evokes the audiovisual spectacle of the Bollywood film *Khal Nayak*'s enormously popular dance number performed to the song of the same name. The phrase, as Devi reminds us, is already burdened by the weight of false morality and female modesty. Subsequently in the story, when we read descriptions of Upin's (absent) photos of Gangor, which highlight her breasts, they carry with them the sonic frequencies of the Bollywood number, as if providing the answer to that leering question, "Choli ke pichhe kya hai?" This connection brought on (both within the logic of the story as well as for Devi's readers familiar with the song and the subsequent debates about female modesty that it raised) by Upin's centering of Gangor's breasts in the images, then makes them the direct cause of her gang rape and brutalization. Abandoning the oft-celebrated power of the visual, Devi instead celebrates Gangor's sayability, represented by her powerful and defiant voice in the story's dramatic climax.

Upin first photographed Gangor nursing her child and, to his surprise, she stuck out her hand asking him for money in lieu of the photograph saying, "Sir, rupees? Snap a photo so give me cash" (144). Upin "crumpled up all the money in his pocket and gave it to her" (144). While his sidekick Ujan is shocked, Upin understands Gangor's behavior, saying, "They are not dumb beasts Ujan, they understand that even when the gentlemen distribute relief they have some hidden agenda" (144). Though they intend to shed light on the plight of the marginalized, elite photographers like Upin also have a profit motive; we are told that Upin's photographs sell for "top rates abroad and at home" (141). He photographs Gangor incessantly, trying to capture the "authentic" beauty of her breasts. Devi describes his photos of her as follows: "A highbreasted rural woman sits slack with her breast shoved into an infant's mouth. The breast is covered with the end of her cloth. The same girl is walking with many girls carrying water on her head. Breasts overflowing like full pitchers" (143).Whether photographed as a young mother or a girl carrying water on her head, Gangor's breasts (and not she herself) form the center of the images. The fine line between objectification of the female body and its aestheticization is thus crossed and Upin's photographs of Gangor completely objectify her body as well as her sexuality. Upin's gaze as the photographer of these images commands his depiction of Gangor, as evidenced by Gangor's name for him – "Camera-Sir." This name combines the source of the capturing gaze, namely Upin, with the instrument of the gaze, his camera. The violence perpetrated by Upin on Gangor's body simply by photographing her is akin to the violence perpetrated by the policemen who later rape her, in that Upin essentializes Gangor's femininity by making her breasts representative of her authenticity, her naturalness as a rural woman, and her womanhood. His photographs unleash the violence of gang rape on her. Even Caretaker, the manager of the bungalow where Upin stays when he visits the village, directly blames Upin's photographs for the rape: "You ruined her with your pictures Sir, otherwise how would she dare" (152). Although Caretaker identifies Upin's photographs as the catalyst which set in motion Gangor's rape, in typical fashion he places the blame on Gangor's "daring" behavior rather than in the masculine lust provoked by the images. His claim that the photographs somehow emboldened her to act in uncharacteristically assertive ways suggests that the images objectified Gangor. As Gayatri Chakraborty Spivak argues in her introduction to the story, "Upin made Gangor self-conscious about the unique beauty of her breasts without any thought of the social repercussions" (1997: xiii). His photographs therefore set in motion the physical violation and brutalization of her body. Thus, while Upin does not in effect rape Gangor, he assaults her violently by photographing her.

Upin is a responsible photojournalist who has brought to light many of the issues plaguing the people of Jharoa – "drought," "pesticide in the river water," "famine conditions," etc. – and his photographs have appeared in the "national press. Also in *Lens Magazine*" (143). However, he also aestheticizes poverty for the Indian elite through his photography. On his fifth trip to cover Jharoa, Upin becomes obsessed with the idea of saving Gangor, which somehow becomes equated for him with saving the breast. The "ace photographer" takes a photograph of Gangor breastfeeding her child. To him, the image represents the authentic femininity of the tribal woman. He hopes that by photographing Gangor's "*statuesque* [...] *mammal* projections" (145) he can save her. Unlike the "breasts of the girls at Elora, [which] are eroding" (147), Upin believes that his photographs will preserve Gangor's breasts and save her, ironically, from rape. However, as Spivak points out, to "preserve the breast as aesthetic *object* by photography or implant is to overlook its value-coding within patriarchal social relationship: it is 'natural' that men should be men" (1997: xiii, emphasis original). In Devi's story, absent images take on multiple connotations. Upin's photograph is used on a banner proclaiming that "The halfnaked amplebreasted [*sic*] female figures of Orissa are about to be raped" and exhorting people to "Save them! Save the breast!" (142). This synecdochic equating of Gangor's breast with all (tribal) female figures of Orissa, is grossly essentializing and deprives her of any individuality.

Ironically, in attempting to speak for Gangor, represent her plight through his photographs, and thereby save her and others like her, Upin creates the way for her subsequent brutalization. Her photograph is used to proclaim the imminent rape of women like her and this proclamation becomes prophetic as it leads to Gangor's horrific gang rape. Instead of her breasts being preserved, they disappear, hacked off leaving "two dry scars. Wrinkled skin. Quite flat" (157). The absence of Upin's photographs within the pages of the story severely undermines photography's indexicality, what Christopher Pinney has called its "stern fidelity" (1997: 17) or its power to tell a fixed truth. It allows Devi to conflate Upin's perception of Gangor with his photographs of her. Beside the images of Gangor described in the story, there are other absent images that Ujan recalls and equates with images of her in Upin's obsessed mind: "Gangor enters Upin's head. No, *those pictures are not here*" (145, emphasis added). Through this double absence – within the materiality of the text as well as the logic of the story – Devi equates the manifestation of Upin's scopophilic gaze with his photographs of Gangor. Ujan goes on to describe these imagined photographs: "Gangor at night, roasting doughballs on a dried cowdung fire, bent slightly forward. Under the dirty red cloth the cleavage of her Konarak chest, resplendent. A train passing, Gangor's crowd looking at it. Her breasts like the cave paintings of Ajanta, against the backdrop of the sky. Dirty choli. Dirty red cloth, hair full of lice, filth ... filth ..." (145, ellipses in original). Devi's ambiguous language suggests that instead of performing their documentary function, Upin's images are constructions of his already sexualized gaze. By comparing Gangor here with the eroticized female portrayals on the walls of the Konarak temple and the cave paintings of Ajanta, Devi momentarily elevates her to the divine. However, we are reminded almost immediately that her *choli* is "dirty [...] hair full of lice, filth." Almost as if to foretell her brutalization later in the story, Gangor's absent image is fractured in these lines – her breasts are elevated to those of mythic origins known for their powers of attraction and seduction while we are simultaneously, somewhat contradictorily reminded of her impoverished and filthy condition.

Despite Upin's intention of capturing Gangor's authenticity, his photographs of her do not provide an authentic representation. Instead, they fix and objectify her in very sexualized ways. As Mary Louisa Cappelli has argued in her analysis of this story, "Upin's frozen image exposes not only the Western gaze of the exotic natural woman's sexuality, but media construction of the breast as a commercial site of patriarchal fetishization and fascination" (2016: 50). Devi depicts Gangor throughout the story as an independent, assertive, and feisty woman. Gangor even attempts to subvert Upin's passive objectification of her by demanding money from him. Instead of capturing Gangor in all her complexity, Upin's photographs emblematize "the halfnaked amplebreasted female figures of Orissa (who) are about to be raped" (142). Ironically, the circulation of these images lead to Gangor's rape and brutalization as they attract the lustful attention of the local police, tempting "everyone to sin against God" (152). The absent presence of Upin's images then serves two functions: on the one hand, it allows Devi to critique Upin's essentializing, scopophilic gaze, which first causes Gangor's commodification and then her desecration and mutilation; on the other, it allows Devi to offer a powerful counternarrative to Upin's photographs through her post-rape depiction of Gangor, which does not fit mainstream portrayals of the traumatized victim. Therefore, the absent image, despite its power, disallows Upin from speaking for Gangor let alone saving her; instead, she powerfully speaks for herself in the story's dramatic denouement.

Devi's depiction of the traumatized Upin and the emboldened and defiant Gangor in the post-rape narrative of "Behind the Bodice" suggests Upin's utter failure to document her rape or even exercise the active gaze that Azoulay speaks of, which could acknowledge Gangor's rape and demand justice on her behalf. When confronted with the devastating consequences of his photography, Upin is utterly powerless to evoke change. When he returns to Jharoa and hears of Gangor's rape, he is still obsessed with saving her. Although the Caretaker directly blames him for the events following his visit, identifying his photographic eye as the main instigator of Gangor's rape – "Who knew Jharoa? You took photos many times. You put us in the news" (153) – Upin fails to comprehend the role his photographs played in causing her brutalization. Instead, ironically using language similar to that of the Caretaker, Upin reasserts his faith in the power of photography to bring justice: "What can the Seopura police do? [...] I'll put pictures in the news" (155). However, the trauma of witnessing Gangor's ravaged body causes him to question the effectiveness of his profession. In a semi-delirious state, unable to fathom the consequences of his actions, he acknowledges his profound failure. Speaking in the third person, as if unable to accept full responsibility for the consequences of his actions, he says, "Upin is a *failure*. What was the good of taking so many pictures of Jharoa, on so many different trips? [...] And nothing has changed. There are more warehouses. A new police station, they harass the women" (154, emphasis original). He recognizes the foolishness of his endeavors: "Gangor's breasts are natural, not manufactured. Why did he first think they were the objects of photography? Why did it seem that that chest was endangered?" (154). Although he does not fully accept his responsibility in Gangor's rape, he now thinks of his act of photographing her as "craziness" (154).

Critics have often alluded to the commonalities between photography as a medium and the effects of trauma. Margaret Iverson suggests that the "automaticity of the process, the wide-open camera lens, and the light sensitivity of film all lend themselves to this association" (1). Photography has the unique capacity for infinite reproduction of the moment it captures and freezes in time. Technical advances enable a photographic negative to be reproduced infinitely. Vijay Mishra has defined trauma in similar terms, alluding to its infinite recurrence without progression: "Trauma repeats itself compulsively and has a historical presence without historical teleology. History cannot be written without trauma, but trauma cannot be part of historical form because trauma disrupts the linear flow of historical narrative with its, history's, basis in an originary moment" (2007: 118). Photographs are similarly grounded in an originary moment, but once a photograph has captured that moment and isolated it from the living stream of history, it can be repeated endlessly with no sense of progression or change. Upin's photographs of Gangor eternally fix her in particularly sexualized modes of excess. These images are then consumed through repetitive cycles of circulation, which ultimately lead to her rape and brutalization. Though her rape is the story's key traumatic event, Upin's act of photographing her may be seen as the originary act of violence and trauma, perpetuating further traumatic acts. As Barthes suggests, in photography, history becomes *hysteria* (1981: 65), analogous to the endless repetition of the originary moment of trauma. In Devi's story, the absent photographs launch the originary moment of trauma. They provide the indisputable answer to the question "Choli ke pichhe kya hai?" Though we never see them, every time the refrain "Choli ke Pichhe" appears in the story, it acts sonically to evoke Upin's photographs, which represent the Barthesian hysteria or endless repetition of Gangor's trauma: "very busy video palace, very loud 'choli ke pichhe', national anthem of these times – Gangor knows what's behind it" (154). When Upin returns to Jharoa to find Gangor, he seems to constantly hear the song playing somewhere in the distance. When he finally encounters Gangor, "suddenly 'choli ke pichhe' starts playing" (155). Upin is shocked to realize that Gangor is "doing whore work" (156) and asks her why. She retorts angrily, "Don't you hear? Constantly playing it, singing it, setting the boys on me ... behind the bodice ... the bodice ... choli ke pichhe ... choli ke ..." (156, ellipses in original). The refrain and its visual counterpart in Upin's photographs have come to be inescapably linked and together encapsulate Gangor's trauma.

In Devi's delineation of the post-rape narrative we see an angry and vengeful Gangor and a nervous and regretful Upin. The roles of the passive rural woman and the powerful postcolonial intellectual attempting to capture her essence with his objectifying gaze seem now to be reversed as "Upin and Gangor look at each other" (155). His gaze is reciprocated and is no longer the active gaze that fixes the passive woman. Ironically, Gangor has been transformed radically from the mother in Upin's photographs to a prostitute. She now invites the sexualizing gaze; as they look at each other a "sharp experienced smile blooms on Gangor's lips" and she now actively returns his look "as if she [were] say[ing] to Upin with her beckoning finger, Get thee behind me!" (155). "Upin offers himself, lets himself go" (155). The two of them enter a shack and notably he is the one who has difficulty seeing: "Upin *can't see* what else there is in the room" (156, emphasis added). When he realizes that Gangor has now become a prostitute, he haltingly demands she take off her blouse. When Gangor finally takes off her *choli* or bodice, Upin does not see her body directly. Her nakedness is mediated to him through the silhouette cast by the hurricane lantern. He is unable to look at her body and she commands him to look at her. Instead of being the passive recipient of the look, Gangor now directs Upin's look toward herself. However, this time it is not to arouse an erotic impulse but rather to evoke horror and guilt in Upin. She says, "look, look, look, straw – chaff, rags – look what's there" (157). Gangor's command – "look what's there" – highlights what is absent, namely her breasts, that Upin had thought of as endangered and had made into the object of his photography in his desperate attempt to save them. This stark absence contrasts sharply with Upin's absent (present) photographs of Gangor, in which her breasts were prominent. Here she is powerfully using her body as a weapon to draw attention to her abuse and exploitation. Urvashi Butalia writes about this phenomenon while discussing a 2004 protest of a young woman's rape and murder by the army in Manipur. A group of naked women marched down the streets of Imphal holding banners inviting rape. Through a self-commodification of their bodies, the women subvert notions of sexualization and the gaze in order to demand justice. Butalia argues that this abandonment of social propriety by middle-class women as a form of protest, the use of their bodies as weapons designed "not to harm but to shame and humiliate" (2017: n.pag.), left society unable to react. Butalia notes that despite the sensational nature of the protest, very few media outlets carried photos of the naked women: "Either they didn't have them – which seems unlikely – or they could not stomach the thought of showing middle-class Indian women (read 'mothers') naked!" This underscores photography's failure to record demands for justice against the most egregious forms of gender violence in the postcolonial nation. Gangor's act of stripping is at once an invitation for transactional sex – "Do your stuff, twenty rupees. Spend the night, fifty, tell me quick" (156) – but also a demand that Upin exercise his active gaze and thereby reconstruct her brutalization and acknowledge it as rape, as suggested by Azoulay. The photojournalist, who wanted to save the breast, is now utterly powerless to document the ravaging of the breast. What Upin sees are not Gangor's fantastic and resplendent breasts but instead:

> Two dry scars, wrinkled skin, quite flat. The two raging volcanic craters spew liquid lava at Upin—*gang rape* ... biting and tearing *gang rape* ... *police* ... a court *case* ... again a *gang rape* in the *lockup* ... now from

> Jharoa to Seopura ... Seopura to Jharoa ... the Contractor catches clients ... terrorizes a *public* ... plays the song, the song ...
>
> Upin stands up weaving, unsteady. (157, all ellipses and emphases in original)

Upin's reaction – his loss for words and his unsteadiness – constitute a crucial moment in the story. It is the moment signifying the transmissibility of trauma or what Dominick LaCapra calls "empathetic unsettlement" (2013: 41). The figure of the bare-chested, breastless Gangor is in sharp contrast with Upin's eroticized portrait of her. Gangor's fierce accusations of sexual exploitation – "But I knew your plans. Otherwise would you have given so much cash?" and "You are a bastard too sir ... you took *photoks* [photos] of my chest, eh?" (156, ellipses in original) – hit home. "Upin runs along the tracks" (157), presumably to his death. Devi harshly indicts the postcolonial artist who distances his creation from the ordinary people and exploits them in order to aestheticize their poverty. She is equally critical of photography itself as an impotent mode that tragically fails to speak for its subjects.

As Upin runs crazed and confused along the railway tracks, the reversal between the traumatized subject and the unwitting agent of the traumatic act that Devi has sustained through the story is now complete. Upin is not only stripped of his photographic and objectifying gaze but is harshly implicated in the violence that has been enacted upon Gangor's body. Gangor's breasts – or their absence – become transformed from the fixed, erotic objects of Upin's portraits to a counteroffensive. She is portrayed in this scene as a fierce and vengeful woman. Her voice is "ragged with anger" (156) and her body emits the "smell of violent resentment" (157). Upin, on the other hand, is wracked by guilt. He feels responsible for Gangor's rape and for the collective rape of the subaltern – "Upin would have known if he had wanted to, could have known" (157). The last reference to him in the story is implied, to "a months-old picture of a dead man" (157) given to his friend Ujan. This is a final photographic reversal between Gangor and Upin, between resilient pride and wracking guilt, between the angrily articulate and the eternally silenced. The (absent) photographic image of the dead Upin is in sharp contrast with the articulate and resilient Gangor in the concluding pages of Devi's story.

The function of the breasts as national allegory comes to be clearly articulated in the last lines of the story – "There is no *non-issue* behind the bodice, there is a rape of the people behind it" (157, original emphasis) – and in the figure of the traumatized Upin running to his death along the railway tracks. In this phrase, Devi radically subverts Upin's photographic essentialism of Gangor's female body. She does so by making the breast symptomatic not of Gangor's womanhood, rural authenticity, and subaltern status, as Upin had hoped to do, but rather by making the violent image of the absence of her breasts symptomatic of the rape of *all* subaltern and dispossessed populations, thereby highlighting the real issue that lies behind the bodice. The figure of the violently raped and disfigured, yet resilient subaltern woman in the concluding pages of Devi's story becomes a severe indictment of violence and exploitation of the dispossessed in the postcolonial democratic nation. In contrast, the figure of the crazed photojournalist who has taken on the trauma of the people after unwittingly causing it, is representative of the ineffectual postcolonial elite and their often fetishizing gaze.

## Conclusion

Postcolonial trauma theory has revealed the many shortcomings of Western trauma theory – its event-based Eurocentric bias, its foregrounding of what Visser calls "an atemporal human (universal) trauma as expressed in [Caruth's] oft-quoted phrase that history is the history of a trauma" (2011: 275), and its emphasis on the impossibility of narrating trauma. Reading Devi's story through a trauma theory lens and contrasting her depictions of the visual and the verbal allows us to question these assumptions. Western psychoanalytic discourses of trauma often emphasize the unspeakability and aporia of the traumatic event. Dori Laub describes a traumatized state as:

> The persistence of an event that has no beginning, no ending, no before, no during and no after. This absence of categories that define it lends it a quality of "otherness," a salience, a timelessness and a ubiquity that puts it outside the range of associatively linked experiences, outside the range of comprehension, of recounting and of mastery. [...] The survivor indeed, is not truly in touch with the core of his traumatic reality or with the fatedness of its reenactments, and thereby remains entrapped in both. (1992: 68–69)

Such psychoanalytic analysis, whose applicability to postcolonial trauma is questioned by Visser, is rendered meaningless in analyzing the trauma depicted in Devi's story. The brutalized Gangor vengefully commands Upin to look at her ravaged body, her breastless torso. Her subjectivity has not been shattered, neither has she retreated to a space of passive, aporetic silence incapable of human communication. Instead, she fiercely articulates her narrative of brutalization and demands justice. Devi's story narrates a post-rape afterlife for her female protagonist that is not envisioned as death, reclusive silence or disappearance. The figure of the photographer Upin and his absent-present images of Gangor, serve to heighten the contrast between his attempts to "save" her, which end in utter failure, and her own defiant voice even in the face of extreme denigration. I suggest that by listening to the (absent) images that take on a sonic connotation in the refrain "choli ke pichhe," and exploring the multiple connotations of the absent images in Devi's story, we can complicate questions of the visual representation of trauma and critique the role of the postcolonial intellectual in documenting the trauma of the subaltern. This in turn offers us opportunities to decolonize trauma theory.

# PART II

# The Absent Image as Metaphor

> "Send pictures," they write. "Send pictures of your new life." "What picture can I send?" She sat, exhausted, on the edge of the bed, where there was now barely room for her. "They think I live the life of a queen, Eliot." She looked around the blank walls of the room. "They think I press buttons and the house is clean. They think I live in a palace."
>
> Jhumpa Lahiri, "Mrs. Sen's," 125

These lines appear after a scene in Jhumpa Lahiri's story, when the eponymous Mrs. Sen takes Eliot, the American boy she babysits at her home, to the bedroom and begins to pull out all her saris from various drawers and closets lamenting the fact that she never has the opportunity to wear these beautiful clothes. The urgent demands of relatives from India for photographs documenting her "new life" are loaded with suggestions of economic prosperity and a life of leisure for Mrs. Sen, which is far from the reality of her mundane and lonely life in the American Northeast. The repetition of "They think" alluding to the relatives in the above lines underscores the falsity of their beliefs. The room is "filled with an intense smell of mothballs" as if to heighten the stasis that plagues Mrs. Sen's life and her failed attempt at preserving the happiness of her past life in Calcutta.

Migrants are familiar with this exhortation of family members to send photographs from the new country. The demand brings with it the unspoken assumption that one would not have left the homeland if it were not for a far better life that surely awaited them elsewhere. Such a view of course elides the travails of immigrant life, erasing any acknowledgment of the struggles that must be endured in order to achieve greater prosperity. This causes Mrs. Sen intense frustration, leading eventually to her emotional outburst.

Here again photography is called upon to serve an indexical function, that of providing evidence of a better life and economic prosperity. Scholars like Tina Campt (2012), Sigrid Lien (2018), Anthony Lee (2014), Bakirathi Mani (2020), and others have studied the intersections of photography and migration. Sigrid Lien begins her book *Pictures of Longing* with a discussion of a faded photograph of her grandfather who had left Norway to live in the United States, but was later forced to return home when his wife died. She concludes that the photograph brought with it "proof" that "grandfather had been a cowboy in America" (1). Photographs like these, sent back home by immigrants, have become a particular photographic genre that scholars have read as careful constructions producing a particular version of history (Trachtenburg 1990: iii).

Photography has documented the migrations and lives of diasporic people and has helped to construct diaspora by making visible commonalities amongst various diasporic communities (Sheehan 2018: 14). Scholarship on photography and migration produced in the wake of the resurgence of diaspora studies and a celebration of hybridity, "imaginary homelands" (Rushdie 1991), multiple belongings and fluid identities, also celebrates a "multiple viewpoint" (Mirzoeff 2002: 208). Nicholas Mirzoeff has argued for an "intervisual" approach since the diasporic visual image is "necessarily intertextual," lacking a single, easily recognizable visual rhetoric as we find in the visualization of national cultures (209). Bakirathi Mani (2020) has written eloquently about the ways in which South Asian Americans seek affirmation of themselves in photographic representations of diaspora. Yet such racialized depictions remain haunted by photography's history of documentary and surveillance uses in the service of empire.

Moving away from the role that real photographs play in the lives of immigrants while also returning to an older understanding of diaspora as a catastrophic loss of the homeland, I turn to photography as metaphor. Jhumpa Lahiri's work with its frequent use of photography either in the form of narrated images or characters who are photographers, provides the object of my study. In this part, I analyze photography as metaphor in two of her texts – her three-part "Hema and Kaushik" story cycle and her 2013 novel *The Lowland*. Although these texts lack any real images, I argue that they engage with the trope of photography in a variety of ways. This allows Lahiri to delineate the diasporic identities of her characters in ways different from what the text may suggest. The discussion of photography as metaphor is not new and can be found in the works of Sigmund Freud (see Smith and Sliwinsky 2017). Deeply influenced by Freud's work, Walter Benjamin developed one of the most influential concepts in photography theory, namely the optical unconscious or the idea that by making visible what remains invisible to the naked eye, photography also opens up new realms of experience. Benjamin also notes a loss of authenticity in the reproducibility of photography due to its distance from the originary moment (1986). Shawn Michelle Smith (2013) builds on Benjamin's theory to suggest that photography's intense desire to see produces an excess that paradoxically heightens awareness of the lack inherent in it. The absent presence of photographs in Lahiri's texts analyzed in this part of the book, and photography's many parallels with diaspora – distance from an originary time and place, a heightened awareness of lack, etc. – allow me to consider the affordances of photography, in particular its absent presence, as metaphor.

# 4

# Diaspora's "Darkroom": Photography and the Vision of Loss in Jhumpa Lahiri's "Hema and Kaushik"

What I see [...] has been here, and yet immediately separated; it has been absolutely, irrefutably present, and yet already deferred.

Roland Barthes, *Camera Lucida*, 77

Photographs contain a realization of loss in the fundamental sense that every photograph represents a past real moment that actually happened but is no longer. It is a myth that photographs bring back memories. Photographs show not the presence of the past but the pastness of the present. They show the irreversible passing of time.

Jay Prosser, *Light in the Dark Room*, 1

## Introduction

Diaspora has come to be celebrated in late modernity as engendering hybrid, cosmopolitan identities. While early scholars like James Clifford (1994) and William Safran (1991) described it as dispersal from the homeland, the term's scope has now broadened to include any kind of migration to geographical spaces outside the originary home. Understandings of diaspora have veered away from earlier notions of a lamentable and "catastrophic" loss (Cohen 2008: 6). Along with the shifts in our understanding of diaspora and the identities it fosters, attitudes toward home and homelessness have also undergone changes. Early definitions of diaspora, such as Walker Connor's "that segment of a people living outside the homeland" (qtd. in Safran 1991: 83), take "home" for granted and essentialize a fixed home, as though to suggest that "home" can be created only within the homeland. William Safran adds to Connor's definition by assigning certain characteristics to diasporic communities: movement from a center to a peripheral region, retention of a collective memory of the homeland, the hope of eventual return, and so on (1991: 83–84). Hobsbawm, too, argues that home represents both "the place from which we set out and to which we return, at least in spirit" (qtd. in Rapport and Dawson 1998: 23). However, as dislocation and displacement have come to be celebrated, home and placement have come under suspicion and theorists have problematized conceptions of an originary home. Avtar Brah, for example, describes home for diasporic people as "the lived experience of locality" (1996: 192). Lucinda Newns has critiqued the way in which for immigrants, "any attachment to home spaces can be figured as embracing insularity and segregation and a resistance to integration or cultural syncretism" (2020: 4).

Much of Jhumpa Lahiri's writing is concerned with the loss of homeland for first- and second-generation Bengali immigrants to the US. She does not subscribe to the liberatory and celebratory models of diasporic identity-formation that have found currency in recent times. Most of the first-generation immigrant characters in her works, whether it be Ashima from *The Namesake* or the eponymous Mrs. Sen, are deeply haunted by the loss of homeland. Her second-generation protagonists are arguably more ambiguous about the loss of a home they never knew. Yet many of them attempt to confront this loss in their own way and remain marked by it in very tragic ways.[1] The loss of home is often doubled for second-generation immigrants who must confront their own indirect loss of homeland as well as try to apprehend the loss felt more acutely by their parents. As Robin Field has noted, in "When Mr. Pirzada Came to Dine" Lahiri uses the perspective of the ten-year-old Lilia to "underscore the psychological as well as the physical distance of the second generation from their parents' land and culture" (2004: 169). However, Lilia's own sense of unease is attributed to her realization, thanks to Mr. Pirzada's watch, which was set to keep Dacca time, that "life was being lived in Dacca first" (30), and connects with her own unprocessed loss of homeland and her consequent "bicultural identity crisis" (Wilhite 2016: 84). In this chapter, through a close reading of Lahiri's three-part story cycle "Hema and Kaushik," I argue that photography provides an effective trope for her to discuss questions of home and belonging for her second-generation immigrant protagonist Kaushik.

This chapter begins with the premise that photography reflects the unconscious. In doing so, it cannot avoid gesturing toward the work of

[1] For example, it may be argued that Shoba and Shukumar's marriage in "A Temporary Matter" is always already weakened by their lack of rootedness and simply cannot withstand the loss of a child.

Walter Benjamin, the most influential, though not the first (Freud preceded him), thinker to explore the ways in which photography reflects the human unconscious. He coined the phrase the "optical unconscious" to suggest that which the camera reveals. In his landmark essay "The Work of Art in the Age of Mechanical Reproduction," Benjamin reflects on the profound changes in our perception of art brought about by the possibility of mechanical reproduction. Photography is even more profoundly affected by these innovations since mechanical reproduction dismantles all hierarchies between the original and the copy in photography, something it manifestly cannot do in the case of fine art. Consequently, mechanical reproduction allows a work to appear beyond the domain of its presence. Though impressed by the reproducibility of art that the technological age affords, mechanically reproduced art ultimately falls short because for Benjamin reproducibility is incommensurate with authenticity. In the case of photography, this is not because the reproduced image is necessarily lacking or inferior. In fact, Walter Benjamin concedes that the reproduced image may bring out more than is visible to the human eye – mechanical processes like enlargement can capture what the naked eye fails to register. The reproduced image may then be more detailed or nuanced, but it lacks the authenticity of the original. The second aspect in which the reproduced image is lacking for Benjamin concerns the question of distance: he writes, "technical reproduction can put the copy of the original into situations which would be out of reach for the original itself" (1968: 220). Together, these two aspects result in "withering" (Benjamin's term) what Benjamin has famously called the "aura" of the artwork. He has described aura in various ways in his writings; here he describes it as "the unique phenomenon of a distance, however close it may be" (222). What we most value in photography – its ability to bring to us people, places, and events from another time and place – is what Benjamin fiercely disapproves. He believes that the original has a "uniqueness and permanence" that cannot be matched by the "transitoriness and reproducibility" (223) of the copy.

I find in Benjamin's analysis of photography a perfect metaphor for exploring questions of diasporic identity and belonging in Jhumpa Lahiri's novella "Hema and Kaushik." Lahiri uses the absent presence of photography in crucial ways to delineate the sense of loss felt by the twice-displaced Kaushik and his failure to deal with the shock and trauma of these displacements. Benjamin's concept of the "optical unconscious" allows me to explore what remains unspoken yet subtly suggested in Kaushik's engagement with photography. I read Benjamin's second quibble with photography, the question of distance, as a way of spatializing the optical unconscious. I argue that Kaushik attempts to engender a sense of rootedness and belonging through photography but, given photography's always already lost origins and lack of emplacement, he ultimately fails to find in it a sense of place. I read what Reshmi Dutt Ballerstadt has called Kaushik's "exilic nomadism" (2012) as akin to photography's detachment from a specific, unique place. Photographs, then, can be present anywhere but are not located anywhere in particular. Kaushik deliberately stays away from both of the places he has called home – India and the US – seeking belonging elsewhere.

## Photography and Second-Generation Diasporic Identity

A few pages into Jhumpa Lahiri's three-part story "Hema and Kaushik," which comprises Part 2 of her collection *Unaccustomed Earth* (2008), we encounter a scene of recollection. Hema, now thirteen, recalls her earliest memories of Kaushik at a farewell party that her parents threw for his family seven years previously, when they decided to move back to India. The immediate stimulus for this recollection is that Kaushik and his family are now returning to Cambridge. Hema looks at pictures in an album taken the night of the farewell party:

> There was my father, his stiff jet-black hair already a surprise to me by then. He was dressed in a sweater vest, his shirt cuffs rolled back, pointing urgently at something *beyond the frame.* Your father was in the suit and tie he always wore, his handsome, bespectacled face leaning toward someone in conversation, his greenish eyes unlike anyone else's. The middle part in your mother's hair accentuated the narrow length of her face; the end of her raw silk sari was wrapped around her shoulders like a shawl. My mother stood beside her, a head shorter and more dishevelled, stray hairs hanging by her ears. They both appeared flushed, the color high in their cheeks, as if from drinking wine, even though all they ever drank in those days was tap water or tea, the bond between them clear. There was no evidence of you, the person I was most curious about. Who knows where you had lurked in that crowd? I imagine you sat at the desk in the corner of my parents' bedroom, reading a book you'd brought with you, waiting for the party to end. (230–231, emphasis added)

This photograph represents more than a slice of immigrant life frozen in time; it also implies a fracture between first-generation immigrant parents and second-generation children growing up in a culture that is familiar and comfortable for them in a way that it will never be for their parents. Hema describes her parents and Kaushik's as relics from a different time and place, somewhat uncomfortable in this foreign land. Their appearance and attire are marked by a difference that Hema is acutely aware of because she looks at them the way other Americans might. The things that stand out for her in the photograph – her father's surprisingly jet-black hair, his habit of wearing a sweater vest with his shirt cuffs rolled back, Kaushik's father's suit and tie which he "always wore," suggesting probably that it is the only one he has (231), and their sari-clad mothers with their flushed cheeks, not from drinking wine as one might expect – are things that an American may notice about them. Like the ten-year-old Lilia in "When Mr. Pirzada Came to Dine," thirteen-year-old Hema's gaze underscores her distance from her parents' culture. Lahiri chooses to open the story a few pages earlier with Hema's recollection of the night the photo was taken. At that time Hema was only six, still an extension of her parents, being raised as an immigrant child in America. She remembers being dressed that night in an outfit that her grandmother had sent from Calcutta, "white pajamas with tapered legs and a waist wide enough to gird two of me side by side, a turquoise kurta and a black velvet vest embroidered with plastic pearls" (224). She recalls fretting about the purple letters stamped on the pajama and "wanting to wear something else" (224). The psychological distance between Hema and her parents' culture that is in evidence in the later scene of Hema looking at the photograph was clearly absent on the actual day and only developed in the intervening years as Hema developed her own Indo-American identity uncomfortable with many aspects of her immigrant life such as having to wear Kaushik's hand-me-downs for many years until she outgrew them: "I found these clothes ugly and tried to avoid them, but my mother refused to replace them" (226).

In the above scene, the reader's attention is also drawn to what lies "beyond the frame" of the photograph – the thing at which Hema's father points, as well as Kaushik, the other second-generation protagonist of the story, for whom Hema constructs an alternative space as if he cannot be contained within the frame of the photograph. She imagines him beyond the frame, sitting "at the desk at the corner of my parents' bedroom, reading a book you'd brought with you, waiting for the party to end" (231). The thirteen-year-old Hema looking for the then nine-year-old Kaushik, presumably aligns him in her imagination more with herself and imagines him doing what she might have done if made to attend a party thrown by her parents' friends. Her imagined construction of him beyond the frame links them as second-generation immigrants different and at a distance from their parents captured in the frame.

Lahiri uses the photograph to underscore the generational distances in immigrant identity that have emerged between the time the photograph was taken and the moment when Hema looks at it seven years later. Photographs capture and freeze memories, thus preserving them; they arrest the flow of time in which the event photographed once existed; and they almost always hint at something lying outside the frame. There is inherent in photography a paradox of time. While photos capture the past, in doing so they also gesture toward a futurity. Hema looking at a photo taken seven years earlier as she waits to meet Kaushik, who is now returning to Massachusetts with his family, connects the past to the present. Within that photograph, we can find the kernel of the present moment. Here Lahiri uses photography's multi-temporality in order to comment on the theme of diaspora that is so central to her wider corpus. The paradoxes inherent in photography offer Lahiri a useful trope to articulate second-generation diasporic identity. Suggesting that Kaushik is haunted by a double loss of homeland, I posit that photography offers him a way to create an alternative history, a way out of mourning the traumatic loss of homeland. However, ultimately, this proves to be a false promise and Kaushik fails to make his way out of what I have here called "diaspora's darkroom."

It is a truism that photographs never lie, yet they are carefully constructed compositions, omitting as much as they contain. Roland Barthes has suggested that a photograph, reproduced potentially to infinity, has nevertheless occurred only once. As soon as the click of the shutter takes place, the subject is transformed into object (1993: 4). John Berger and Jean Mohr concur in their book *Another Way of Telling*: "A photograph arrests the flow of time in which the event photographed once existed. An instant of the past is arrested, so that unlike a lived past it can never lead to the present" (1989: 86). This sense of capturing a moment for posterity, memorializing and objectifying it by plucking it from the living stream of continuity, provides me with a productive way of engaging Lahiri's work and to argue that she uses the trope of photography to impart to her second-generation immigrant characters a sense of rootedness and belonging that ultimately proves to be tenuous. The notion of home and return remains fraught for second-generation immigrants. Since the children of immigrants have no firsthand experience of migration, for them migration involves a phantom loss of homeland. I contend that Lahiri deliberately foregrounds the trope of photography in this story because of its double edge: its ability to capture a moment and preserve it for posterity and, conversely, its inalienable connection with absence, loss, and even death. The contradictions within photography provide Lahiri with the means to reflect the ambivalent nature of home, belonging, and diaspora for characters like Hema and Kaushik.

As a means of mechanical reproduction and therefore more realistic than painting, photography can, according to Benjamin, capture the secrets of the photographed object that may not be visible to the human eye; thus "the camera introduces us to unconscious optics" (1968: 237). A more detailed expression of this can be found in his earlier essay, "A Small History of Photography":

> No matter how artful the photographer, no matter how carefully posed his subject, the beholder feels an irresistible urge to search [...] a picture for the tiny spark of contingency, of the Here and Now, with which reality has so to speak seared the subject, to find the inconspicuous spot where in the immediacy of that long forgotten moment the future subsists so eloquently that we, looking back, may discover it. For it is another nature that speaks to the camera than to the eye: other in the sense of a space informed by human consciousness gives way to a space informed by the unconscious [...] Photography [...] reveals the secret. It is through photography that we first discover the existence of [the] optical unconscious, just as we discover the instinctual unconscious through psychoanalysis. (1985: 243)

For Benjamin, photography does not simply freeze a moment in time, it also projects the future from the past that is captured in the photo. The "spark of contingency" that the future viewer sees in it resides beyond the presence of the moment photographed. If we return to the narrated photograph in the opening pages of "Hema and Kaushik," we can see that Hema finds the spark of contingency in the absent presence of Kaushik. She imagines him sitting in another room reading a book, "waiting for the party to end" and thereby already imagining a moment past the immediate temporality of the image she is studying. Benjamin's theorization attributes to photography a paradoxical, Janus-faced quality. Photographs capture a moment that has passed, yet they gesture toward a futurity and can thus be read as metaphoric of both loss and hope. Christopher Pinney has also noted the ability of photographs to invite a backward glance while also being oriented toward a future (in Pinney and Punjabi 2014: 64). In this chapter, I argue that this double-edged quality of photography allows Lahiri to use it as a trope in delineating her second-generation protagonist Kaushik, who is haunted by a double displacement from both of the places he has called home.

## Twice Removed: The Trauma of Kaushik's Double Displacement

Vijay Mishra begins his book *The Literature of the Indian Diaspora* (2007) with the following striking sentence: "All diasporas are unhappy, but every diaspora is unhappy in its own way" (1). Mishra uses psychoanalysis, particularly trauma studies and Freudian conceptualizations of mourning, to theorize diaspora as a traumatic event. One of the cornerstones of trauma theory is that trauma can be transmitted to those who may not have experienced it firsthand in such a way that it has a lasting presence in the lives of subsequent generations. Mishra conceives of the moment of originary trauma as the loss of homeland, which creates an eternal wound that is transmitted generationally until all memory of the homeland is obliterated or until the migrant is able to reintegrate it into their psyches. Return as an act of healing is impossible because as Mishra reminds us, in an ironic twist of its epistemic origins, "diasporas do not return to their homeland (real or imagined)" (2). Nor can the loss be ameliorated since there is no substitution for it via the nation-state. For Mishra the "primal loss" (9) of the homeland can never be cured because the diasporic condition is one of "an impossible mourning that transforms mourning into melancholia" (9). This melancholia is heightened for the second generation, who can only experience the loss of homeland as a phantom loss.

Although Jhumpa Lahiri's fiction features many protagonists who are second-generation immigrants, only a few scholars have paid attention to questions of these characters' diasporic identity-formation in her writing. Delphine Munos's book-length study of second-generation diasporic subjectivity in Jhumpa Lahiri's work, *After Melancholia* (2013), uses psychoanalytic theory to explore the ways in which the second generation is impacted by their parents' separation from the originary homeland. Most of the book offers a close reading of Lahiri's triptych which powerfully explores transgenerational forms of mourning and melancholia. Dutt Ballerstadt has proposed that the rupture and dislocation felt by Indo-American subjects is not due to the clash of cultures they experience but rather by the untimely passing of a parental figure, a death that then becomes the site of mourning and melancholia for characters like Kaushik (162). In her article "Writing the Second Generation," Robin Field comments on the "transience of 'ethnic American' identity" (2004: 167) for Lahiri's second-generation immigrants, who attempt instead to form their diasporic identity by moving toward a "transnational, post-ethnic ethos" (167).

In many ways, second-generation immigrants have a more vexed process of identity-formation in diaspora than that of their parents. They are born and raised in a national and cultural space that is not autochthonous to them. They have a secondhand understanding of their native culture which is passed on to them by their parents, who are themselves often holding on to arcane and fixed notions of cultural identity arising from their calcified memory of the home country. The second generation learn about their roots either in brief visits "back home" or in a familial setting, rarely through any formal education. Recognizing themselves as different from their parents in crucial ways, second-generation immigrants are faced with the difficult choice of performing their ethnic identity or disavowing it completely. Despite frequently celebrated notions of hybridity, fluidity, and cosmopolitanism that shape immigrant identity, the second generation often face a dual alienation, never fully belonging in either homeland. In addition, children of immigrants may experience intense pressure to perform the expectations of model minorities and to find economic success. Susan Koshy has used the term "filial gothic" to connote these pressures resulting from the "deformation of filiality in economic migration" (2013: 355).

Lahiri's *Unaccustomed Earth* opens with an epigraph from Nathaniel Hawthorne about human nature not flourishing "any more than a potato, if it be planted and replanted, for too long a series of generations, in the same worn-out soil." While this seems to allude to the advantages of migration and the possibilities it offers for hybrid identities, many characters in this collection (as in Lahiri's earlier work) feel anachronistic and disempowered as they attempt to strike root in "unaccustomed earth." As Koshy has argued, Lahiri's adoption of Hawthorne's optimistic metaphor of the benefits of transplantation is "pensive, ironic" (2013: 356). Even "hyphenated" second-generation children of immigrants are unable to assimilate fully into American culture. Of Lahiri's second-generation protagonists, Kaushik from "Hema and Kaushik" is somewhat different. he is particularly affected by two tumultuous upheavals – his move away from America as a child and his subsequent return as a young adult. He was born in Massachusetts but lived there only until the age of nine, when his parents moved back to India. He returns to Cambridge, Massachusetts with them seven years later when his parents decide to relocate back to the United States. Therefore, the loss of the originary homeland for him is both a phantom loss (experienced via his parents when he was a child) as well as a real one, experienced once again when he is sixteen. This double displacement from the originary homeland, coupled with a temporary displacement from the United States, exacerbates his sense of homelessness and lack of rootedness. He at once feels kinship with Hema, a second-generation immigrant like him, but also with his stepsiblings, the two young daughters of Chitra, the woman from India whom his father marries and brings back to Massachusetts after Kaushik's mother dies. At first, as we may expect, he finds little in common with them – "I felt separate from them in every way" (272), yet he is forced to confront that which binds him to them. Surprisingly, this is not the father they now share but the sense of displacement that is equally familiar to them. Kaushik says, "Like them, I'd made that journey from India to Massachusetts, too old not to *experience the shock of it*, too young to have a say in the matter" (272, emphasis added). This is the only moment in the story when Kaushik acknowledges the pain of the second upheaval, the choice of his words seeming to suggest that he might have remained in India if he had "a say in the matter."

Some have argued that in negotiating the two homelands, second-generation youth often identify more with the American side of their identity, which is comparatively far more real, accessible, and lived. Mary Mathew for example, has suggested that these youth remain at a distance from their bicultural parents as their "imaginations construct the homeland as a series of absences and negations" (2007: 218) or, as Lahiri says of one of her most memorable second-generation immigrant protagonists, Gogol, he "never thinks of India as *desh*. He thinks of it as Americans do, as India" (2004: 118). For Kaushik, however, the concept of *desh* has some meaning since he has experienced life in Bombay for seven years. Lahiri's story is firmly located in the diasporic space of the United States and we never hear about Kaushik's life in India in the interim years between the Chaudhuri family's departure from Cambridge and their return seven years later. This, I contend, is deliberate on Lahiri's part; Kaushik feels the loss of homeland even more acutely than other second-generation characters in Lahiri's fiction. He is unable to articulate the "shock" of that departure or even speak about the time he spent in India. This is in keeping with Vijay Mishra's contention, following Freud's characterization of mourning and melancholia, that the object of mourning (in this case, the memory of the homeland) remains unrepresentable. According to Mishra it "defies representation" (2007: 9). The trope of photography, I argue, allows Lahiri to represent Kaushik's sense of loss. In pursuing a career as a photojournalist, Kaushik embraces an exilic nomadism that takes him away from both of the places he has called home. I contend that he seeks in photography a sense of rootedness and belonging, which he desperately craves. Photography with its double edge of loss and enlightenment, pastness and futurity, ultimately fails Kaushik.

Mishra has argued that the diasporic imaginary is characterized by an impossible mourning. He writes

> the truth of mourning in literature, as figurative language, effectively implies that true mourning can never be defined, except as an absence [...] The normal working of mourning is precisely this, an idealization of absence because it is prior to the possibility of mourning ... True mourning becomes impossible because we do not accept the truth, the textuality of mourning. (8)

Thus, it is the attempt to represent mourning that precludes true mourning. Kaushik's attempts to photograph things around him may be interpreted as the desire to capture what is absent, thereby falsely attempting to define a loss to be mourned. For second-generation immigrants like Hema and Kaushik, migration is tied to an originary moment that they cannot access in memory. They are condemned to eternally memorialize the haunting absence, or, in Mishra's terms, to idealize the absent. The photograph is often described in similar terms. Eduardo Cadava, for example, defines the photograph as "the return of what was once there," which "takes the form of haunting" (1998: 11). Kaushik's desire to photograph everyday occurrences during his adolescence and his later, brief career as a war photographer are, I argue, a means by which he attempts to retrieve the past. However, his efforts are constantly undermined by the fact that representing a moment photographically takes the form of a haunting: photographs ironically heighten loss by resuscitating memory. Instead of providing him with roots and access to the past that would give him a secure sense of diasporic identity, photographs and photography simply exacerbate Kaushik's sense of phantom loss and diasporic mourning.

## Photography's Double Edge

Kaushik attempts to deal with his lack of rootedness and belonging by celebrating his itinerant life as a photojournalist who visits war-torn areas documenting the destruction with his camera, in an attempt to defy the need for a place of belonging. Lahiri uses photography's double edge – its power to confer truth and legitimacy upon a moment, but contradictorily also to contain within it the loss of that moment forever – as a metaphor in the characterization of her doubly displaced protagonist. As a war correspondent based in Rome and sent on assignment to South America, Africa, and the Middle East, Kaushik becomes the quintessential translocated citizen of the world, occupying a number of fractured spaces. He virtually severs connections to both his originary home (India) and his diasporic home (the US): he does not return to either place for years and feels no need to do so. "As a photographer his origins were irrelevant" (310), Kaushik, thinks, although the naiveté of this is exposed in the very next line: "And yet, in Rome, in all of Europe, he was always regarded as an Indian first" (310). Susan Sontag suggests that "photographs give people an imaginary possession of a past that is unreal, they also help people to take possession of a space in which they are insecure" (1977: 9). Photojournalism gives Kaushik a sense of control over his existential reality, perhaps combating the rootlessness he feels as a twice-displaced individual. He finds comfort and meaning in the power that comes with the ability to document events, thereby granting them legitimacy, coupled with the detachment he feels as a photojournalist. However, the double edge of photography constantly makes us aware of the falsity and ultimate failure of attempts to find meaning and belonging through the act of photography.

Photography has been described as a noninterventionist act, "The person who intervenes cannot record; the person who is recording cannot intervene," and the photographer as "someone moving through a panorama of disparate events with such agility and speed that any intervention is out of the question" (Sontag 1977: 12). Kaushik strongly identifies with this noninterventionist role. It allows him a sense of detachment. One of his first published photographs was taken when he is living in Guatemala, of a man who had been shot in the head: "When he thought back to that afternoon, he remembered that his hands were shaking but that otherwise he felt untouched by the situation, unmoved once he was behind the camera, shooting to the end of the roll" (304–305). Lahiri's suggestion, however, seems to be that photography is not entirely noninterventionist; it also functions as a form of participation that offers Kaushik a way to confront his own isolation and lack of power: "though he had not saved the man's life, he had *felt useful,* aware that he had *done* something to mitigate the crime" (305, emphasis added). Photography temporarily provides Kaushik with a sense of making a difference. He does not acknowledge this easily, instead choosing to remain dispassionately detached as he documents horrific war crimes and acts of torture: "He could no longer remember all the corpses he had photographed" (305). Sontag points out that "To photograph is to appropriate the thing photographed. It means putting oneself into a certain relation to the world that feels like knowledge – and, therefore, like power" (1977: 4). Although Kaushik does not acknowledge his acts of appropriation through photography, his work gives him a sense of purpose and meaning. As he travels the world seeking the latest news story, photography also allows him to avoid the US, the unacknowledged site of both displacement and belonging.

A certain power relates also to conferring importance on an event by (not) photographing it. When Kaushik comes home from college to visit his father and his new family over Christmas, he deliberately does not bring his camera with him, "knowing that I would not want to document anything" (280). It is as though by not photographing this particular Christmas, he is denying it legitimacy. Later, when he is a professional photojournalist and Chitra and his father visit him in Rome, he takes them to the popular tourist sites, and takes pictures of them, "handing his father the rolls of film before they left as if it had been any other job" (307). This cold professionalism disavows his pain at not being able to make himself part of the new family unit with Chitra at its center. Giving away the photographs also enables him to obliterate the memory of their visit to Rome, replaced by memories from a much earlier trip to Rome – a trip made when he and his family were returning to Massachusetts from Bombay. Although he had no photographs of that visit, his recollection of those days from almost a quarter century ago is sharp and vivid: "He remembered the look of the hotel where they stayed [...] The strong shaft of light that poured through the dome of the Pantheon [...] He remembered [...] seeing clusters of swallows [...] swiping the sky" (307). He remembers these beautiful yet innocuous moments in time, cast in melancholia by the memory of his mother who, though only forty, was already dying. Ironically, the vividness of Kaushik's memories of that visit is unaided by any photographic documentation, while although he took pictures of his father and Chitra's visit to Rome, "they had left no dent on the place, and he never thought of their presence on the streets of Rome as he continued to think, now and again, of his mother's" (307). The contrast throws into relief photography's inability to keep certain moments alive in our memory. Kaushik becomes a photographer hoping to find in his work a sense of groundedness and presence. Instead, it becomes the thing that distracts him from confronting the traumatic experiences of his early life – his double displacement by the time he is sixteen and the subsequent death of his mother.

Unlike his mother, who "had set up households again and again in her life [...] always given everything to make her home beautiful, always drawn strength from her things, her walls," Kaushik "never fully trusted the places he'd lived, never turned to them for refuge" (309). He is haunted by memories of his family's moves every time he visits a refugee camp and sees life reduced to and ultimately defined by a few earthly possessions. Living in a rented apartment with furniture and even sheets and towels that are not his own, he likes to believe that he is different, "that in ten minutes he could be on his way to anywhere in the world" (316). Hema identifies in him (notably through photographs he has taken of strangers, capturing moments of their quotidian) a willingness and a need "to disappear at any moment"

(316). Dutt-Ballerstadt has interpreted Kaushik's way of life as "embracing a state of nomadism and wandering that is provoked by his mother's untimely death" (2012: 167). I argue that Lahiri's use of the trope of photography belies Kaushik's pride in his lack of rootedness and brings to light the cracks in his seemingly dispassionate and aloof personality. Although he dismisses Hema's question about being affected by the things he photographs, he later confesses, "It does affect me [...] Taking pictures. Not always, but sometimes. Sometimes in ways I don't like" (317). He proceeds to tell her about a time he came upon a car accident and immediately began to take a picture "before even asking if they were okay" (317). This rare confession from Kaushik that he uses photography to suppress his emotions signals the Benjaminian unconscious coming to the fore. Questions of the visual here open up larger philosophical and ontological questions of wanting to belong, to connect in meaningful ways with others. Kaushik recognizes that photography distances him from people, making the act of documenting clinical and dispassionate, rather than humane. Although as a photojournalist he craves the thrill of chasing after news, there is something deeply unsatisfying in his life and he seeks to fill this void through photography. Despite living a sparse life with few belongings, through his photography he collects things – "he knew that in his own way, with his camera, he was dependent on the material world, stealing from it, hoarding it, unwilling to let it go" (309). Photography makes the man of few belongings a hoarder, it makes the seemingly detached man unwilling to let go of the world. Tragically though, through his photography Kaushik does not gather the kinds of objects his mother used to decorate her home and shape her identity wherever she was. His are impersonal objects capturing slices of other people's lives, sometimes horrific, ordinary at other times. They are ultimately of no use to him. Seeking the stillness of a photograph, Kaushik finally decides to stop running, to let go of his nomadic existence and embrace a stillness instead. Ignoring his friend's unknowingly prescient warning that such a job meant "death to the photographer" (308), Kaushik accepts a position as photo editor of an international news magazine in Hong Kong, due only to "The promise for the next few years at least, that he would be still" (308). In fact, this stillness is attained tragically when Kaushik drowns on holiday in Thailand in the devastating 2006 tsunami.

In *Camera Lucida*, Barthes writes, "In photography I can never deny that *the thing has been there*. There is a superimposition here of reality and of the past" and "Every photograph is a certificate of presence" (1993: 76, 87). Although Kaushik is predominantly positioned in Lahiri's story as photographer rather than photographed subject, I posit that the verifiability of the referent to which Barthes alludes can be applied by extension to

Kaushik. As a photojournalist, he bestows a "certificate of presence" upon everything he photographs; but, in doing so, he himself is authenticated and made present as documentarist of the moment. There are several moments in the story when Kaushik's photographs "stand in" metonymically for him. Traveling the world, he consciously distances himself from his family, not even going back for graduations and weddings: "And yet ... thanks to his work, Kaushik continued to wash up on his father's doorstep, in the form of his photo credit in one of the news magazines his father read, announcing that he was alive, indicating where he'd been and what he'd seen" (306). Kaushik's photographs bestow upon him the Barthesian certificate of presence, rooting him to a particular time and place. A poignant instance of the same phenomenon occurs at the end of the story when Hema goes to the newspaper stands in Calcutta the day after the tsunami "and bought the papers, studying every picture, looking for your name in one of the credits, hoping that you had been lucky and had continued to do your work" (332). Obviously, she fails to find any photos credited to him – the absence of "the certificate of presence" here signifying death.

## Photograph as *memento mori*: Death and the Apprehension of Loss

Kaushik is not the only character to die in this story: his mother dies of breast cancer half way through the novella (which we later learn is the real reason for the family's return to the US). Death is linked to migration in complex ways. Kaushik's mother returns to her immigrant home, America, "not so much for treatment [...] as [...] to be left alone" (250). For her, diaspora provides a sheltering cocoon in which she can wait for death removed from the attention of friends and family. Kaushik dies on his way to live in yet another foreign land, the journey of translocation cut short by a premature death. The "presence" that a photograph supposedly provides is, in fact, spectral. Looking at a photograph of himself, Barthes argues, "Death is the *eidos* of that photograph"; in other words, no matter how life-like a photograph may be, an apprehension of death always lies beneath it. A photograph is a kind of "flat Death" which both exposes what has passed and precedes actual death (1993: 15, 92). In a crucial episode in Lahiri's story, photographs can be read both as a return of the dead and as a threat to the fragile stability of the present. As if to dispel the reality of Kaushik's mother's existence and all memory of it, the day Kaushik and his father return from the hospital after her death, his father takes every photograph of her and puts them in a shoebox, which he seals with tape and places in a closet.

After her death, his father returns to India to bring back his new wife, the recently widowed Chitra, and her two young children. The newly formed family, to which Kaushik never fully belongs, imposes a new reality on him.

The shoebox reappears later in the story, in a painful clash between Kaushik's past and new reality when Chitra's curious daughters disinter it. He discovers them surreptitiously exploring the contents of the box:

> They leapt apart, startled, realizing I was there. Spread out on the gray carpet, arranged like a game of Solitaire, were about a dozen photographs of my mother taken from the box my father had sealed up and hidden after her death. Even from a distance the banished images assaulted me: my mother wearing a swimsuit by the edge of the pool at our old club in Bombay. My mother sitting with me on her lap on the brown wooden steps of our house in Cambridge. My mother and my father standing before I was born in front of a snow-caked hedge in Cambridge. (285–286)

It is as though Kaushik's repressed and "boxed up" grief for his mother is laid bare upon the carpet: the images assault him because they encapsulate an inescapable realization of loss which banishing the images had served to suppress. Kaushik feels deeply violated and reacts violently, shaking one of the girls and saying hurtful things about their mother, whom he describes as inferior to his own. He – strikingly – puts the pictures "face down" on the dresser and drags one girl "away from the shoebox as if her proximity would contaminate it [...] thrusting her aside [...] I wanted to remove the pictures from the house as far as I could" (286). In this moment of confrontation, two alternate realities collide – the reality of the past, which Kaushik's father sought to obliterate or at least repress, and the present reality of life with his new family. Through the revelation of the photographs, Kaushik's mother and all that she meant to her family is brought to light. As such, the images threaten to depose a newer and, for Kaushik, less legitimate reality. He sees this reality as tarnishing his mother's memory; he is overtaken by the impulse to hide the photographs from the corrupting gaze of the girls and to remove them from the house now occupied by the woman and children who have replaced his mother.

In *Camera Lucida*, Barthes describes a strangely analogous scene of going through some photographs of his mother shortly after her death. He is not "assaulted" by the images as Kaushik is; rather, he has no hope of "finding" his mother in them. Quoting Proust, he writes, "I expected nothing from these 'photographs of a being before which one recalls less of that being than by merely thinking of him or her'" (1993: 63). These images lack a *punctum*, which Barthes describes variously as the prick, disturbance, or sudden wound that makes a particular photograph epiphanic to a particular viewer and which he finds much later in the "Winter Garden" photograph of his mother. For Kaushik, by contrast, the photographs stir up emotions of grief and loss that he has suppressed since his mother's death: the force of their impact, the Barthesian *punctum*, is overwhelming.

Kaushik then drives for days along the eastern coastline into a desolate, cold, and unforgiving landscape, until he finds a spot close to the Canadian border with cliffs overlooking the Bay of Fundy. There, he watches the waves, "their thick caps crashing apart against the rocks, that eternally restless motion having an inversely calming effect on me" (292). He returns to the same spot the following day, bringing the shoebox with him, and begins going through the pictures: "But there were too many pictures, and after a few I, like my father, could no longer bear their sight" (292). Neither can he stand to let them fly into the sea below. Finally, he digs a hole with a sharp-edged rock and his bare hands and buries the box in it. The decision to bury the photos suggests the suppressive force in Kaushik's largely unprocessed grief over his mother's death; but it also suggests the possibility of returning to unearth the photographs (and all that they represent) at a later date.

In a powerful article on death in Lahiri's fiction, Mridula Nath Chakraborty reads death as a way for migrants to fix and root themselves into the adopted country as a means of making "a claim final and irrefutable" to belonging (2011: 814). To have to assert belonging through the loss and erasure signified by death is tragic; perhaps in an attempt to ameliorate this tragedy, Kaushik wishes they were not Hindus so that his mother "could be buried somewhere" (249). It could be argued that Kaushik seeks to give his mother a grave in the scene where he buries her photographs, digging the ground with a rock – the scene immediately recalls another, much earlier, where Kaushik gets down on his knees to uncover the Simonds family tombstone (249). This desire to leave a physical marker of presence in absence (death) is denied to Kaushik himself as he meets a watery death on foreign shores far from America. Lahiri often thinks of photographs as tombstones or the markers of presence in death. In *The Namesake*, Gogol realizes on the anniversary of his father's death that the "closest thing his father has to a grave" is the framed portrait that hangs in the hallway of his childhood home (Lahiri 2004: 189), what Chakraborty in her analysis calls "the portable tombstone" (2011: 820).

Eduardo Cadava argues that photography is a "mode of bereavement. It speaks to us of mortification" (1998: 11). In Lahiri's story, we encounter not only the deaths of Kaushik and his mother; we also learn of the death of a minor character, Chitra's first husband, and of the countless deaths that Kaushik witnesses as a photojournalist. There are many instances in the narrative where the act of photographing is juxtaposed with death. The first occurs when Kaushik and his family return to the US and are staying with Hema's family until they find a home of their own. Hema and Kaushik go for a walk in the woods because he wants to show her something; he has his camera hanging around his neck and often stops to focus it. After walking some distance, he suddenly goes down on his knees and begins to dig: Hema realizes that what he wants to show her is a half-buried tombstone of a family of six, the Simonds. At this moment, confronted with the inevitability of death, Kaushik tells Hema about the cancer in his mother's breast. The thirteen-year-old Hema feels neither sorrow nor sympathy, "only the enormous fear of having a dying woman in our home" (250). Although Kaushik photographs neither the graves nor Hema in the woods, his power to capture that moment is highlighted by Hema's fear "that you would lift the camera and capture me that way" (250). Later in the story, as a war photographer, Kaushik takes innumerable pictures of "bodies with faces smashed and throats slit and penises hacked from between their legs" (305).

The process of making photographs is likened explicitly to death in one of Kaushik's poignant memories of his mother, when he recalls setting up a darkroom at home during his last year of high school:

> There were times my mother came down and kept me company, sitting quietly in the blackness as I struggled to load film onto the developing reel. Together we would breathe in the chemical smells, their corrosiveness, from which my hands were protected by rubber gloves, nothing compared to what was taking place inside her body [...] "It must be something like this," she said once in that perfectly dark, silent, sealed up space, and I understood without her saying so that she was imagining what it might be like to be dead. "This is how I want to think of it." (278)

Photography's darkroom is a contradictory space, a space of utter darkness in which a photographic plate or film preserves traces of light that, after several chemical processes, result in prints. It is a space of creativity, illumination, meaning-production, and beginnings, yet Kaushik's mother finds in "that perfectly dark, silent, sealed up space" (278) the perfect analogy for death, and one that seems comforting for her. The chemicals coursing through her body and destroying both healthy and diseased cells are compared with the chemicals necessary in the creation of the photograph; the former struggle to delay her inevitable death, while the latter are necessary elements in the creation of art. Jay Prosser finds in photography a similar paradoxical duality – while making acutely real the sense of loss, photography also "makes possible the apprehension of loss" and in doing so, for Prosser, it holds out "the promise of a kind of enlightenment" (2005: 2). Lahiri extends the duality of photography's darkroom to what I am calling "diaspora's darkroom."

During their brief yet intense relationship in "Going Ashore," the concluding part of the triptych, Hema and Kaushik visit Volterra, the ancient city of the Etruscans.[2] At the Guarnacci Etruscan Museum, they see the urns in which the Etruscans stored the ashes of their dead: "The sides were covered with carvings showing so many migrations across land and departures in covered wagons to the underworld, so many fantastic beasts and fish-tailed gods of the sea" (320). Later we see Kaushik uploading photographs of Volterra onto his website. These prove to be the last photographs he uploads and they reappear when Kaushik himself has made that final journey from this world to the next. Hearing of the tsunami in Thailand and knowing that Kaushik was there at the time, Hema goes to an Internet café in Calcutta and opens up his website. There she sees "A faint sliver of the shoreline we had seen in Volterra. Three blackened faces, supposed to be Etruscan divinities that loomed over our heads" (332). She looks at these photos in an attempt to confirm Kaushik's continued existence, despite intuitively knowing that he is dead.

## The Impossibility of Return

"Hema and Kaushik" ends, as it begins, with Hema's narrative voice, but thirty years have passed since the beginning of the story. Hema, pregnant and married to another man, is mourning the loss of Kaushik and wondering if her unborn child might be his. This juxtaposition of life and death is akin to the contradiction that lies at the heart of photographs, as signs of presence but also as evidence of absence. Photographs recall a moment to which we may never return. This impossibility of return, always implicit in a photograph, lends further poignancy to the phantom loss of homeland felt so acutely by Hema and Kaushik. The title of the triptych's final section, "Going Ashore," suggests a homecoming, a return, reflected in Kaushik's

[2] The Etruscans built elaborate tombs to store the urns in which the people of Volterra stored the ashes of the dead.

adult relationship with Hema: "She was the first person he had ever slept with who'd known his mother, who was able to remember her as he did" (313). Although they have led separate lives for many years, their brief relationship in Italy is imbued with a sense of returning to a place (or, in this case, person) to which (whom) one belongs. Ironically, though, Kaushik will die because he *fails* to come ashore. Alternatively, his death can be read as bringing to an end his itinerant and restless life, bestowing the stillness he so desperately craves: as such, he comes to the shores of the afterlife, as the Etruscans believed, by making a final migratory journey, which, like all diasporic journeys, forecloses the possibility of return and must necessarily be linear.[3]

The subtle recurrence of aspects of the past during Hema and Kaushik's time in Italy implies a cyclical structure, but signifies a return that proves ultimately to be temporary and tragic. In Volterra, Hema wears Kaushik's pea coat, which recalls his coat that was handed down to her when she was a girl, "back when they were nothing but already something to each other" (319). The first night they spend together in Italy, Kaushik recognizes the bangle Hema used to wear as a child, a gift from her grandmother that she has had enlarged so that she can continue to wear it. Kaushik "hooked one of his fingers, lightly but possessively, around the gold bangle on her wrist, causing her hand to shift slightly in his direction" (312). The bangle returns a few pages later when Hema inadvertently leaves it in the plastic tray as she passes through security at the airport on her way to India, where she is to be married:

> It would be replaced ten-fold in the course of her wedding. And yet she felt she had left a piece of her body behind. She had grown up hearing from her mother that losing gold was inauspicious, and as the plane began to climb, in those moments she was still aware of it moving, a dark thought passed through her, that it would crash or be blasted apart in the sky. Then the fear turned numb. Already on the screen at the center of the plane there was a map with a white line emerging away from Rome, creeping toward India. And this simple graphic composed her, making clear the only road available now. (324)

The linear inevitability of this concluding cartographic image indicates the impossibility of return for characters like Hema and Kaushik. They

[3] Although this is the commonly held assumption, I have argued in "Revisions, Rerouting and Return" (2009) that this linear teleology of diaspora may be reversed under certain conditions.

return not to an originary place, but rather to an originary moment that was captured in the photograph that opens the story. That first moment of parting is repeated in the above passage when Hema "returns" to Kaushik briefly and then leaves him forever, the bangle left behind signifying the part of herself that she leaves behind with him. The foreboding she feels as the plane takes off portends Kaushik's untimely death. Lahiri thus poignantly suggests that Hema can never return to an originary homeland. She is on her way to India, but this is a temporary return to solemnize her marriage with someone who is essentially a stranger, thus rendering it hollow and meaningless.

Eduardo Cadava writes about the haunting quality of photographs:

> The image bears witness to an experience that cannot come to light. This experience is the experience of the shock of experience, of experience as bereavement. This bereavement acknowledges what takes place in any photograph – the return of the departed. Although what the photograph photographs is no longer present or living, its having-been-there now forms a part of the referential structure of our relationship to the photograph. Nevertheless, the return of what was once there takes the form of a haunting [...] the possibility of the photographic image requires that there be such things as ghosts and phantoms. (1998: 11)

By recalling a moment to which we may never return, photographs invoke a sense of loss and cause us to be haunted by that phantom loss. This is analogous to the phantom loss of the homeland felt by Lahiri's second-generation protagonists and the originary moment of departure from the homeland, a moment to which they have no access. Akin to the impossibility of returning to the moment captured in a photograph, the inaccessibility of the originary moment of departure, and the necessarily linear teleology of diaspora, eternally and painfully occlude the possibility of return for second-generation immigrants like Kaushik and Hema.

## Conclusion

Shortly before Kaushik accidentally meets Hema in Italy, we are told that he notices something wrong with his eye:

> [A] faint gray speck, smaller than the head of a pin, began floating across his left eye. He first noticed it in the afternoon they went to

> Testaccio, his father wanting to visit Keats's grave. In the lush grounds of the Protestant Cemetery, Kaushik had thought that a gnat was circling his head, and he kept swatting at it [...] But the speck continued to accompany him wherever he went, quietly tormenting him, and he realized it was within him, that it was not possible to remove it or make it stop. He was told he would grow used to it, and he had, more or less, not bothered these days unless he were in a bright room with white walls, or outside without his sunglasses. It did not affect his driving or his picture-taking. And yet it felt like an invasion of the part of his body, the physical sense that was most precious: something that betrayed him and also refused to abandon him. (307–308)

The seemingly insignificant affliction acquires symbolic weight in relation to my analysis of photography as metaphor in the story. The photographer "sees" with his/her camera. Although the gray speck does not affect Kaushik's ability to take pictures, it might be interpreted in terms of his failure to "see" (himself) fully. The speck becomes symbolic of his (non)-immigrant identity, that impossible-to-mourn aspect of himself. Interestingly, the speck bothers him only when he is in bright spaces. A well-lit room with white walls provides the perfect conditions for the projection of images, for perception followed by (re)cognition, neither of which Kaushik is willing to do.

It is also significant that Kaushik first becomes aware of the gray speck beside John Keats's grave in the Protestant Cemetery in Rome. Keats's last request was to be buried under a tombstone without his name, bearing only the words, "Here lies one whose name was writ in water." Death and water are conflated once again:

> Kaushik lifted the camera to his face, took a picture, and set the camera down at his feet [...] He took off his sunglasses, leaving them in the boat next to his camera. The speck in his vision rose and fell, erasing its random trail. He held on to the edge of the boat, swinging his legs over the side, lowering himself. The sea was as warm and welcoming as a bath. His feet touched the bottom and so he let go. (331)

This passage, quietly suggestive of Kaushik's death by drowning, echoes the concluding section of T.S. Eliot's *The Waste Land*, "Death by Water":

> Phlebas the Phoenician, a fortnight dead,
> Forgot the cry of gulls, and the deep sea swell
> And the profit and loss.

A current under sea
Picked his bones in whispers. As he rose and fell
He passed the stages of his age and youth
Entering the whirlpool. (77–78)

Eliot's phrases – "the deep sea swell," "a current under sea," and "entering the whirlpool" – assume a tragic resonance in the context of Kaushik's death. In Eliot's poem, it is Phlebas that "rose and fell" while in Lahiri's story it is the gray speck, metonymy – according to my reading – of Kaushik's (unacknowledged) self. Lahiri's reference to two things that provide an altered vision – sunglasses and camera – subtly implies Kaushik's inability to see himself even moments before his final annihilation. His last act is to take a photograph, and so to seek presence and rootedness. This sense of security and mooring proves as illusory as his feet temporarily touching the ground beneath the sea.

Through her foregrounding of the trope of photography, so riddled with contradictions, Lahiri has always already suggested the failure inherent in attempting to provide a sense of belonging or a possibility of return for her itinerant protagonist(s). The artificiality of the medium, the unbridgeable abyss between the moment of recording and the moment of looking at the photograph, and the impossibility of returning to the originary moment captured in the photograph, all combine to render it a most appropriate trope through which to represent diaspora consciousness. Hence the void and absence alluded to in the concluding lines of the story: "It might have been your child but this was not the case. We had been careful, and you had left *nothing* behind" (333, emphasis added).

5

# Finding Gauri: *Allo*-Portraits of a Mother in Jhumpa Lahiri's *The Lowland*

> One November evening, shortly after my mother's death, I was going through some photographs. I had no hope of "finding" her.
>
> Roland Barthes, *Camera Lucida*, 63

> At every moment the past is there, appended to the present.
>
> Jhumpa Lahiri, *The Lowland*, 275

## Introduction

Photography is often celebrated for its power to see acutely and thus expand the range of human vision. One of the many paradoxes of photography has to do with its heightened powers of perception. In recording that which may not be visible to the human eye, photography also makes us acutely aware of what remains unseen, what lies outside the frame or out of focus, or simply beyond photography's ability to capture. Photography's power to reveal is therefore constantly undermined by its inability to capture the unseen world. Despite its technological advantage over human vision, it also has limitations of its own and constantly reminds us of what remains invisible. In what Shawn Michelle Smith calls photography's faulty start, she writes that the first photograph produced in 1826, Joseph Nicephore Niepce's pewter plate, is shadowy and hard to see. For her this underscores "at the very heart of photography, both an intense desire, and a failure, to see" (2013: 2). This intense desire often also works in faulty ways by producing an excess. Photographs routinely capture the unintended – shadowy things in the background, unwanted or unseen things that have come into the frame.

Smith describes the ability of photography to capture an excess while paradoxically making us aware of the lack inherent to it as photography's "capacity to make the invisible visible and to reveal what we don't see" (19). When writers incorporate photographs only as narrated images in a novel, this invisibility is doubled, heightening the performativity of the absent-present image. On the one hand, the image itself is absent or invisible while, on the other, the narrated image makes us aware of the unintended or the invisible within the absent image. This provides the novelist with a metaphor of photographic absent presences. In this chapter, I provide a close reading of the absent images in Jhumpa Lahiri's 2013 novel *The Lowland*. I return repeatedly to the exclusions and inadvertent inclusions in these images and argue that they provide us with alternative ways of reading Lahiri's characterization of one of the central characters in the novel. Most critics have argued that *The Lowland* provides a rather harsh portrayal of Gauri, a diasporic mother, described somewhat uncharitably by Esha Shah as a "hyper contemporary individual" ( 2014: 31), who abandons her daughter and husband in pursuit of personal success. I argue that the absent presence of a few images in the novel allows Lahiri to offer an alternative and far more sympathetic portrayal of Gauri as a deeply tragic figure who is misunderstood, othered, and denied a place within the family; she remains tragically haunted by her past, unable to become a part of her family.

In her book *Family Frames* (2012), Marianne Hirsch has extensively studied the ways in which "photography's social functions are integrally tied to the ideology of the modern family" (7). She begins by analyzing the iconic photograph called the "Winter Garden photo" in Roland Barthes's *Camera Lucida*. Writing after his mother's death, Barthes describes his attempt to find a photograph that captures her real essence. He despairs as he goes through many images, unable to find one that satisfies him. Finally, he sees a photograph of his mother aged five standing with her brother in the garden of their family home. For Barthes, this is the only image that captures the fundamental essence of his mother. Though it depicts his mother as a child, long before he knew her and not easily recognizable to him, for him the child in the photograph connects with the frail woman he had nursed in the last days of her life. Although this is a very important image for Barthes, he does not include it in his book and it remains an imagetext or prose picture, described by him but invisible as a photograph to the reader. Barthes's reason for not including the image is that it is an intensely personal photograph.

Hirsch develops an ideological reading of family photographs where the camera, the photo album, and the familial gaze become the instruments of the ideology. She argues against a hegemonic familial ideology to suggest instead that the ideology of a family is shaped by its particular sociohistorical contexts and the lived reality of the family. In her reading Hirsch has also privileged what she calls "meta-photographic texts which place family photographs into narrative contexts, either by reproducing them or by describing them" (2012a: 8) like Barthes's Winter Garden photo of his mother, because the "work of contestation" appears more in such texts rather than in actual family photographs. Novels that include narrated images that are absent from their pages provide good examples of such meta-photographic texts. These narrated images provide an alternative mode of characterization. I analyze absent images used by Lahiri to resist familial ideologies in diaspora.

Lahiri's *The Lowland* has been variously described by reviewers as "the bleakest story Jhumpa Lahiri has ever told" (Sestanovich 2013: n.pag.) and "Jhumpa Lahiri's book for unhappy mothers" (Malone 2013: n.pag.). The family saga begins with the story of two brothers, Subhash and Udayan, growing up in a middle-class family in Tollygunge, a Calcutta suburb, in the 1970s. However, the novel's trajectory changes with the tragic murder of Udayan soon after Subhash leaves to study in America. Subhash returns to Calcutta and decides to marry Gauri, Udayan's pregnant widow, and take her back with him and raise her child as his own. However, his grieving mother's warning – "Udayan's wife, [will] never love you [...] [she is] too withdrawn, too aloof to be a mother" (114) – proves tragically prophetic. Gauri abandons her family, leaving Subhash to raise their daughter, Bela, on his own.

Although *The Lowland* is essentially Subhash's story, for many readers Gauri is the most memorable character and yet the least likable. Though the novel was received very well and nominated for a number of literary awards, most critics find Lahiri's portrayal of Gauri deeply problematic. Machiko Kakutani characterizes her as "a folk tale parody of a cold, selfish witch" in her *New York Times* review of the novel, lamenting Lahiri's failure to give us any "real insight into Gauri's decision-making or psychology" (2013: n.pag.). Noreen Malone writing for *The New Republic* concludes, "Gauri isn't just ambivalent, she is stunningly selfish" (2013: n.pag.). Like Kakutani, Malone attributes this to Lahiri's failure to "delve into Gauri's interior life." Clare Sestanovich labels her "a bad wife and a bad mother" and even goes on to suggest that she is a "more troubling menace" than Subhash's radicalized militant brother Udayan. Sestanovich concludes that Gauri's "rootless loneliness – more than Udayan's radical zeal – is the scariest brand of extremism in the book" (2013: n.pag.). Shoma Sen finds it unconvincing that "the mother who abandons her child, never once attempts to look her up [...] this extremely cold response to the only relatives and friends she had in the US [...] is difficult to swallow" (2013: 141). Still others have found Gauri's portrayal as a brutal and cruel character, and Lahiri's insistence on engaging the reader's sympathy for her, infuriating. James Lasdun writes:

> As a minor character, or as a full-on study in cruelty, Gauri might have been interesting. If there were an ounce of irony or humour in her portrayal, or of unabashed wickedness in her spirit, she might have been fascinating to follow. But her depiction is relentlessly solemn and insistently – actually infuriatingly – compassionate. While acknowledging the brutality of her deeds, Lahiri also wants to enlist our sympathy for Gauri as a person of tragic emotional integrity. She charts her lonely intellectual progress with a scrupulousness that seems intended to confer a kind of martyred dignity upon her, though to me it just intensifies the unpleasant effect of pious sadism that emanates from the book whenever she appears. (2013: n.pag.)

I disagree with Lasdun and argue instead that Gauri is indeed worthy of our sympathy as a marginalized, haunted, and misunderstood character.

Given the wide agreement amongst critics about Gauri's selfishness, her aloofness, and her brutality, it is safe to say that Lahiri's portrayal of her has failed to evoke sympathy. I suggest that paying attention to Lahiri's use of the photographic trope makes a sympathetic reading of Gauri possible. By reading the unintended excesses and accidents captured in the margins of the narrated images and analyzing them through the Hirschean model of ideologically invested familial gazes within the novel, I propose an alternative reading of Gauri.

Gauri's portrayal as what Malone calls the "un-motherly mother" makes her unsympathetic as a character to most readers. Going against the grain of such readings, I will instead argue that Gauri fails as a mother in diaspora because she is haunted by the past and unable to recover from it. I will further suggest that photography offers us an analytical trope to recognize Gauri's marginalization and her ultimate failure as a wife and mother. My starting point for the analysis of motherhood and the themes of diasporic mourning and loss in the novel are several absent photographs that Lahiri describes at significant length. These, I argue, offer us valuable insights into Gauri's character and the possibility of viewing her more sympathetically. Using photographic theory in general and Marianne Hirsch's work on family photographs, the familial gaze, and the connection between photography and motherhood, I will argue that Gauri is a more sympathetic character than critics have suggested, one who fails to fulfill the role that hegemonic familial ideology imposed upon her. The trope of photography, I suggest, allows us glimpses into Gauri's inner life and provides a more nuanced portrayal of motherhood in diaspora, of a woman who fails to mother because she is in perpetual mourning, haunted by the past, rather than the monstrous mother that Gauri is often simplistically assumed to be.

Marianne Hirsch discusses the role of family photographs at length in *Family Frames.* She begins with the common assumption that for today's modern family, the family photograph displays the cohesive nature of the family and functions as the instrument of its togetherness (2012a: 7). However, photographs can also self-consciously disrupt their own documentary authority and create a space of contestation. Hirsch argues that this is particularly true of imagetexts, "which place family photographs into narrative contexts, either by reproducing them or by describing them" as in novels and short stories (8). Imagetexts often resist the conventions of family photography and undercut their implied hegemonic familial ideals. Hirsch concludes that "Only in the context of this metaphotographic textuality and in this self-conscious contextuality can photographs disrupt a familiar narrative about family life and its representations, breaking the hold of a conventional and monolithic familial gaze" (8). I find this approach particularly useful in analyzing Lahiri's imagetexts in *The Lowland.* Hirsch's "hegemonic familial ideology" is of course not a fixed, ahistoric ideology. When applied to a reading of Lahiri's novel, it refers to the ideology of the assimilated, heteronormative diasporic family that one would be hard pressed to find in Lahiri's fiction.[1] In Gauri, named after the Hindu goddess of Shakti or female strength, Lahiri creates for her readers a fiercely independent, rootless, and intensely lonely woman haunted by the past who ultimately refuses to be bound by the hegemonic ideology that governs the lives of South Asian immigrant families. Through my analyses of several absent photos in the novel using photographic theory, I will demonstrate how Gauri is simultaneously (m)othered – becomes a mother but is also othered – throughout the novel.

This chapter is divided into four sections. The first, "The Othered Self," turns to Gauri's portrayal before she was married to Udayan. Lahiri introduces her in the novel through a photograph that Udayan sent to Subhash in America

1 See Gayatri Gopinath's (2018) discussion of the ways in which the aesthetic practices of queer diaspora powerfully repudiate heteronormative notions of the family, often mandated by the state. She does this via an analysis of New York City-based visual artist Chitra Ganesh, whose parents emigrated from Calcutta in the early 1970s. Ganesh's work titled *13 Photos* reconstitutes the traditional family album by selecting and recontextualizing several photographs that never made it into the original family album (66–71).

to introduce his brother to the woman he loves and has married. I argue that Gauri is denied her individuality as she is "consumed" by the masculine gaze in the brotherly transaction of her photograph. In the second section, "The Ghostly Mother," I focus on a series of photographs of Subhash's life in America, which he shows to his mother on a visit back to Calcutta. I posit that Gauri is left out of the circuit of familial gazes in these photos and is thus denied her own identity and presence within the family. The third section, "Masculine Maternity" uses Roland Barthes's suggested connection between photography and maternity to demonstrate how Gauri's motherhood is gradually usurped by Subhash. Finally, in the last and most extensive section, "A Devastating Doubling," I analyze Udayan's death portrait to suggest that Subhash and Udayan are inextricably "twinned" in the novel such that Gauri remains eternally haunted by the past, unable to recover from it, and her memories of Udayan even after she comes to America.

## The Othered Self

As mentioned above, Gauri is first introduced to us through an absent photograph. Udayan sends Subhash a photograph of her along with a letter announcing their marriage. The photograph, and Udayan's accompanying description of Gauri, contains within it the kernel of her true character, which is much misunderstood later in the novel. Lahiri describes the scene of Subhash looking at the photo:

> Subhash [...] found a small black-and-white photograph of a young woman, standing. Her slender arms were folded across her chest.
>
> She was at ease, also a little skeptical. Her head turned partly to one side, her lips closed but playful, her smile slightly askew. Her hair was in a braid, draped over the front of one shoulder. Her complexion was deep.
>
> She was compelling without being pretty. Nothing like the demure girls that his mother used to point out to Udayan and Subhash at weddings, when they were in college. It was a candid shot, somewhere on the streets of Calcutta, in front of a building he did not recognize. He wondered if Udayan had taken the picture. If he'd inspired the playful expression on her face. (45–46)

This description of Gauri marks her in many ways as atypical. Subhash finds something "compelling" in her, but it is not her beauty. Her arms are described as “slender,” her smile is “slightly askew,” her complexion “deep.” A reader familiar with the traditions of Indian arranged marriages may be reminded of the portraits of women used in marriage negotiations that were quite popular at the time depicted in the novel. These portraits are by no means candid shots like this one, but they bear similarities to Gauri’s portrait – the figure of a woman standing with her hair in a traditional braid, draped over the front of her shoulder, like Gauri, thus displaying the length of her hair. Yet the woman depicted in this photograph is no demure bride-to-be. She is a “skeptical” woman wearing a “playful” expression. She has already defied the familial expectations of an arranged marriage, marrying a man of her own choosing. In the words of her husband, she “prefers books to jewels and saris.” In evoking the genre of the photograph used in arranged marriages, yet utterly defying that genre in the depiction of Gauri, Lahiri creates ambiguity for her heroine and sets her up as an atypical woman, simply through the description of her photograph accompanied by Udayan’s comments about her.

Rather than being impressed by Udayan’s choice of a bride or his unconventional means of going about his marriage, or even simply being happy for his sake, Subhash is quite upset to receive the photograph and the letter. He sees this “as another example of Udayan forging ahead of [him], of denying that he’d come second. Another example of getting his way” (47). The date, from a year ago, on the back of the photograph provokes in Subhash the thought that “all that time, Udayan had kept Gauri to himself.” Through no fault of her own, then, Gauri becomes not a real person or a new member to welcome into the fold of the family, but instead a trophy of brotherly rivalry. Though Subhash destroys Udayan’s letter, he keeps the photograph inserted at the back of one of his textbooks, “as proof of what Udayan had done” (47). Although this makes Udayan’s simple decision to marry the woman he loves seem like an act of grave betrayal, Subhash’s action reveals his sense of being bested once again by his more charismatic and enterprising brother. He secretly admires Gauri for the kind of girl she is and “a part of him felt defeated by Udayan all over again, for having found a girl like that” (47).

Gauri’s photograph “is in lieu of a formal introduction,” as Udayan writes; consequently, she is silenced here and does not get to “see” the other person in this introduction. It is a one-sided introduction where Subhash gets to see her and admire her beauty through the photograph (over and over again since he takes out the picture from “time to time” and looks at it), learn some facts about her from Udayan’s letter, and form an impression of her. Yet she remains passive and objectified through her photograph. His gaze fixes her with the weight of his assumptions about her. Gauri's photograph and Subhash's reaction to it serve to do a number of things – unbeknownst to her she is introduced to Subhash, gazed upon, even desired by him, and finally assigned by him as a trophy for his brother in this round of fraternal competition, which Udayan has clearly won. She also becomes emblematic of what Subhash sees as Udayan's betrayal of him and his family – her photo serves as "proof of what Udayan had done" (47). The scene denies Gauri any agency of her own.

Although Subhash does not set eyes on Gauri for another fifty-odd pages, the above scene suggests that her photograph sets up certain expectations about her. She intrigues him; he "wondered when he would meet Gauri, and what he would think of her, now that they were connected." (47) Curiously, he does not wonder what she might think of him, thus again denying her agency even in anticipatory encounters. I would suggest that by introducing Gauri to Subhash, as well as to the reader, through an imagetext, Lahiri denies her the agency she deserves, her agency as a woman and later as a mother, which she is never able to claim for herself in the novel.

When Subhash finally meets Gauri after Udayan's death at the family home in Tollygunge, he immediately recognizes her from the photograph. He is impressed by her beauty and calls into question the truth-value of the photograph – he realizes that she wears glasses (something the photograph had withheld) and notices "another thing the photo had not fully conveyed. The frank beauty of her eyes" (94). In the initial moments of this encounter, the photographic referent and Subhash's active gaze as that which looks and fixes seems to continue to operate: "He took her in, but did not speak to her, watching her eat some dal and rice" (94). Subhash's immediate recall of Gauri's photo and his desire to almost consume her ("take her in") as he "watches" her continues the othering begun in the earlier scene of passively fixing Gauri in his gaze while denying her any agency of her own.

According to Marianne Hirsch, this kind of exchange of gazes "reveals the self as necessarily relational and familial, as well as fragmented and dispersed [...] the self-portrait always includes the other, not only because the self, never coincident, is necessarily other to itself, but also because it is constituted by multiple and heteronomous relations" (2012a: 83). She thus concludes that self-portraits have a "double-edged otherness – combining multiplicity with alterity" (83) and borrows Philippe Lacoue-Labarthe's term *allo*-portrait (from the Greek *allos* meaning "other, different") for this kind of self-portrait. Gauri's self-portrait becomes an *allo*-portrait as it travels through the screens created by Udayan's description of her, which accompanies the photo, and Subhash's desiring gaze as he consumes it.

Through Lahiri's use of photography, Gauri is therefore firmly established as a familial Other even before we encounter her in the novel. When we finally meet her, she is already a (m)other to be.

## The Ghostly Mother

When Subhash visits India with Udayan and Gauri's daughter Bela, whom he has raised as his own, he brings some photographs for his mother Bijoli. The purpose of the photographs is presumably to create a narrative of their life in America for her. These are not family photographs but rather photographs of their house – "the dining table, the fireplace, the view off the sundeck" (191). This in itself is not surprising or telling in any way. Immigrant families often want to show their relatives back home the trappings of their comfortable life in the host country. However, Bijoli is neither impressed by nor interested in these photos. She studies the pictures "as if each one showed the same thing" and eventually reveals what she has really been looking for by asking, "Where is Gauri?" Marianne Hirsch has argued that family photographs are not always meant for public consumption: "Family albums include those images on which family members can agree and which tell a shared story. Pictures that diverge from the communal narrative tend to be discarded as 'bad' or 'unrepresentative'" (2012a: 107). Subhash's photographs do not really have a communal narrative or a shared story because Bela's family does not have a shared story. These photos tell a different story – of a comfortable immigrant life, a child growing up. However, notably absent from the photos are Bela's parents. Gauri appears, almost as if by accident, "in the background" of a picture of Bela in her Red Riding Hood Halloween costume. Subhash is absent from them because he is present behind the camera, the one who has documented their life together. Hirsch has argued that a network of looks operates in photographs which often allow us to see more than what was intended in a family photo and familial subjectivity is constructed through the familial gaze, which is "affiliative and identificatory" (9):

> Both through images and through the stories they elicit and contain photographs reveal looks that circulate in multiple ways among different familial subjects and thus offer a point of entry into the family's unconscious optics. Pictures enable us to see the constitution of the subject in relation to mother, father and siblings, to non-oedipal as well as to oedipal processes. They stress separation, distance, and

> misrecognition as well as mutual recognition as fundamental aspects of subject-formation and familial interaction. (129)

The only photo that includes Bela with at least one of her parents is the one in which "her mother appeared [...] inadvertently. The picture was of Bela from several years ago [...] But there in the background was her mother, leaning slightly over the kitchen table, in the process of clearing the dinner plates, wearing slacks and a maroon tunic" (200). Bela shares a gaze with her father who is absent from the photo itself but still within its broader compass as the photographer. Although her mother is in the photo, there is a complete absence of the familial gaze and therefore of any possibility of affiliation and identification between Bela and Gauri. Bela's affiliation with Subhash, albeit outside the circuit of the familial gazes, is stronger as she is the object of his camera lens. Gauri simply remains a ghostly presence in the photograph.

We can see the multiple ways in which Gauri is marginalized and ultimately excised from the ideological narrative of family life in this scene. She is unrepresented as a wife and mother in the photos and merely appears as a ghostly revenant in one of them. Even with the wisdom of an eleven year old, Bela recognizes the injustice of this. She laments the fact that although she spent most of her time during the week with her mother, there were no photographs documenting the time her alone with her, "no evidence of Bela watching television in the afternoons, or working on a school project on the kitchen table, as her mother prepared dinner or read through a pile of exam booklets with a pen in her hand" (200). The memories Bela conjures up of her time alone with her mother are unremarkable; one may even get the impression that Gauri is simply fulfilling her duty as the person providing adult supervision to a child. In most of the scenarios, Gauri goes about her own work as Bela trails behind her "through various buildings as her mother met various professors" (200). However, for Bela, these moments have a certain significance and she seems disappointed that there is no photographic evidence of the time she has spent with her mother. The absence of any photographs of Bela's time alone with her mother denies their relationship a certain legitimacy, which Bela's silent musings also fail to provide.

This is in keeping with Hirsch's discussion of the conventions of family photography which, "with its mutuality of confirming looks that construct a set of familial roles and hierarchies, reinforce the power of the notion of 'family'" (2012a: 47). Hirsch goes on to demonstrate the exclusionary power of photographs, the way in which, on the one hand, they consolidate family and group identity, while simultaneously, on the other, asserting "boundaries of difference" (47). Though in Hirsch's case such otherness comprises of racial differences, we can extend her analysis to our readings of Subhash's atypical family photographs. As a ghostly figure appearing inadvertently in one of the photographs, Gauri is excluded and othered from the expected ideological framework of the photograph. Rather than asserting her inclusion in the family, her accidental presence serves to reinforce her exclusion. When asked by Bijoli why Gauri is absent from the photographs, Subhash's response is telling: "She doesn't like to pose for the camera [...] She's been busy teaching her first class" (199). His response betrays the fact that these are "posed" photographs, not a genuine photographic representation of their family life, as they are purported to be. This undermines their truth-value. Bela's musings on what these photographs fail to document also undermine their truth-value. However, since photographs always already come with the implication of truth, what they show – an absent mother at worst and a ghostly one at best – is established as the absolute truth. The Barthesian "certificate of presence" (1993: 76) ironically becomes a "certificate of absence," echoed in Bijoli's question, "Where is Gauri?" Photographs are a signifying system which produces an ideological subject. Victor Burgin argues that

> The intelligibility of the photograph is no simple thing; photographs are texts inscribed in terms of what we may call "photographic discourse", but this discourse, like any other, engages discourses beyond itself, the "photographic text", like any other, is the site of a complex "intertextuality", an overlapping series of previous texts "taken for granted" at a particular cultural and historical conjuncture. (1982: 144)

Thus, Burgin goes on to argue, domestic photographs "serve to legitimate the institution of the family" (144). As the viewer/reader of these photographs, Bijoli brings to them all her ideological baggage of the heteronormative family with its prescribed, gendered roles. However, as atypical family photos, these images flout all the conventions of family photography and she does not find in them what she is looking for – proof of Gauri's mothering. She quickly loses interest in them, it is as if "each one showed the same thing" (199).

In discussing the various types of looks involved in a photograph – the look of the camera, the look of the viewer, the inter-diegetic looks, and the look of the actor – Burgin writes: "The effect of representation (the recruitment of the subject in the production of ideological meaning) requires that the stage of the represented (that of the photograph as object-text) meet the stage of the representing (that of the viewing subject) in a 'seamless join'" (1982: 150). Bijoli as the viewing subject looks at the photos her son shows her as object-text and tries to produce ideological meaning – of family and motherhood – from them.

However, in the absence of the seamless join between her and the photograph, she is unable to do so. This failure compels her to avert her gaze and return the photos to her son. He wants her to keep them but she hands them back, "loosening her grip so that a few of the pictures fell to the floor. I've seen them already, she said" (201). Burgin has argued that looking at a photographic image for a prolonged time results in the loss of the look's command: "As alienation intrudes into our capitation by the image we can, by averting our gaze [...] reinvest our looking with authority" (1982: 152). Bijoli's gaze carries with it the ideological power of an idealized heteronormative family. By averting her gaze from the pictures rather quickly, she denies the photographs the opportunity to claim an alternative narrative in lieu of her master narrative, which they have failed to narrate. She even denies them the opportunity of a later, second look by refusing to keep them, even though they are meant for her. Instead, she decisively closes the circuits of looking by asserting that she has already seen them. Thus, the photographs are incontrovertibly established as evidence of Gauri as an absent mother.

As my analysis of this brief scene in the novel indicates, Subhash's sharing of the photographs with his mother alienates Gauri in a number of ways. Before Bijoli even begins to look at the photographs, Gauri is always already fixed as the mother in them. However, it turns out that Subhash, as the author of these photos, the eye behind the capturing lens, has denied Gauri a presence. She is merely a ghostly presence appearing accidentally in one of the photos. Although Bela silently recalls her memories of the time spent with her mother, there is no photographic evidence of this and so it remains uncorroborated and therefore, invalidated and meaningless. Finally, Bijoli brings to her viewing of these photographs the full ideological weight of familiality in general and motherhood in particular. Not finding in them what she had hoped to, she refuses them the possibility of an alternative, redemptive narrative. Gauri is thus preordained to be the absent or barely present mother in this entire scenario, although Subhash's intent was presumably merely to show his mother a slice of their family life in America.

Bela and Subhash return to Providence from this trip and discover that Gauri has left their home. This is not without significance since it means that the last they see of Gauri is the ghostly presence in the above photograph. She leaves what Barthes would call "a trace." Heartbroken and incredulous, Bela remembers her mother as a shadowy figure who has left something of herself behind in her:

> What else had her mother left behind? On Bela's right arm, just above the elbow, in a spot she had to twist her arm to see, a freckled

> constellation of her mother's dark pigment, an almost solid patch at once discreet and conspicuous. A *trace* of the alternative complexion she might have had. (213, emphasis added)

Just as Gauri appears as a mere trace in Bela's Halloween photograph, so also does she remain as a physical trace marked forever on Bela's body. Bela also feels her presence everyday in a shadow that briefly appears on a section of the wall of her room: "In this shadow she saw the impression of her mother's forehead, the slope of her nose. Her mouth and chin. Its source was unknown [...] She never saw it form or fade" (213). This is akin to a photographic transparency, which suggests the bare yet faintly recognizable outlines of an individual's features but gives no concrete image until it is further developed into a photograph.

In speaking of the photographic referent, Roland Barthes has used the analogy of the umbilical cord, thus forever linking photography to motherhood. Analyzing the photograph as the emanation of the referent, Barthes writes: "A sort of umbilical cord links the body of the photographed thing to my gaze: light, though impalpable, is here a carnal medium, a skin I share with anyone who has been photographed" (1993: 80–81). Her fleeting presence in the Halloween photograph is for Bijoli proof of Gauri's failed motherhood. However, for Bela it has far greater significance and is rendered even more poignant by the loss of her mother soon afterwards. Just as Roland Barthes reads his own life and his mother's death in the Winter Garden photograph, so that it becomes a scene of mourning, so the Halloween photograph becomes for Bela a scene of loss and mourning rather than proof of Gauri's failure as a mother. Ironically, when Bela sees this photograph in Calcutta, Gauri has probably already left their Providence home and become forever lost to her daughter. By looking at it and recalling what it fails to document – the time she spent with Gauri alone – Bela establishes the maternal bond, which ironically has also been severed, as the photograph itself proves. In Barthesian terms, "The referent is both present (implied in the photograph) and absent (it has been there but is not here now). The referent haunts the picture like a ghost: it is a revenant, a return of the lost and dead other" (Hirsch 2012a: 5). Bela's later ruminations on the bodily traces her mother has left behind as markings on her own body are reminiscent of Barthes's phrase "a skin I share with anyone who has been photographed" (1993: 81). Although it appears that Gauri is marginalized and vilified as a selfish and absent mother through her ghostly depiction in the Halloween photograph, a Barthesian reading such as the one I have provided redeems her as a lost and deeply mourned mother rather than a vilified one. A scene establishing the hegemony of the familial ideology is transformed into a scene of maternal mourning.

In the two sections of this chapter so far, I have discussed a portrait of Gauri and some unconventional family photos where she appears fleetingly. Marianne Hirsch has brought the self-portrait and the family photo together in her theorizations in order to "explore the continuum on which these genres uneasily define themselves" (2012a: 84). This continuum allows us to trace the subject's constitution in the familial and the family's visual reflection of the individual. What we get through this continuum is the process of subject-formation. Even before Gauri appears in the novel, she is introduced to the reader and the protagonist through a photograph. My analysis above shows that the consumption of her portrait presages her marginalization within the family. Her subject-construction occurs relationally through the plural exchange of familial looks filtered through ideological and heteronormative screens of desire. However, she is denied her own gaze and kept firmly out of this circuit of looks.

## Masculine Maternity

Barthes's metaphor of the umbilical cord forever linking the photographed object to the photographer's gaze underscores what Hirsch has called "a frightening connection between photography and maternity" (2012a: 170). Ironically, Hirsch argues, Barthes's Winter Garden photograph resurrects his mother, giving birth to her, "thus actually displacing her own maternity" (170). Logically following this argument, Hirsch concludes that "Barthes's camera technologizes and instrumentalizes the function of giving life, shaping a masculine maternity or a paternal form of generativity, a techno-birth" (171). Applying a similar reading to the scene I have discussed from Lahiri's novel, we can see that by photographing Bela as a child, Subhash takes on a masculine maternity. Barthes's likening of the photographic process to a birth process allows us to read Subhash as a maternal figure birthing Bela through his photographs and not simply photographing her. Where does that leave Gauri, Bela's real mother? A closer look at the text allows us to see that such a reading of Subhash usurping Gauri's motherhood is not far-fetched.

A scene as early as that of Bela's birth is depicted by Lahiri as Bela's separation from Gauri and affiliation with Subhash: "The cord was clipped and suddenly the child was no longer a part of Gauri. Others were handling her, cleaning, weighing, and warming her. A little later, when Subhash was called up from the waiting room, Bela was placed in his arms" (144). In the initial days of Bela's life, Gauri suffers from the anxieties often experienced by new mothers – she feels overwhelmed – "the nurse in the hospital had been right, she could not do it all by herself" (144). Gauri even imagines that Bela will somehow meet a horrific death, and she would be responsible:

> She began to imagine scenarios, unbidden but persistent. Grotesque images of Bela's head snapping back, her neck breaking. When Bela fell asleep at her breast, Gauri imagined falling asleep also, forgetting to unlatch her from the nipple, Bela's capacity to breathe put to an end. At night, alone with her in the bedroom, Gauri started to worry that Bela would fall to the floor, or that Gauri would roll on top of her, crushing her. (145)

These are common anxieties among new mothers, but for Gauri they lead to a gradual withdrawal from Bela, enabling Subhash to take on some of her maternal responsibility, even necessitating that he do so. She attempts to assuage the feelings of guilt this raises in her by reminding herself that all mothers need assistance, that Bela was her child and Udayan's, and Subhash "was simply playing a part" (146). As Gauri distances herself from Bela, Subhash becomes essential to Bela's life. I am not suggesting that Subhash maliciously usurps Gauri's motherhood from her, but a closer look at the text reveals that he becomes both a father and a mother to Bela long before Gauri leaves. Lahiri's delineation of the early days of motherhood for Gauri when she feels insecure and vulnerable sets the tone for the distanced and aloof mother we see later in the novel. If Subhash had not simply taken over the role of Bela's caregiver so early in her life, we may have witnessed a different mother in Gauri.

## A Devastating Doubling

Late in Lahiri's novel, when Subhash learns that Bela is pregnant and has decided to raise the child on her own, inspired by his success as a single parent, he is wracked with guilt for not telling her the truth about her parentage. He remembers a conversation between them from long ago:

> Why aren't there two of you? She'd asked, sitting across from him.
> The question had startled him. At first he had not understood.
> I have two eyes, she'd persisted. Why do I see only one of you?
> An innocent question, an intelligent one. She'd been six or seven. He'd told her that in fact each eye did take in a different image, at a

> slightly different angle. He'd covered one of her eyes, then the other, so she could see for herself. *So that he'd appeared to double, shifting back and forth.*
>
> He'd told her *the brain fused the separate images together.* Matching up what was the same, adding in what was different. Making the best of both. (265, emphasis added)

This scene of the child Bela's simple question about visual optics, answered by Subhash with the analogy for photographic seeing, allows me to suggest that he is curiously "doubled" in this novel. Again, using the analysis of a single absent photo as my starting point, I will go on to suggest that Subhash is doubled or twinned with his dead brother Udayan and "becomes" Udayan in many ways. This doubling of the brothers affects Gauri's ability to love Subhash and to form a family with him; he becomes a constant reminder of a past from which she is unable to escape no matter how wide the spatial and temporal gulf between her present life and her past back in Tollygunge. Again, Lahiri uses the trope of photography to delineate her themes of death, loss, and mourning.

Subhash returns from America after receiving the news of his younger brother's untimely demise. As he enters the family home, his parents take him to see Udayan's framed photograph. Lahiri describes the scene as follows:

> In spite of the picture that hung in his parents' new room which they took him to see, he could not believe that Udayan was nowhere. But here was the proof. The photo had been taken nearly ten years ago by a relative who owned a camera, one of the only pictures of the brothers that existed. It was the day they had gotten the results of their higher secondary exams, the day his father said had been the proudest of his life.
>
> *He and Udayan had posed side by side in the courtyard. Subhash saw an inch of his own shoulder, pressed up besides Udayan's. The rest of him, in order to make the death portrait, had been cut away.*
>
> He stood before the image and wept, his head cradled in his arm, in an awkward embrace of himself. But his parents, beyond the shock of it, observed him as they might an actor on stage, waiting for the scene to end. (91, emphasis added)

I have quoted this passage in its entirety because it is an important scene in the novel – a scene of excision – the excision of Udayan from life but also the forced excision of Subhash from the photograph and therefore from his bond with his brother. Instead of simply telling us that Subhash was taken to see his brother's death portrait, Lahiri describes the photograph and its origins at great length. The image performs a number of functions in this scene – it provides "proof" of Udayan's death, a Barthesian *memento mori*; it ironically and painfully recalls a happy moment from the past; and its alteration into a death portrait underscores the finality of the severance of the close bond the brothers shared.

Clare Sestanovich writes in her review of the novel that the brothers' "oneness crumbles – first into twoness, then into many unhappy pieces" (2013: n.pag.). This moment marks the final crumbling. However, because Lahiri uses a photograph to delineate this scene, the implied crumbling of the relationship takes on a layered complexity that also contradictorily suggests a doubling. Until this point, the relationship of the brothers had been developed as a very close one. Though their personalities were quite different – Subhash is cautious and obedient while Udayan was the rebellious one – they were constantly confused with each other, "so that when either name was called both were conditioned to answer" (11). When Subhash decided to leave for America, Udayan had said with love and need in his voice, "You're the other side of me, Subhash. It's without you that I'm nothing. Don't go" (31). Although they were brothers fifteen months apart in age, they were like twins, voices indistinguishable, complexions identical, mirror images of each other – "Irish twins" as one reviewer wrote (Sestanovich 2013: n.pag.). Even reviewers of the book have erroneously referred to them as "twin boys" (Marquardt 2014: n.pag.). None of that oneness now remains. Yet, as if in utter defiance of the abrupt and untimely rupturing of oneness, an inch of Subhash's shoulder remains pressed up against Udayan's in the photograph. This could symbolize that a part of Subhash died with Udayan or that the two of them could never be fully separated. Though most have read the death of Udayan as a rupture of the oneness of the brothers, I will argue that they are twinned and doubled in a number of ways throughout the novel and although Udayan dies early in the narrative, his oneness with his brother never really dies but rather continues through this doubling. Lahiri uses this absent image, along with all the implied connotations of photography, to suggest death's failure to rupture the brothers' relationship, as well as the constant impinging of the past upon the present and the repetitive doubling of the brothers. Subhash's gesture of mourning as he weeps with "his head cradled in his arm, in an awkward embrace of himself" is also a kind of doubling, the self-embrace becoming an embrace of his brother *in absentia*. Udayan's death leads to a number of events – Subhash marrying Udayan's widow and becoming his unborn daughter's father. Thus as far as Subhash's familial identity is concerned, he does in fact "become" Udayan or his double.

Udayan's death portrait recurs a few more times in the novel and creates acts of (mis)recognition. On a visit back to Calcutta with Subhash, Bela sees the photo and Bijoli tells her it is of her father. Bela assumes it is a picture of Subhash and to her it is "proof of him from the time before she was born" (197). Later her father tells her that Bijoli is mistaken and the photo is of her uncle who died. The secret of her paternity and the doubling of Subhash and Udayan causes Bela's misrecognition. Her confusion with the photograph is reminiscent of the earlier childhood scene where Subhash demonstrates to her how the human eye processes what it takes in, by covering one of her eyes, then the other. At the time, Subhash had "appeared to double, shifting back and forth" and had explained that the brain fuses "the separate images together." Similarly, Bela's perception of Udayan's portrait shifts back and forth, fusing together and doubling her father and her uncle in her mind's eye.

Photography has an inherent and undeniable connection with death. According to Roland Barthes, the "ça a été" ("what has been") of the photograph creates the scene of mourning for those who are left to look at the picture. In many ways, as Marguerite Duras argues, a photograph is "a confirmation of death" (qtd. in Hirsch 2012a: 20) since the fleeting moment captured in the photograph has already passed and cannot be revived. Photographs function in contradictory ways – they "bring the past back in the form of a ghostly revenant, emphasizing at the same time, its immutable and irreversible pastness and irretrievability" (20). The photograph of Udayan is not just any photograph, but his death portrait. Therefore, its function as proof of Udayan's death overrides all other functions. However, the presence of life signified by the marginal presence of Subhash within the frame jarringly brings together the past and the present, creating a disturbing continuity as well as the doubling of the brothers. This doubling has a profound impact on Gauri, for whom Subhash, the doubled and surviving brother becomes a constant reminder of Udayan, the man she loved and whose child she bore.

I wish to suggest that Gauri is not the inherently selfish person reviewers have made her out to be; however, she is unable to love Subhash and form a family with him in diaspora because she remains deeply haunted by memories of the past. Subhash is an intense reminder for Gauri of Udayan and the life she could have had with him. The doubling of the brothers prevents her from memorializing Udayan and living her new life with Subhash. The one constantly reminds her of the other. Even their voices are identical: "Almost the exact pitch and manner of speaking. This was the deepest and most startling proof of their fraternity. For a moment she allowed this isolated aspect of Udayan, preserved and replicated in Subhash's throat, to travel back to her" (123). Just as Udayan's death portrait will forever be accompanied by a trace of Subhash, so being with Subhash will always painfully remind Gauri of being with Udayan. Driven by ambition, she tries to surge toward the future leaving the past behind. But like the photograph which collapses time and erases differences while also asserting them, Gauri remains trapped in time, haunted by the past and unable to embrace the future: "the future haunted but kept her alive; it remained her sustenance and also her predator" (151).

What haunts Gauri the most and to varying degrees all the characters in the novel is of course Udayan's violent death at the hands of policemen, in the lowland in front of their house, one dark night at the height of the Naxalite movement. Gauri had witnessed his death along with his parents. Time and space afford her some respite from the vividness of those memories, "but she knew they were there. What was stored in memory was distinct from what was deliberately remembered, Augustine said" (152). Gauri cannot deny the memory of that time, "a time she'd crushed between her fingertips, leaving no substance, only a protective residue on the skin" (153). The past and the present jarringly collide again in a dream Gauri has in which she sees herself in the present as a fifty-six-year-old being seduced by Udayan, as she remembers him. Her husband's touch feels forbidden as "she is coupled naked with a boy who appears as youthful as her son" (230).

The trauma of the past remains vivid in Gauri's consciousness, surfacing at the slightest provocation, however unrelated or remote. This is most disturbingly portrayed in a scene when Bela is afraid to cross the street to her school bus because the path is covered with hundreds of dead earthworms. Gauri's mind immediately returns to Tollygunge at the height of the Naxalite rebellion, when "the bodies of party members were left in streams, in fields [...] to shock people, to revolt them" (169). Troubled by these memories and accusing her child of being a coward, Gauri drags the screaming Bela to the waiting school bus. "I watched your father killed before my eyes, she might have said" (170). Gauri's hardening as a mother is not evidence of her monstrous maternity, but the consequence of her inability to escape the past.

Perhaps Gauri's most incomprehensibly cruel act as a mother is what may be read as a test run of her eventual abandonment of Bela. During the long summer afternoons when Subhash is away at the university and she stays home with Bela, Gauri begins playing a dangerous game. She sets up the six-year-old Bela on the kitchen floor with her toys and books and leaves her, telling her she is going to check the mailbox. The first time she does this, she simply wants to run across to the grocery store next door to get some milk and Bela does not want to go with her. However, Gauri gradually begins to extend the length of the time she is gone, setting Bela up more elaborately each time – now with food and water on the counter in case she gets hungry – and straying increasingly far from their apartment each time. This continues for a while until one afternoon Subhash returns home unexpectedly in the afternoon and finds Bela alone. He is understandably appalled by this act of maternal negligence and irresponsibility. It marks a watershed moment in their relationship and from that day onwards, Subhash distances himself from Gauri, giving her the "wide berth for herself that she had been seeking in their marriage" (176). This is Gauri's most egregious act as a mother, second only to abandoning her family. I read it as a subconscious attempt to test the ramifications of her future abandonment of Bela. It is a symbolic execution of that later abandonment carried out in order to test whether she is indeed capable of this act of monstrous maternity, as well as gauge its consequences for Bela. Although her final abandonment does not leave Bela alone as these afternoon escapades do, when Gauri finally leaves their Providence home, Bela withdraws completely and Subhash is of little comfort to her for the first few years. So this smaller act of parental neglect could be read as Gauri's subconscious and symbolic act to test the ramifications of her final abandonment.

Gauri feels incapable of loving Subhash or Bela: "it was not turning up; after five years [...] the love she'd once felt for Udayan refused to reconstitute itself. Instead there was a growing numbness that inhibited her, that impaired her" (164). This reader finds Lahiri's use of the word "reconstitute" significant here. I would argue that it suggests that Gauri sees Udayan and Subhash as inseparable doubles and she must reconstitute the same love she had for Udayan in order to love Subhash. Unable to do this, her growing numbness inhibiting her, she becomes deeply impaired and debilitated by her loss. Love and sex become disconnected for her as she sleeps with Subhash in order "to extinguish Udayan's ghost. To smother what haunted her" (161).

Haunted by a past which constantly impinges upon the present not only in the form of memories but also in the image of her dead husband reflected in the man she has now married, Gauri is unable to shape her identity in diaspora. Although she has not returned to India for more than three decades, she never overcomes the trauma of leaving her homeland. Overcoming that trauma would necessarily entail eschewing her identity as Udayan's wife and widow; it would entail the erasure of the memories that continue to haunt her in diaspora. Her departure from Calcutta was marked not only by the pain of leaving her homeland, something felt by all immigrants, but also by the upheavals of personal and political trauma. Unable to relinquish her first role as Udayan's wife, she systematically begins to eschew every other familial role she had taken on:

> [H]er role had changed at so many other points in the past. From wife to widow, from sister-in-law to wife, from mother to childless woman. With the exception of losing Udayan, she had actively chosen to take these steps.
>
> She had married Subhash, she had abandoned Bela. She had generated alternative versions of herself, she had insisted at brutal cost on these conversions. Layering her life only to strip it bare, only to be alone in the end. (2014: 240)

In theorizing the concept of family in Lahiri's writing, Ambreen Hai distinguishes between the *natal*, the family and culture into which one is born, and the *non-natal* or the family one creates or chooses to be a part of. She posits the notion of the *alternatal* for diasporic individuals to include "alternative affiliations that can in the best of worlds enrich individual emotional lives, and multiply an individual's commitments and communities, even as they require a coexistence with, and reassessment (though not a rejection) of those primal or prior natal bonds" (2012: 185). In *The Lowland*, Gauri hardly has a natal family – we only hear of her brother Manash, through whom she met Udayan. Her parents disapprove of her romance and break all ties with her. By marrying Udayan, she creates her non-natal family, which quickly dissipates with his tragic death. Her marriage with Subhash and the attempt to create a family with him in diaspora is akin to creating the alternatal. However, Gauri's alternatal is tragically doomed to failure even before it comes into being. The attempt blurs the lines between the natal, the non-natal, and the alternatal by overlapping or multiplying the roles of the individuals involved – "from wife to widow, from sister-in-law to wife," and from uncle to father. Bela's misrecognition of her father in Udayan's photo is emblematic of this blurring of boundaries, this collapsing of the alternatal. Citing an example from Lahiri's collection *Unaccustomed Earth*, Hai also argues that "the natal family can destroy the alternatal if kept secret and unresolved" (2012: 194). The question of Bela's paternity remains a secret until very late in the novel, when Subhash feels compelled to tell her that he is not her real father. It could be argued that the burden of this secret weighs heavily on Gauri. Although she promises Subhash that she will never reveal the truth to Bela on her own, "she felt the weight of it, sinking down inside her [...] A weight always settling instead of surfacing" (171). When Bela finally learns the truth about her father's identity, she immediately connects this family secret to her mother's abandonment; she is now able to understand her mother's actions and feel sympathy for her. She realizes that when her mother left their home, "she'd taken her unhappiness with her, no longer sharing it, leaving Bela with a lack of access to that signal instead" (269). Bela feels relieved of the burden she had carried with her since the day Gauri left: "What had seemed impossible had taken place. The mountain had gone" (269). It is significant that at this moment, Bela recalls Udayan's portrait in Tollygunge, for the first time recognizing it for what it is – a portrait of the father she never knew. However, time has faded the image: "she no longer remembered the face in detail. After being told it was not her father, she'd stopped paying attention to it" (268).

## Conclusion

Monstrous and absent mothers are not uncommon in literature. Victorian literature in particular is replete with examples of powerful, angry, even mad mothers, and mothers that are trivially inconsequential and silenced or absent. Joan Manheimer has argued that the terrible mothers that populate nineteenth-century women's writing should be read as a scathing critique, "an indictment, like an open wound" of the impossible social institution of motherhood with its rigidly codified demands (1979: 545). Fast-forwarding to more contemporary ethnic or immigrant North American literature, we see an oft-repeated pattern whereby patriarchy and gendered familial norms often inhibit diasporic women's search for selfhood and identity. Women characters in South Asian diasporic novels by writers like Shawna Singh Baldwin, Chitra Banerjee Divakaruni, Ginu Kamani, Anita Rau Badami, and others often find themselves trapped in their traditional familial roles of wife and mother by patriarchy and strictly gendered expectations.

Jhumpa Lahiri's writing is not without its fair share of absent, dying, dead, or childless mothers and motherless daughters. We have Shobha in "A Temporary Matter," damaged forever by the stillbirth of her only child; Ruma in "Unaccustomed Earth," who has recently lost her mother and is herself a conflicted and alienated mother; Kaushik's mother, who dies of cancer in "Hema and Kaushik"; and the intensely lonely, eponymous protagonist of "Mrs. Sen's," who becomes a surrogate mother to the little American boy she babysits at her home. However, contrary to what we see in earlier South Asian diasporic fiction, what we cannot find in Lahiri's writings are one-dimensional portrayals of hyper-masculinized, repressive, and abusive patriarchs. Instead we find "nuanced and sensitive depictions of Bengali American male characters who are amiable, intellectual, caring, sensitive, thoughtful, often nurturing, and certainly not villainous" (Hai 2012: 141). For example, in the stories listed above, we see sympathetic and caring characters like Shukumar, Ruma's father, Kaushik, and Mr. Sen. Lavina Dhingra attributes this to a number of things – Lahiri's focus on the male point of view, thus eliciting empathy (even from female readers) for her male characters; her challenge and transcendence of "the Asian American gender troubles paradigm" (Dhingra, 136) that earlier writers modeled; and her attempt to evoke new definitions of Asian American masculinity.

Subhash is a representative example of Lahiri's sensitive, thoughtful, and nurturing male characters. Thus Gauri's failure as a mother (if we see it as a failure) cannot be attributed to patriarchal oppression. In fact, Subhash is the facilitator and enabler of her escape from a life of marginalization and gendered oppression as a widow in India. Despite his love and support, Gauri fails as a wife and mother, finally abandoning her family in search of selfhood. Though moving to America as her former brother-in-law's wife is a bold move, the trauma of her husband's death, coupled with the doubling of her familial roles, proves too much for her. She is irrevocably altered by her past. She is subtly portrayed early in the novel through her photograph as an independent, intellectual, ambitious, and self-assured woman. Her traumatic past, which never ceases to haunt her, coupled with her strongly individualized character and her search for selfhood, creates a debilitating numbness and a drive to be alone, shorn of her devastatingly doubled roles that deeply impair her as both a wife and mother.

Gradually coming to accept the failure of their marriage, Subhash recalls Gauri's photograph that Udayan had sent him by way of an introduction: "She never expressed any unhappiness, she did not complain. But the smiling, carefree girl in the photograph Udayan had sent, that had been Subhash's first impression of her, that he had also hoped to draw out – that part of her he'd never seen" (259). His disappointment and frustration is akin to Barthes's frustration as he looks through photographs of his mother, encapsulated in the epigraph of this chapter – "I had no hope of 'finding' her" (1993: 63). "That's *almost* the way she was," Barthes says later, his frustration growing. Though these scenes are somewhat analogous, Lahiri's captures the reverse of Barthes's – Subhash tries to find in Gauri what he had seen in the photograph, while Barthes tries to find in the photograph what he had seen in his mother. Juxtaposing the two allows us to see the paradoxes of photography – its failure to capture the essence of a person, and its attributes of truth-telling. Barthes is ultimately able to find his mother in the Winter

Garden photograph, which achieves for him "utopically, *the impossible science of the unique being*" (71, emphasis original). So too, I argue, can we find Gauri only if we look differently, through the photographic trope so subtly employed by Lahiri. Lahiri's use of the narrated photograph allows her to create what may be the most complex character in her writing so far. The "ça a été" ("what has been") of the "smiling, carefree girl in the photograph Udayan had sent" is undeniable. However, as I have shown, that part of her has been destroyed by the circumstances of her migration and the hauntings of her past, leaving her desperately alone. Like Subhash, we can only mourn the unfulfilled potential of the girl in the photograph.

# PART III

# The Absent Image as Trace

Classical theorists of photography have defined the photograph as a trace. André Bazin writes, "photography is altogether something other [than the pre-photographic plastic arts]. Not at all the image of an object or being, but more exactly its trace" (quoted in Pettersson: 189). Similarly, Susan Sontag has written of photographs as traces, arguing that a "photograph is not only an image [...] it is also a trace, something directly stenciled off the real, like a footprint or a death mask" (1977: 154). This idea of the trace in photography comes from what may be called the "proximity effect" of photography – the sense that photographs make us feel close to the object photographed regardless of how distant the photographed object may be in time and place. However, critics have also pointed out that the proximity effect occurs only in the case of personal photos or photos that have an affective import for the viewer. Others like Janne Seppanen have argued that the basic assumption of the absence of the represented in all forms of representation is contradicted in photography because the trace "establishes a physical connection to the represented subject" (2017: 122), creating confusion in the observer over whether the photograph is a representation or the represented entity itself. This, for Seppanen, lends a contradictory agency to the trace – the photograph providing a visual representation of an absent object but the photograph's own materiality at the same time, undermining that absence. Seppanen concludes that "photographic representation is haunted by the desire for truth but inhabits an unresolvable epistemological aporia" (123).

This aporia is heightened in my reading of the photographic trace; in the novels discussed in this concluding part of the book, the photographic trace is suggested in different ways – either through hauntings and evocations of particular photos that lie outside the text or through an intense spectatorship of an absent photo. While the absence of the material image weakens the proximity effect, the suggestions of the photographic trace in other ways allows us to think of photographs in less dualistic ways. No longer do we think of subject and object, model and copy – my purpose in this part is to dismantle the humanistic construct of photography and think of it in terms of entanglements and doublings by reading the absent image as trace.

Interestingly, both the novels discussed in this last part of the book – Indra Sinha's *Animal's People* and Siddhartha Deb's *Surface* – include as their epigraph the following words from Joseph Conrad's *Heart of Darkness* – "Do you see the story? Do you see anything?" – thereby underscoring questions of visuality. These are Marlow's words describing Kurtz to his fellow seamen. The lines in Conrad's novel preceding the ones chosen for Sinha and Deb's epigraph are: "He was just a word for me. I did not see the man in the name any more than you do." "Kurtz" is just a word and we cannot see the man in the word. Of course, this remains true throughout the novel, even when Kurtz appears, because he is presented with words on the page. The epigraph chosen by both Sinha and Deb underscores sight but also the relationship between word and image, one key concern in *Traces of the Real.* It invites us to "see" in the traces of the absent presence of photographs more than meets the eye, to engage our civil imagination as spectators.

6

# Imagistic Haunting: Posthuman Photography and Photographic Traces in Indra Sinha's *Animal's People*

Photographic images are persistent, fugitive bodies that remind us of our obligation to look, to think, and to act.

Lee Mackinnon, "Toward a Materialist Photography," 157

## Introduction

Much of the scholarship about Indra Sinha's 2011 novel *Animal's People*, which is loosely based on the Bhopal Gas Tragedy of 1984,[1] centers around two main issues – environmental justice for the poor and the spectacularization of abject bodies. Sinha's protagonist, the eponymous Animal, encapsulates both these themes in his personhood. A slum-dweller in Khaufpur, Sinha's stand-in for Bhopal, Animal has a horribly twisted spine, which compels him to walk on all fours. In refutation of his humanity, he has claimed the name "Animal" for himself. He blurs the boundary between human and animal, not only through his name, but also through his deformed body and aggressive sexuality. In his deformity, he is easily spectacularized. Consequently, visibility and questions of looking, seeing, gazing, and staring have also been central to the scholarly discussion of this novel. Chattopadhyay and Nayak (2014) discuss the valencies of the stare in disability studies and contrast this with the colonial gaze. Andrew Mahlstedt analyzes what he calls the "spectacular invisibility" of the poor in the context of this novel. He argues that "Part of the project of *Animal's People* [...] is to make visible the invisible people; though this is insufficient for justice and recognition, it may be an essential precondition" (2013: 62). Sinha himself centers the novel on the question of looking vs. seeing by

[1] https://en.wikipedia.org/wiki/Bhopal_disaster.

framing the story through the "eyes" of the readers. Animal speaks directly to the listener and an Australian journalist who had visited Khaufpur years earlier and left a "tape mashin" for Animal to record his story, transcribes his narrative. Imagining the invisible auditor, Chunaram tells Animal to "look at him, see his eyes. He says thousands of other people are looking through his eyes. Think of that" (7). Sinha rejects the voyeuristic readers' gaze as well as any empathetic impulse on the part of the reader. However, as Mahlstedt argues, Sinha still hopes we may see "*a bit more* ethically by being aware of our distance" (Mahlstedt 2013: 65). Using Julia Kristeva's notion of abjection, Délice Williams argues that "such representations encode the author's conceptions of and responses to the marginalization of environmental justice communities in modern India and the Global South" (2018: 586). This chapter contributes to the discourse of invisibility and seeing that has developed around the scholarship on *Animal's People* by arguing that the absent presence of photography in the novel plays a powerful role in furthering Sinha's social justice agenda.

Given Sinha's own human rights activism and the humanitarian aspects of his novel, other critics have studied *Animal's People* as representing a particular genre of writing having to do with humanitarianism. Jennifer Rickel (2012) considers Sinha's novel a posthuman rethinking of literary humanitarianism, while Julietta Singh ascribes the term "post-humanitarian fiction" to it; she describes a novel of this genre as "a postcolonial literary text that pressures humanitarian action by revealing its dehumanizing functions" (2015: 138). Both critics engage with recent scholarship on posthumanism and Singh briefly touches on new materialist studies. For Rickel, the posthumanist approach helps to ameliorate the hierarchizing tendencies of literary humanitarianism, which is grounded in humanist ideas that center the civilized subject. Similarly, Singh calls for a more vulnerable reading of post-humanitarian fictions, which allows for a transformation of agency, a reframing of "the act of reading itself in such a way that allows for other agencies to emerge and to affect the vulnerable reader" (141). Heeding calls like Rickel's and Singh's for a less dialectical approach to humanitarianism, in my reading of Sinha's novel I adopt a twin approach using posthumanism and new materialism to suggest that although photographs are absent in the novel, Sinha uses the absent presence of photographs that take on a new materialist agency as they become part of a posthuman assemblage. This strategy, I argue, allows Sinha to avoid the spectacularizing gaze, which often silences the recipients of humanitarian aid by appealing to the generosity of the privileged via a highly binarized framework of humanitarian appeal, one that follows a rescuer/rescued model.

Photography has long been viewed as a humanist project dominated by the notion of the primacy of the human subject and its emphasis on the subject-object dialectic. The message of photography has always been that humans are an exceptional species, possessing a rational view of the world with the power to discern between the real and the representational or what we might call a copy. The role of the human has long been central to photography, in particular the role of the photographer. As Hugh McCabe points out, "the emphasis is always on how the meaning of the photograph is to be located with respect to the relation between the image and a human subject or subjects" (2013: 9). The subject-object dialectic that underpins photography also considers a universal subject to be at the center of an anthropocentric worldview. It is only very recently that critics of photography have moved away from such humanistic understandings of photography in order to de-emphasize the role of the human. Daniel Rubinstein has posited the notion of posthuman photography, which he defines as "concerned with the photographic image that is based not on the patriarchal politics of identity and subject-object dualisms but on establishing the multiversal: a rhizomatic assemblage of interconnected fragments" (98). Rubinstein's framework, although suggested in the context of the digital age, can be adopted to read Indra Sinha's novel *Animal's People*, where the absent presence of iconic photos together form an assemblage. This includes the nonhuman characters in the novel, namely Animal and Khã-in-the-Jar, the double-headed fetus in a jar, and the digital in the form of the website Sinha designed for Khaufpur (www.khaufpur.com). I argue that this unique assemblage based on the absent presence of photography enables Sinha to draw attention to issues like environmental toxicity and degradation, humanimality and disability without provoking the distancing gaze or spectacularizing the suffering of victims, contrary to what photographs of disasters might achieve.

Sinha's own long engagement with the photography of Raghu Rai, India's most influential photojournalist, haunts this novel in various ways and usefully offers us an example of the spectacularizing approach to humanitarian aid. In the first half of this chapter, I trace the trajectory of Rai's iconic photos to underscore the ways in which they have been used, including by Sinha himself for his own humanitarian work raising money to build a free clinic for the Bhopal Gas Tragedy's survivors. I suggest that while these photographs have often been used in spectacularizing ways, the absent presence of the very same photos in Sinha's novel draws attention to the victims in a nonspectacularizing manner. Rai was one of the first photographers to arrive in Bhopal the morning after the leak and he took many photos in the aftermath of the tragedy. The photo called "Burial of an

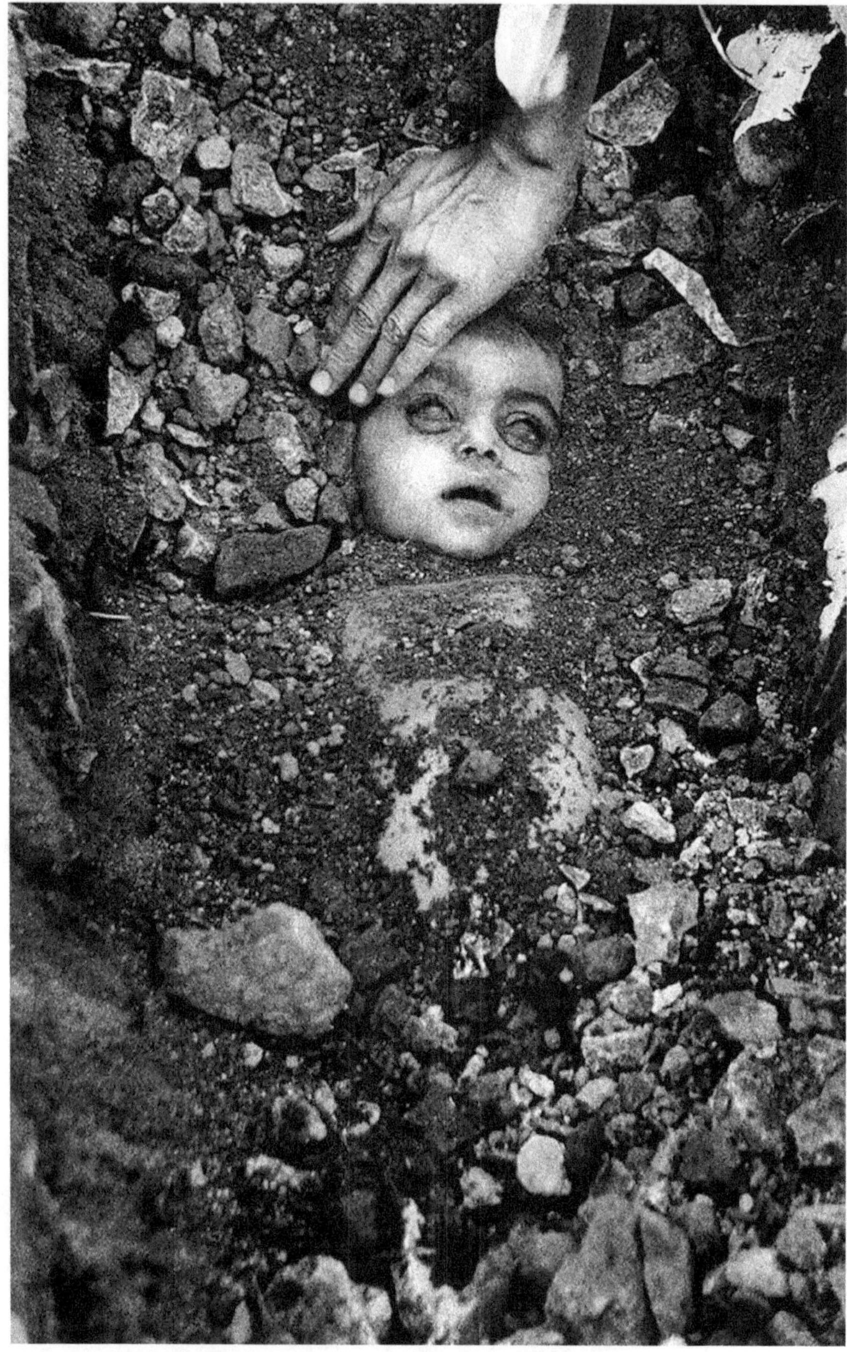

Figure 4. Reproduced with permission from Raghu Rai

Unknown Child" (Figure 4) is a striking image that has become emblematic of the disaster.

In addition to this photo, which Sinha used in his own ad campaigns published in *The Guardian*, Raghu Rai's image of a fetus in a bottle, another iconic photograph taken in the aftermath of the Bhopal tragedy, haunts Sinha's novel. Animal's imaginary friend Khã is a two-headed fetus in a jar that Animal had seen as a child in the doctor's office. *Animal's People* is profoundly haunted by both these images though they never actually appear in the novel. Finally, images of Khaufpur, the imaginary setting of Sinha's novel, exist outside the pages of the novel at www.khaufpur.com[2] and https://khaufpur.wordpress.com/about/. Adopting a new materialist, posthuman approach to photography in my reading of the novel, I argue that Sinha uses photography to present a posthuman postcoloniality made up of assemblages of the human, the animal, the nonhuman, and the digital, animated by the haunting of real images which never appear within the work. Instead, these images are evoked and create a nexus of sensations and new assemblages; this enables Sinha to critique neoliberal slow violence (Nixon 2011) and offer posthuman, postcolonial alternatives. The next section traces the circuits that Rai's photos have traversed and the ways in which they have been deployed in order to tell the story of the Bhopal Gas Tragedy. The subsequent sections of the chapter propose the posthuman assemblage suggested by the absent presence of photography in Sinha's novel.

## Spectacular Trajectories

*Animal's People* has its roots in photography and goes back to Sinha's work fighting for the rights of the Bhopal tragedy's survivors and victims, which was a particularly challenging task for him. In an interview he says:

> For months, Raghu Rai's famous picture of a baby's burial stared at me from my office wall. I was unable to find words to go with it. Finally, with the 10th anniversary of the disaster approaching, I wrote a double page ad and took it to Carolyn McCall at *The Guardian*, explaining that we hadn't a penny, but the appeal was so important she had to publish it. It ran on a personal guarantee to stump up if it failed. (Mahadevan-Dasgupta 2007: n.pag.)

[2] Unfortunately, this website is now defunct and the images are no longer accessible. However, I was able to obtain images of the pages from Indra Sinha who reconstructed the pages as they had appeared on the website. See Appendix.

This appeal was a success and led to the establishment of the free Sambhavna clinic, which provides medical care to the survivors of India's worst environmental disaster. The photograph he refers to is one of Raghu Rai's most iconic images capturing the tragedy of the disaster. What has come to be known as the Bhopal Gas Tragedy took place on the night of December 1, 1984, when 40,000 tonnes of methyl isocyanate leaked from the Union Carbide pesticide factory in Bhopal, Madhya Pradesh. The leak is the worst chemical disaster of the century, affecting nearly half a million people, by some accounts. Twenty thousand people are said to have died and another 150,000 were harmed by the toxic leak. The long-term effects of the disaster are evident even today, more than three decades later, in the maimed bodies of the survivors.

Eminent Indian photographer Raghu Rai received a phone call late on the night of December 2, 1984 from his editor at *India Today* informing him that there had been a gas leak in Bhopal and he should take a flight early the next morning to get there as soon as possible. A short while later he received a similar call from the Paris office of Magnum Photos. Representing both *India Today* and Magnum Photos from India, Rai flew from Delhi to Bhopal the next morning. He soon realized the magnitude of the Bhopal tragedy on his drive from the airport into the city; the streets were strewn with bloated bodies, dead animals, and people being taken to the hospital. He recalls that the entire international press had descended upon the city, "looking for dead bodies, dying ones … like vultures" (qtd. in Krishnan 2014: n.pag., ellipses in original). The predatory instinct in his choice of words is somewhat undercut when he goes on to say that in the midst of an unfolding tragedy on such a scale, "the situations themselves were so strong that you didn't have time to think or organize your image."

During this visit to cover the Union Carbide gas leak in Bhopal, Rai took what probably came to be the most iconic photo of the tragedy – the photograph titled "Burial of an Unknown Child." Describing how that came about in an interview with *The Economic Times,* he says:

> You see, the Hindus were burning their dead. There was mass cremation. There were huge piles of wood and bodies were put on top of that and then burned. The Muslims … their graves were almost like three-tier kind of graves … they were digging, putting a body, then some mud, another body, then some mud. This was the situation in that case. These two babies … actually I've got another photograph where there are two babies one below the other. This is the one that they were going to put the mud on. And the baby's eyes were open and that's why I thought it

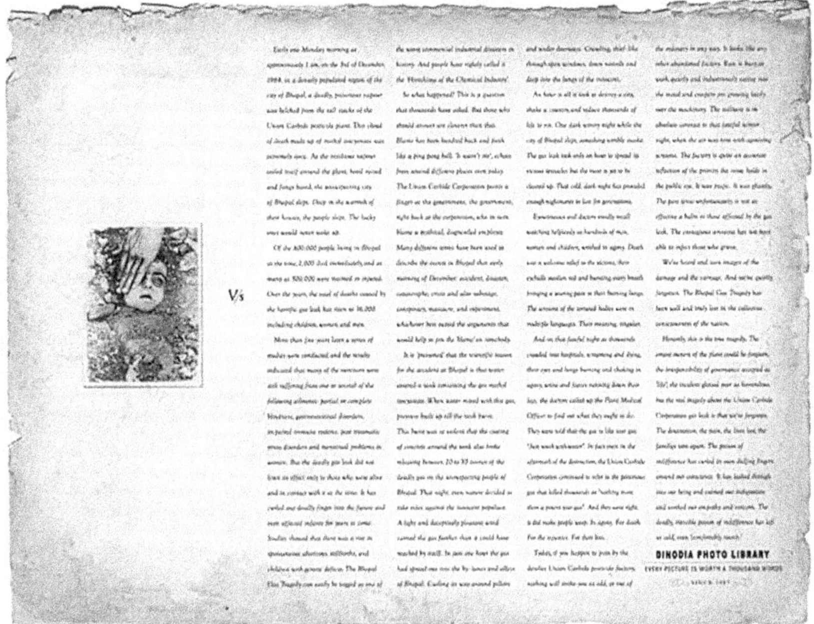


Figure 5. Reproduced with permission from Raghu Rai and Dinodia Photos

> was moving and very touching because [of] that innocent face, the opened eyes and the man's hand. I said, "Can you just move the mud a bit?" because they were about to bury them. So this is the one that became an iconic image for Bhopal. (Krishnan 2014: n.pag., all ellipses in original)

As with many iconic photos, particularly those taken in times of great human tragedy (such as the image of the Afghan girl that graced the cover of *Time* magazine or the photo of the "Napalm Girl"), a mythology has developed around this image. The photo has sometimes been used inappropriately in various circuits. For example, Dinodia Photo Library[3] used Raghu Rai's iconic

[3] Dinodia Photo Library is a stock image company founded in 1987 with a collection of over thirty-nine million images ranging from historical photographs from as far back as 1870 to contemporary images. It represents one hundred and seventy-five image libraries from various parts of the world but its focus remains on images that are uniquely Indian in nature. Prints of all their images are available for sale.

image "Burial of an Unknown Child" for its own ad campaign "Every picture is worth a thousand words" (Figure 5).[4]

The ad campaign was designed to juxtapose a single powerful image from Dinodia's collection to a write-up of exactly one thousand words. The ad appears on a single page, looks like parchment from a photo album, frayed and stained at the edges. The thousand-word write up is printed in very small script and ends with the words "DINODIA PHOTO LIBRARY: EVERY PICTURE IS WORTH A THOUSAND WORDS. SINCE 1987" in boldface. The placing of "vs" between the image and the writing seems to suggest that this is a competition between image and words. However, the subtext hinted at not so subtly in the punchline, "Every picture is worth a thousand words" suggests that in terms of economy of expression, visual impact, and immediacy, a single picture clearly wins over a thousand words. The art director and typographer of the ad, Santosh Padhi, remarked, "we adopted the route that no amount of words can match up to a single picture" (in Joshi 2006: n.pag.). Leo Burnett, Mumbai, the ad agency responsible for this particular ad, earned a bronze prize at the US-based Andy Awards for its press entry titled "Bhopal Gas" in the category Newspaper: Industrial/Building Products and Services in 2006. Interestingly, the news item reporting this award does not mention Raghu Rai anywhere (Joshi 2006: n.pag.).

Indra Sinha used the same photograph for his own advertisement (Figure 6), accompanied by a thousand words that seemed inadequate to tell the story of the tragedy and its long-lasting effects on the people of Bhopal. The money raised through his ad campaign enabled Sinha to establish the Sambhavna Free Clinic in Bhopal, which has provided free medical treatment to tens of thousands of people. Sinha's ad was designed with Rai's photograph in the middle of the page.

The piece is titled "Union Carbide, May God Forgive You" and the text is an open letter to "the directors of Union Carbide." The tone is deeply condemnatory, heaping accusation upon accusation. The "us versus you" binary sets up the people of Bhopal ("us") as victims of a rapacious, secretive, and remorseless company interested only in profiteering even when it comes at the cost of human death and misery on an enormous scale. Sinha accuses the directors of knowing long before the actual leak that "there was a threat of toxic chemicals leaking into the ground water and thus into our wells." He vividly portrays the terror of that fateful night when "our lungs caught fire" and "we fled from our houses into the yelling and

[4] https://www.adsoftheworld.com/campaigns/bhopal-gas.

# Union Carbide, may God forgive you

REPORT BY
INDRA SINHA
www.indrasinha.com

*To the directors of Union Carbide: You have known for more than ten years that your derelict factory in Bhopal is lethally contaminated and that there was a threat of toxic chemicals leaking into the ground water and thus into our wells. You did not warn us. We found out from your own secret documents after a court in New York last month ordered you to hand them over. Because of your gases, our people are ravaged by illness, but for years we have puzzled why people who weren't in Bhopal when your factory blew up were getting ill with symptoms like those of the gas survivors. You knew, but did not tell us. What kind of people are you, to keep quiet when you must have known that the poisons leaking into our water could cause cancers and birth defects among the very same people whose families your gases killed eighteen years ago?*

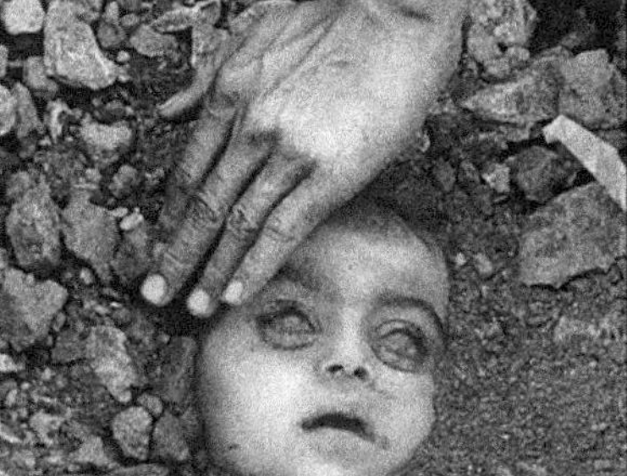


WHEN YOU BUILT your factory, you promised us it was for good. You told us – those of us who lived in the shadow of your steel towers and could smell their stench – 'We are making *kheti ki dawai*, medicine for the fields'. You never said you were making poisons.

It's eighteen years since that night, the night no one who survived it will ever forget. You did not wake with your eyes burning to tell your crying, innocent children, 'Go back to sleep darling, it's only someone burning chilis.' You weren't there when it did not stop and our lungs caught fire, as if someone had thrust live coals down our throats. You weren't with us when we fled from our houses into the yelling and screams and confusion, the cows running too and trampling us in their terror.

Where were you when we began falling, thousands of us, to lie like rag bundles, like the sacks of poison you used to employ our men to stack with bare hands in your factory?

Only on that night did we learn the truth about that factory of yours. It was manufacturing death. The deaths you'd planned were those of insects, but you killed us instead. Was there much difference, to you?

We saw you, coming from Shamla Hills in your big cars, looking neither left nor right as the gates of your factory opened and the guards saluted. You did not see us, our houses, our lanes, shops, strings of washing, signs for Ganesh Beedis and Shalimar Dry Cleaning. For you we didn't really exist.

You certainly never treated us as people, because you wouldn't tell our doctors what had leaked or how to treat it. You said these were 'trade secrets'.

You were interested, but not in us. You sent a man to Bhopal to question our doctors. We know all about him now, but for years he was a sinister legend. He'd worked with chemical weapons, hadn't he? – testing them on animals and people too. He was interested in the effects of cyanide. That's why he came. Not to help us, but to watch us die and make notes about how long it took.

Your man didn't stay to see what overtook us in the months that followed, nausea, breathlessness, headaches, giddiness, aches that seemed to bend our bones. He left, but these things didn't. As months became years, you showed no further interest in us – in our cancers, the epidemic of menstrual problems, the terrifying births – none of these things did you ever enquire about. You never thought of us again.

You did your best to avoid paying compensation. Your gases injured half a million people in our city and you threatened to cross-examine every one of them. You asked the court to allow a day per witness. It would have taken 1,500 years. Isn't this why the Supreme Court settled with you, so we would at least get something before all of us were dead? You ended up paying a pittance. Over eighteen years it works out at enough to buy one cup of tea per day. It doesn't even buy aspirin. Meanwhile we were still dying. How we died! To date, you have achieved at least 20,000 victims.

You didn't just take our loved ones. You took our livings. Most of us worked very hard – pulling loads, carrying things – long hours on meagre diets. We were among the poorest people on earth, you among the richest, but you turned us into beggars and then turned your back on us.

You locked the gates of your factory and left. But the stink still hangs there, eighteen years later. You never bothered to clean it up. We know, you see, because we've been in. We've gone through the gaps in the wall to stop our children playing among the heaps of brown rocks that have tumbled from rotting tanks. They're not rocks, they're lumps of poison.

You've never been back – you didn't come even when our court ordered you to appear. You were Americans, you said. Indian courts had no powers over you.

So you don't know that in your factory, no birds sing. This isn't magic. There's nothing for the birds to eat. The ground is poisoned. In many places, drops of mercury lie gleaming on the ground. In your solar evaporation ponds are thousands of tons of toxic sludge. When the rains turned them into lakes, children used to splash in them and cows drank there. No more. Since we got hold of your secret papers, we know you filled the ponds with some of the most dangerous chemicals ever made. We know that drinking from the wells you contaminated can cause cancers, liver damage and birth defects.

If it seems surprising that people who never went to school have taught themselves chemistry and medicine, the reason is that we learned a long time ago to expect nothing from the giant US corporation that killed our families, ruined our lives and now hides like a toxic Jonah inside Dow Chemical's whale. We had to help ourselves, so we started our own clinic, where gas-affected people are treated free.

It is called Sambhavna, 'possibility', and is run for survivors by survivors – most of our staff are gas-affected. No one is turned away. The poorest are welcomed with dignity. We offer modern medicine along with traditional Indian ayurveda. We pioneered the use of yoga breathing and massage for lung patients. (See www.bhopal.org)

Sambhavna has just won the Margaret Mead award, which is given to small groups of people who make a real difference in the world. The prize also belongs to the readers of this newspaper.

Guardian readers gave the money to start Sambhavna and have kept it running for six years. Thank you, God bless your good hearts.

Our need this year is urgent as ever.

The people we treat cannot be cured, but their suffering can be eased. Please be as generous as you were last year. We value your support as much as your donation. There may be no justice in this world, but there are a lot of good people.

That alone keeps us alive.

PRESENCE OF TOXIC INGREDIENTS IN SOIL/WATER SAMPLES INSIDE PLANT PREMISES

The matter has assumed significant importance in view of recent reports in local and national news papers. The seriousness of the issue needs no elaboration. It is earnestly suggested that the subject be given due consideration and studies initiated without further delay. If the situation so requires, the work may be carried out primarily for our own understanding of the situation, in the first phase. In the following paragraphs a summary of preliminary work carried out in 1989 is described.

1. Analysis of samples drawn by plant personnel in June-July 1989.

SECRET CARBIDE DOCUMENT

Samples drawn in June-July '89 from land-fill areas and effluent treatment pits inside the plant were sent to R and D. They consisted of nine soil/solid samples and eight liquid samples. The solid samples had organic contamination varying from 10% to 100% and contained known ingredients like naphthol and naphthalene in substantial quantities.

Majority of the liquid samples contained naphthol and/or Sevin in quantities far more than permitted by ISI for inland disposal. All samples caused 100% mortality to fish in toxicity assessment studies and were to be diluted several fold to render them suitable for survival of fish.

*Carbide knew of the danger to water in 1989, but kept denying there was a problem. People did not know they were being poisoned until the Greenpeace report in 1999.*

*torture me*

AIM A BLOWTORCH AT MY EYES
POUR ACID DOWN MY THROAT
STRIP THE TISSUE FROM MY LUNGS
DROWN ME IN MY OWN BLOOD
CHOKE MY BABY TO DEATH IN FRONT
OF ME, FORCE ME TO WATCH
HER STRUGGLES AS SHE DIES –
CRIPPLE MY CHILDREN, LET PAIN
BE THEIR DAILY AND ONLY PLAYMATE –
SPARE ME NOTHING
RUIN MY HEALTH SO I CAN NO LONGER
WORK OR FEED MY FAMILY –
WATCH US STARVE – SEE MY CHILDREN
DRINKING WATER AT NIGHT TO FILL
THEIR HUNGRY BELLIES

THEN POISON OUR DRINKING WATER
NEVER WARN US OF THE DANGER
CAUSE MONSTERS TO BE BORN AMONG US
MAKE US CURSE GOD
STUNT OUR LIVING CHILDREN'S GROWTH
SAY IT'S NOTHING TO DO WITH YOU
DON'T EVER SAY SORRY
FOR EIGHTEEN LONG YEARS IGNORE
OUR CRIES AND TEACH ME
THAT MY RAGE IS AS USELESS AS MY TEARS
PROVE TO ME BEYOND ALL DOUBT
THERE'S NO JUSTICE IN THIS WORLD
YOU ARE AN AMERICAN CORPORATION
AND I AM A WOMAN OF BHOPAL

*— the survivor's poem —*

FREEFONE 0800 316 5577 TO DONATE NOW WITH A CARD *or visit www.bhopal.org/donations*

*'There may be no justice in the world, but there are good people, and that alone keeps us alive'* - BHOPAL SURVIVOR

1. I'd like to give £5☐ £10☐ £20☐ £50☐ £100☐ £250☐ £500☐ £1,000☐ £2,000☐ £5,000☐ Other........
Here's a cheque payable to PAN-UK(Bhopal Medical Appeal) / Please charge my credit/debit card. Valid from ☐☐ / ☐☐
Card No ☐☐☐☐☐☐☐☐☐☐☐☐☐☐☐☐ Expiry date ☐☐ / ☐☐ Issue no. (Switch/Solo only) ☐☐

2. ☐ Please Gift Aid my gift. (This increases its value at no cost to yourself as we are able to claim back the tax you've already paid on it. Please tick the box if you can confirm that you've paid UK Income Tax or Capital Gains Tax.)

3. ☐ Please contact me about making a standing order.
☐ I would like to receive email updates about Bhopal - (no more than one email every three or four months)

4. Please fill in your details and sign where indicated
Name........
Address........
........
........Postcode........
Signature........Date........
Email........

4. Please post the completed form to: Gua0904
Pesticide Action Network/Bhopal Account
49 Effra Road, FREEPOST, London SW2 1BZ
No stamp needed but if you use one it saves us the cost.
You can also donate direct to:
PAN-UK/Bhopal Account No 61752312, NatWest Bank, Sort Code (60-03-36), 504 Brixton Rd, London SW9 8EB

Bhopal Medical Appeal

A PROJECT OF PESTICIDE ACTION NETWORK UK, CHARITY 327124

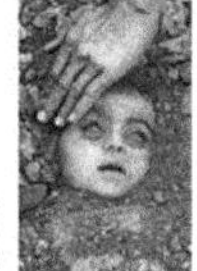

Figure 6. Reproduced with permission from Raghu Rai, Indra Sinha, and *The Guardian*

screams and confusion." The company is accused of turning a blind eye to the continuing suffering of the people years after the leak by avoiding the payment of compensation, inhibiting the cross-examination of witnesses, and finally entering a settlement with the Supreme Court which had them pay "a pittance [...] It doesn't even buy aspirin." In a scathing indictment of the company's crimes Sinha writes, "How we died! To date, you have achieved at least 20,000 victims." Further accusations of abandonment, neglect, and shirking of any responsibility for the horrific tragedy follow. As the text nears its end, Sinha's attention shifts to the people who have had to "help ourselves," thus allowing him to introduce his free clinic, "Sambhavna," a Hindi word meaning "possibility," run for survivors by survivors, where the "poorest are welcomed with dignity." The text ends with an expression of gratitude to *Guardian* readers who have already donated to start the clinic and contributed to keeping it running for six years and with an urgent call for further generosity. The last lines read: "There may be no justice in the world, but there are good people, and that alone keeps us alive." The bottom of the page includes a two-inch donation slip with Rai's photo reprinted in a tiny box on the right.

There are stark differences in the ways in which Rai's iconic image is deployed in the Dinodia Photo Library ad and Sinha's own advertisement to raise money for his free clinic for Bhopal victims. While the former attempts to demonstrate the power of a single photographic image over the written word and thereby promote itself as the repository of other similarly powerful images, the latter uses it in concert with other images as well as an emotional piece of writing to make an urgent plea for funds for a humanitarian cause.

I have spent some time detailing only a few of the visual and rhetorical circuits that Rai's iconic image of the Bhopal Gas Tragedy has traveled and the uses for which it has been deployed. I have done so to highlight several issues that are crucial to this chapter – the ethics of photographic representation, particularly in the context of large-scale human tragedies like the Bhopal gas leak, the relative power of words and images in conveying suffering, the circumstances of the composition of images, and the purposes for which these images are used as well as the affective import of photographic images and the photographer's agency. Describing his experience of taking the iconic photo on that fateful day, Raghu Rai says "it was very moving and touching because that innocent face, the open eyes, the man's hand." He says he asked for the man's permission to "move the mud a bit" (Krishnan 2014: n.pag.). Rai portrays himself as a professional, focusing on deadlines and the need to "go on taking pictures" because "every minute was so intense." Rejecting nostalgia, "good or bad," he says, "As you photograph each situation, you don't compare. You just get into the intensity and expression of the situation – how strong it is coming along – and you try to capture that in its most raw and strongest possible way" (Krishnan 2014: n.pag.). Rai portrays himself as an aloof artist, acutely aware of the intense emotional impact of his work but consciously distancing himself from that emotionality in the service of his profession.

We may ask what makes Rai's photo an ideal one for Sinha's purposes? I would suggest that the answer lies in what Wendy Hesford has called the "spectacular rhetoric" in her theorization of the visual economy of human rights – the way in which "spectacular texts and contexts project identifications onto audiences and how human rights subjects are represented as possessing certain identities" (2011: 9). Rai's photo accompanying Sinha's text enables Sinha to produce the subjects on behalf of whom he is making his appeal as well as his audience (readers of *The Guardian*) in particular ways that Hesford would argue fall along the axes of the "material relations of power and difference" (9). The shift in gaze and agency from that of the photographer in Rai's narrative to that of the reader of the *Guardian* in Sinha's advertisement is indicative of the public/private binary of the photograph. It depicts the spectacularization and publicization of a private moment of intense grief and loss. Our complete lack of information about the identity of the child or the father undercuts the illusion of intimacy. In a sweeping metonymic gesture, the child comes to represent countless Bhopali children who lost their lives that night. Hesford has demonstrated how the visual ecology of human rights often simply reinscribes normative identities in ways that produce and ultimately govern human rights subjects. Western media coverage of humanitarian disasters like the Bhopal gas leak tends to portray those affected as helpless masses deprived of agency, spoken for by the experts or reporters. The use of photographs from these disasters for the purposes of humanitarian appeals heightens this dynamic. Such ads are often designed to shock the privileged out of their passivity and compel them to exercise their moral responsibility based on a shared humanity by donating generously to the humanitarian cause. Sinha's concluding sentence appeals to the assumed goodness of the Western audience as the last hope of those suffering half a world away in the face of the failure of global justice: "There may be no justice in the world, but there are good people, and that alone keeps us alive." However, in doing so it also highlights the hiatus between the privileged readers and the impoverished victims. Agreeing with Lillian Wilkins that such moves are "profoundly undemocratic" Alexandra Schultheis Moore writes: "It empties rights claims of political agency for the claimants and seeks humanitarian assistance in its place" (2015: 126). Advertisements like this often perform a simultaneously spectacularizing and silencing gesture. The implied purpose of such appeals is to make visible the plight of the poor, who often remain invisible; however, in using photographs like Rai's in such appeals, the outcome is one of spectacularization rather than of making visible.

Sinha's novel *Animal's People* may be read as the literary counterpart to his *Guardian* advertisements designed with the same purpose of drawing humanitarian attention to a story of suffering. In this chapter, I propose a somewhat different posthumanist approach to suggest that Sinha attempts an alternative mode of "mak[ing] visible the invisible people" (Mahlstedt 2013: 62), this time by erasing the photo he used so effectively in his advertisement campaign for the Bhopal Medical Appeal, in his novel *Animal's People*. However, it is not a complete erasure, I argue, as this photo, and others, remain in traces. Sinha offers us what I call a posthuman assemblage, which enables us to look differently.

## Photography, New Materialism, and a Posthuman Assemblage

"I used to be human once." Thus begins Sinha's severely deformed narrator. As if to signify the loss of his humanness, he is called Janvaar or Animal. From the very beginning of the novel, Sinha plays with ideas of the human and the nonhuman, thereby subtly drawing attention to the plight of people like Animal who live on the very edge of society in subhuman conditions. As Upamanyu Pablo Mukherjee points out, the Bhopal Gas Tragedy and the legal wrangling over compensation and accountability that followed it "revealed that the idea of 'environment,' and indeed, of the 'human,' carried radically different meanings in the 'global north' of Euro-north America and the 'global south' of the postcolonial nations" (Mukherjee 2010: 134).

Humanism's idealized notion of the Vitruvian Man, embodying the ideals of reason, rationality, and beauty, came to be discredited in the second half of the twentieth century. Fascism, communism, and the Holocaust flouted cherished humanist ideals, precipitating a moment of crisis. It was soon realized that the individualized, self-determined Man of humanism was not an ideal aggregate but rather "a systematized standard of recognizability – of Sameness – by which all others can be assessed, regulated and allotted to a designated social condition" (Braidotti 2013: 26) – or, in other words, the model for a system of othering and discrimination. With antihumanism the Western ideal of humanity was deposed. Going further, posthumanism, more recently, broadened the corpus of subjectivities to include the nonhuman or the more-than-human, such as animals, nature, and machines. Thus anthropocentrism, the core tenet of humanism, came to be replaced by an egalitarianism of species. Postcolonialism has an obvious affinity for antihumanist thought given the latter's questioning of the presumed centrality and superiority of the idealized Western man. However, posthumanism offers a further deposing of man by calling into question the human species's heretofore unchallenged superiority, particularly that of the Western liberal subject. Indra Sinha's novel, with its magic realism and its deliberate blurring of the lines between the human, the subhuman, and the nonhuman, lends itself well to a posthuman analysis.

New materialist studies developed in the area of qualitative research as a direct consequence of the posthuman turn in critical theory, and helped to demonstrate the heretofore-unacknowledged agency and subjectivities of the material world. With terms like "naturecultures" (Haraway 2003), "agential realism" (Barad 2007), "hybrids" (Latour 2007), and "assemblages" (Deleuze and Guattari 1987), the human and nonhuman worlds were brought into closer dialogue and the affective dimensions of objects were explored. Photography's complex nature makes it an apt area of study for new materialism. It already blurs the boundaries between the material and the affective. Photographs are objects that are displayed, produced as forms of identification, preserved in albums, carried in wallets, etc. However, they also derive their value from the use to which they are put and the image displayed in a photograph often takes precedence over the objecthood of the photograph itself. The development of digital photography has further erased the objecthood of photographs, which now exist as a collection of pixels in various devices without which they cannot be viewed or displayed.

With the advance of new materialism, photography studies has seen a materialist turn in recent years. This has taken a number of forms. Scholars have either analyzed the materiality of the medium in the context of the various agents and pieces of equipment that go into the making of photographs. In new materialist terms, this is seen as an "intra-action – of photographer, light, camera, objects, chemicals and or algorithms involved in its digital reproduction" (Lorenz-Meyer 2018: n.pag.). Others like Plummer, Riches, and Wooldridge have seen this development as a more nostalgic and impossible return to the medium's early days, when it was rooted more firmly in its objecthood. Underscoring the impossibility of this return, they draw attention to the tension between the image that a photograph captures and the materiality of the photograph itself. They rightly point out that the materiality of a photograph is often invisible due to the hypervisibility of the image it depicts, thereby underlining the rejection of photography's referentiality in the move toward materialism. Consequently they conclude that the "current interest in photographic objecthood is similar in its rejection of representation and its engagement with surface" (2016: n.pag.). Lee Mackinnon combines both approaches by exploring "photography as event and the materiality of the photographic apparatus" (2016: 149). Elizabeth Edwards argues that photographs are social objects which she calls "relational objects" (n.d.: para 3), whose power is connected to the nature of the medium. Taking my cue from these critics, I will demonstrate the ways in which Sinha's novel creates a new materialist assemblage between Raghu Rai's images, which are manifested in various absent-present forms, the character of Animal, and the digital presence in both text and image of Khaufpur outside the pages of the novel, by queering the materiality of absent photographs.

The materialism of Raghu Rai's images play an important role in Sinha's novel, as I have attempted to demonstrate by tracing the many circuits through which the photographs travel and by which they haunt the novel. However, given their absence from the novel itself, their absent presence is akin to the absent materialism of the photographic event. New materialist studies extend materialism into an arena of relationality such that many actors come into play, not all of whom are necessarily liberal human subjects. I am interested in this aspect of the "intra-action" between Rai's absent images, Animal, and finally Khã, who may be described as a fictional manifestation of Rai's photographs of fetuses in jars. Together the three form an assemblage of queer objects which compels us to look at events of environmental toxicity in posthuman ways and consider the question of environmental justice. This approach does not privilege those who look but instead privileges the elements of the queer assemblage.

Posthumanism and new materialism have enabled us to consider the interconnectedness between the human and nonhuman worlds as well as the nonbinary nature of agency. Jane Bennett encourages us to move away from our "habit of parsing the world into dull matter (it, things) and vibrant life (us, beings)" (2010: vii). We can do so only by becoming more attuned to the agentic role of objects. New materialist critics disagree about the nature of this agency. While Karen Barad (2007) insists that objects acquire their agency from what we map on to them, what she calls "agential realism," Bruno Latour's *actants* (2007) provide objects with a more autonomous agency that may not even be recognizable to humans. I would like to deploy Barad's agential realism to suggest the ways in which various elements related to and influenced by photography interact in Sinha's novel to form a posthuman assemblage. Barad has critiqued the primacy given to the linguistic domain and the discursive over matter and materiality. For her the material and the discursive exist in a relationship of intra-action. I demonstrate how photographs take on an agential realism in *Animal's People* to work in an absent yet interactive way with the novel in order to suggest an alternative human rights framework – one that decenters human exceptionalism and dismantles binaries of privileged and unprivileged and despectacularizes misfits like Khã and Animal who live on the margins of society.

While Rai's iconic images have been appropriated to lesser or greater self-serving purposes by Sinha for his ad campaigns, Dinodia Photos, and many others, the way in which they work in *Animal's People* is markedly different. By not including the physical images within the novel, yet incorporating traces and hauntings of them in various ways, Sinha sets in motion yet another "event" of these photographs. He does so through the plot of the novel, which is a slightly veiled retelling of the Bhopal tragedy where Rai's images originated and by creating a nonhuman character deeply reminiscent of the fetuses in one of those photos. However, this time it is a different sort of event. The photograph was actively used for a particular purpose in the earlier events initiated by the circuits that the images traversed. However, in the novel the absent photographs take on an agency of their own, ironically manifested by their very absence. In this, the human photographer Rai, or even Sinha himself, is no longer the sole agent of the photograph. Instead, the photograph itself acquires agency as part of its own photographic event and Sinha's posthuman assemblage.

## The Posthuman Khã-in-the-Jar

In 2001, Rai returned to Bhopal, invited by Greenpeace to document the lingering effects of the gas tragedy fifteen years on. One of the most striking images from this series is that of fetuses in jars (Figure 7). These fetuses were spontaneously aborted during the disaster. Rai's caption informs us that they were "preserved by Dr. Satpathy, a forensic expert of the State Government's Hamida Hospital to establish the exact cause of death" (Rai n.d.: n.pag.). It is a macabre image showing several jars containing fetuses lined up on a terrace wall with the skyline of Bhopal forming the photograph's backdrop. The disjuncture between foreground and background raises more questions than it answers. Why are these jars not in the hospital laboratory? The picture postcard quality of the photograph, if imagined without the jars, creates a

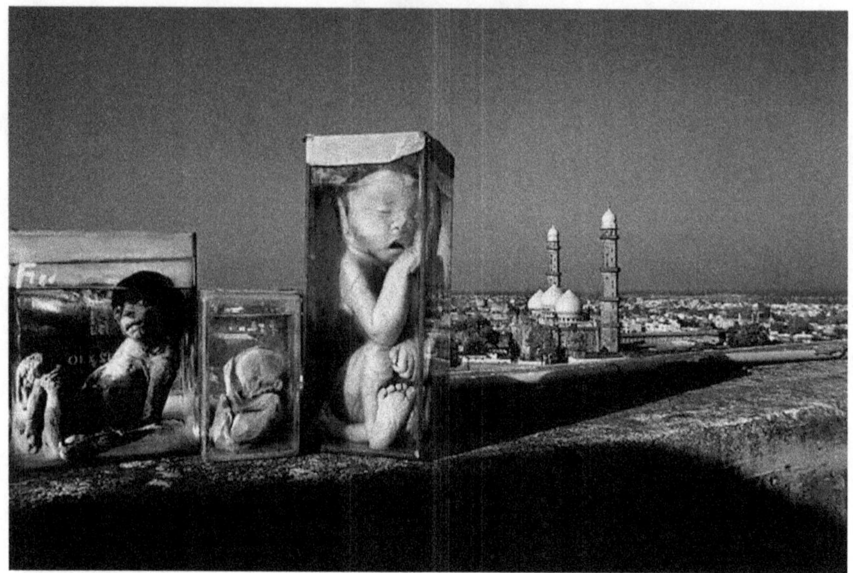

Figure 7. Reproduced with permission from Raghu Rai

further sense of rupture and disquiet, the minarets of the city's mosque in the background in a strange mirroring of the jars containing the fetuses in the foreground.

Raghu Rai's image of fetuses in jars follows a long tradition of specimen photography, also known as "formaldehyde photography." Lisa Cartwright writes in her classic book *Screening the Body: Tracing Medicine's Visual Culture* that the use of still photography in the early twentieth century animated specimens with a new kind of life: "With the emergence of biological modes of representation, we find a historical break between observation (or image) and object of knowledge – a break in which the visualization of 'life' becomes all the more seductive to the scientific eye even as the limitations of representation are made plain" (1995: 10). Images quickly made the fetus one of the most spectacularized specimens in the history of medicine. The fetus is a key figure in the study of reproduction. By the middle of the twentieth century, the collection and preservation of fetal remains became routine. Images of fetal specimens became iconic in the 1960s thanks to the efforts of Swedish photographer Lennart Nilsson (see Nilsson and Hamberger 1990), who pioneered images of unborn life by publishing them in the pages of *Life* magazine in the 1960s. This heralded the entry of fetal photography into popular culture. Ironically Nilsson's photographs of unborn children are in fact fetal postmortems, thus blurring the line between the yet-to-be-born and the dead-before-birth.

Given the proliferation of fetal images in the twentieth century, visual artists began to explore the aesthetics of specimen photography. What has come to be called the bio-art movement arose from increasing scrutiny of the human species as well as the turn to the posthuman. Some of this art has moved toward the grotesque. In *The Pyrotechnic Insanitarium: American Culture on the Brink*, Mark Dery identifies the photographer Joel-Peter Witkin as the pioneer behind the specialized genre of formaldehyde photography and the photographic aesthetic of the New Grotesque that emerged in the mid-1980s (1999: 149). Dery uses Edmund Burke's definition of the sublime as "that which defies rational understanding by evoking a mixture of pleasure and terror in the viewer" to describe this kind of photography as evoking the "pathological sublime" (160). It would be safe to assume that Rai was already familiar with this emerging aesthetic.

While Rai's photo captures the loss of innocence, the untimely and premature end to what could have been a new life, Sinha's Khã-in-the-Jar is more reminiscent of the pathological sublime – he is grotesque, "masculinized, uncouth, unnatural and monstrous" (Moore 2015: 137). Animal first encounters Khã at the doctor's office. He is immediately portrayed as aggressive and confrontational, refusing the spectacularizing glare often evoked by the grotesque:

> I am looking at a shelf in the professor's room. On it is a jar, a big round glass jar of liquid that flashes like it's full of sunlight.
>
> "What did you think, it's that easy?" says a gnarly voice in my ear. "Quit staring by the way it gives me the creeps." Glaring at me from inside the jar is a small crooked man. An ugly little monster, his hands are stretched out, he has a wicked look on his face [...] looks like someone is peering over his shoulder, a second head is growing out the side of his neck. (57)

Sinha describes Khã as a man rather than a child, echoing Animal's own stunted growth. In fact, this doubling is deliberate. On his second encounter with Khã, the creature suggests a kinship with Animal: "'Brother Animal,' says he, 'you and I are not so different. Doublers both, we're. Two of me there's, two also of you'" (139). Khã enables Animal to see his second and better self – the one he aspires to be but which is always already there. Khã continues, "My two heads rise from one neck. From your hips, at the point where your back bends, rises a second you who's straight, stands upright and tall. This second you's there all the time, has been there all along, thinks, speaks and acts, but it's invisible –" (139).

The second Animal that Khã sees is in the image of humanism's man – tall, upright, speaking, thinking, and acting, but invisible. Khã enables Animal to see this second self not as something he can never be or only aspire to become through corrective surgery, but as a self that is always already present. Perhaps it is the belated awareness of this self that enables Animal to ultimately reject the offer of surgery and to choose to remain his crooked but unique self, *"I am Animal fierce and free / in all the world is none like me"* (366, emphasis original). Raghu Rai's images haunt the novel through the depiction of Khã and work in a multilayered way to dissuade us from "staring" at the "abnormal" and instead consider what is normal while also questioning its true worth. Khã lives poised between life and death, between the unborn and the living. As he says to Animal,

> As for you, poor fuckwit, you think you're an animal, I am your mother and father. I was you in your childhood, I'll be you when you're old. Dead am I who never lived, wasn't buried, waits to burn. Tough I'm and tender, now you see me now you don't, I go down into the earth and leap up to the sky. (139)

Khã's duality, the impossibility of categorizing him as human or animal or plain matter, makes him representative of posthumanism in the novel. As a grotesque version of an unborn child, he questions and undermines humanism's understanding of the liberal human subject.

Khã repeatedly calls for his own destruction, complaining that he detracts attention from what actually matters. He urges Animal to "break the jar, with fire, destroy us" (138). His wish fulfillment almost comes true when Elli's clinic is set on fire. Animal enters to save Khã and finds that all the other jars have shattered, leaving their contents scattered on the floor. He wants to save them but Khã informs him, "By burning they'll be freed" (336). Disregarding Khã's injunction to smash his jar as well, Animal escapes the burning clinic tucking Khã-in-the-Jar under his arm and takes him to the factory, which has also been set alight. He attempts to enter the factory by climbing a tree that leans on the factory wall, on which he places Khã. In that moment the "clear light of the moon falls on the jar" (337) and Animal is able to see Khã clearly. The jar slips from his hand and shatters, revealing "the thing that was within, a half-rotted relic of that night" (337). In the fraction of a second before the jar breaks, when Animal places it on the wall backlit by moonlight, Sinha recreates Rai's photograph in the reader's eye. Rai's image is also taken in the dark with the sky illuminated by what could easily be moonlight with the old city visible in the background. Animal has also just escaped from the old city. We briefly see Rai's fetus in a jar in our mind's eye before the jar shatters, making way for Khã's death by fire, which he intensely desires.

In the pages following the shattering of Khã's jar, Animal suffers excruciating pain in his gut and experiences fantastical hallucinations through which he arrives at his final reckoning. In these pages, the novel takes on a truly surreal yet markedly posthuman tenor. Animal escapes the burning factory and sees "the earth alive with snakes and other small creatures, rushing desperate to escape the flames" (339). In dreams and hallucinations brought on by the thirteen *datura golis*[5] he has consumed, Animal sees himself abandoning the human world and returning to the animal kingdom. He walks through a forest hearing the "howra hoora cries of birds" (342) as he himself transforms, "four feet have I my eyes are stars my nose is snakes that lick their nostrils, dream lipless dreams" (342). Instead of "beedi wrappers, orange peels, plastic" (343), the forest floor is covered with grasses, twigs, and leaves. Suddenly he hears voices uttering the exhortation, "Show the animal, show him what he really is" (343) and realizes this is Khã speaking, not dead but released from his jar. Animal feels tormented and is convinced his death is imminent as his body becomes the site for various species – a cobra passes through him sliding out of his throat as "its tail dangles out of my arsehole" (344) and the *datura* growing in his gut "pushes forth leaves and flowers out of my mouth and out my nose." With a mere snap of his fingers Animal is able to make the two-headed creature disappear. His body becomes a composite of the species' world, mocking and utterly destroying humanism's hierarchies. Animal is made to witness horrific visions of a monkey whose flesh slides from his face as his bones are gobbled up by the earth, creating new trees with monkeys on them. The trees become antagonistic as "grasses push sharp needles into my hands and feet" (345). Driven by acute hunger Animal begins to eat grass, berries, roots, and flower petals and even eyes a lizard for food. Eventually the lizard talks him out of eating her and promises to "creep into your dry carcass and lay my eggs around your heart" (347). Through these torments and hallucinations, Animal is confronted by his humanimality, provoking him to ask, "am I man?" to which the only answer he receives is a counter-question, "WHAT IS A MAN?" (347, emphasis original). This surreal and hallucinatory section of the novel gestures toward a posthuman possibility

[5] Pellets made of a poisonous flowering plant.

in the face of environmental degradation wrought by neoliberal corporate greed. Sinha seeks redress for environmental injustices by suggesting a posthuman decentrality of Vitruvian Man. Animal's deformed body has served as a constant reminder of the horrendous effects of toxic chemicals on the people of Khaufpur and raised questions about his humanness while his appropriation of the signifying name "Animal" simultaneously refuted that humanness of which he is deprived. Now in the novel's surreal climax, Animal's body is transformed into a part of the natural landscape where grass grows, lizards lay eggs, and snakes travel through. In acknowledging the absence of his human qualities, Animal becomes something much greater – an organic part of the human universe, himself an assemblage of the living world.

In the remaining pages of the chapter, Animal sees visions of the humans he has known who attempt to right the wrongs they have done to him. His parents appear and want to take him home; Nisha says that she loves him after all and invites him to "fuck me, stick your big cock in me" (349) while Elli, Farooq, and Zafar offer him what he has most wanted from each of them. Animal rejects all these offers and becomes instead a universe unto himself, including within himself mountains, the sun and the moon, the four winds, his body "the earth, lice its living things" (35), a miniature universe with galaxies and his own Milky Way. Ironically, he feels "truly alone" at this moment. The chapter ends with a reminder to him of the power of his phallus and its quick swelling, which has tormented him in the most unexpected moments, threatening to give away his sheer animality. As it grows in his hand, he begins to "close the fingers round its stem, aim it at the stars, pump it like a shotgun to blast the night with living galaxies" (350). Animal's heightened hypersexuality only serves to underscore his animality.

Mel Chen's theory of "animacies" proves to be particularly useful in helping us unpack Sinha's gestures toward the posthuman in the penultimate chapter of his novel. Starting with the assertion that the term "animacy" usefully does not have a single standard definition, Chen loosely defines it as "a quality of agency, awareness, mobility and liveness" (2012: 2). Their book *Animacies: Biopolitics, Racial Mattering and Queer Affect* raises the question, "What if nonhuman animals, or humans stereotyped as passive, such as people with cognitive or physical disabilities, enter the calculus of animacy: what happens then?" (3). The *animacy hierarchy*, adopted from linguistics, replicates humanism's hierarchy with disabled bodies seen as compromised in comparison with able bodied humans. Chen uses animacy to trouble the easy binaries of human/animal, subject/object, life/death, able bodied/disabled, etc. They question the line between fetus and infant as well as the "expulsion of bodies marked as unworthy" (7) of repair when affected by environmental toxicity. Somewhat similarly, Sinha's novel blurs the line between the characters of Khã and Animal. In Animal's surrealist visions, he becomes doubled with Khã. The "ex-of-the-jar" refers to Animal as Khã and this follows the exhortation by the voices in the forest to "Show the animal, show him what he really is" (343) in which the individual Animal becomes the generic animal. Sinha attempts through the assemblage of the non/subhuman to blur the boundaries between these categories. While Raghu Rai's images of Bhopal on that fateful night and in the days that followed are designed to compel us to see the loss of human life and its potential in all its tragedy, by evoking his images through Khã, Sinha urges us to see these marginal creatures as filled with human potential.

## The Afterlives of Khaufpur

Khaufpur, the stand-in for Bhopal in Sinha's novel, means "city of terror" when translated from Urdu. It is of course a fictional place. Sinha has said in interviews that he knew Bhopal too well and setting his novel there would "kill the fiction" (2007b: n.pag.). Instead, he created Khaufpur and imagined it in great detail. He goes on to say that the name of the place is ultimately irrelevant and "Khaufpur is every place in which people have been poisoned and then abandoned." Khaufpur therefore transcends its fictionality and becomes representative of real places like Seveso, Halabja, Minamata, Caracas, or São Paolo. Beyond its depiction within the pages of Sinha's novel, Khaufpur was also featured on a website: www.khaufpur.com,[6] where it was illustrated with images and text.[7] Regarding the website, Sinha says he was often asked if Animal and his friends were real. Being reluctant to admit they were fictions, he created the site so he would not

6 This website was constantly evolving, sometimes inaccessible and more recently seems to have become defunct. What can be accessed now is the Khaufpur Gazette page (https://khaufpur.wordpress.com/about/) with a few textual stories and a number of broken links. All of this gives the Khaufpur of Sinha's novel many afterlives.

7 Indra Sinha said the following in conversation with me while discussing the website: "It is sort of appropriate that the website, the remains of it, are slowly falling apart in the Wayback Machine, just like the factory. There's a sort of poetry in all of this, the factory has never been cleaned or decontaminated, children are born malformed every year and many little children die."

have to “part with Animal and his chums. By now they were my chums too but they had been shut out of the book and needed somewhere else to live” (2007b: n.pag.). However, the Khaufpur of the novel and that of the website have little in common. There is no mention on the website of the toxic spill that is of such central importance to Khaufpur in the novel. Interestingly, contrary to its etymology and the city represented in the novel, the website portrays Khaufpur as offering “the experience of a lifetime” with luxurious hotels and splendid gardens overlooking a lake. Tourists are invited to indulge in the culture and wildlife of Khaufpur or go shopping. There is nothing here to suggest the horrific events that are central to the novel. There is no mention of the factory where the leak took place all those years ago, except for a passing, jocular one when we are told that the Microbudget Cafe Paradise is “Factory ke bilkul aaspass” (“very close to the factory”). From all accounts, Khaufpur is a bustling city with a bright future, in contrast with the Khaufpur of *Animal's People*. The latter is haunted by the now-abandoned factory building to which Animal returns repeatedly and from where one can see “clear across Khaufpur, every street, every lane, gully, shabby alley” and all the neighborhoods – Mira Colony, Khabbarkhana, Salimganj, Phuta Maqbara, and Qazi Camp, “killing grounds all” (31). Heather Snell has commented that the website is “a sham or, alternatively, an inside joke for the novel's interactive readers” (2008: 2). The use of photographs of people and places, alongside text to create this sham and tell the story of the fictional Khaufpur, self-reflexively raises questions about the indexicality of photography. As readers, we know that Khaufpur is entirely fictional. Yet the website includes images of Khaufpur's former rulers and the important sites of the city, such as the Taj-ul Masjid, described as “one of the biggest mosques in India,” and the Chowk, both delineated in some detail with accompanying images. The origins of these images are withheld, thereby perpetuating the myth that these are indeed images of Khaufpur. This sham highlights the manipulative quality of photographs. Those used to illustrate the website are low-quality images and a far cry from Raghu Rai's iconic images which haunt the novel. They are more like stock images – Bollywood posters and advertisements for Kesar Kasturi, the local liqueur, and Faqri's Tonic Oil for all ills. As digital images, they have a fragile and temporary presence. The City of Khaufpur website was perennially “being remade” and visitors were instructed to “kindly avail of features which are available.” Here again Sinha uses photography in a posthuman way – it functions not through its indexicality and representational force as photography often does, but rather forming a network of connections that continually evolves through expansions and contractions. The continued existence of Khaufpur beyond the pages of the novel allows Sinha to further blur boundaries between the fictional and the real and to give his characters continuing afterlives.

## Conclusion

This chapter counters the humanist, representational approach of photography and considers instead the way in which photography can function through absence and via traces in a posthuman manner. In this, my arguments are inspired by new materialist studies of photography and Daniel Rubinstein, who uses the structure of the rhizome in order to understand photographs as "connected to other photographs as well as to objects, entities, processes and organisms, forming a network that continually evolves through expansions and contractions" (99). Rubinstein's "rhizomatic assemblage" (98) is reminiscent of Deleuze and Guattari's *assemblage*, something that is "simultaneously and inseparably a machinic assemblage and an assemblage of enunciation" (2003: 504). Such an approach, Rubinstein argues, is based on connections and proliferation. The posthuman rhizomatic assemblage in Sinha's novel includes Animal himself; Khã-in-the-Jar, the unborn fetus who becomes Animal's friend and is immediately evocative of Raghu Rai's photographs of aborted fetuses taken in the aftermath of the Bhopal tragedy; the website www.khaufpur.com, a now-defunct page mentioned in the Editor's Note at the beginning of the novel; and Sinha's own social justice work to draw attention to the Bhopal tragedy. Through this posthuman assemblage of elements that lie both within the text and outside it – traces of absent photographs, an imagined city made real online with the use of false photographs, characters that challenge human/nonhuman binaries – Sinha suggests an alternative politics of looking and representation. This is not the spectacular invisibility that Mahlstedt critiques so powerfully, but rather the ability to see through other means, through a network of connections, and elements that lie beyond the text.

I find Jennifer Rickel's reading of *Animal's People* as a refutation of what she calls "literary humanitarianism" more compelling than Andrew Mahlstedt's reading of it as an attempt to make visible those who are invisible in their suffering, akin to Sinha's purpose in *The Guardian* advertisements. Rickel powerfully delineates "the novel's challenge to stories that fetishize suffering in the name of literary testimony" (2012: 87), thereby mapping the testifier-of-trauma-versus-witness model onto the narrator versus reader relation. Within the framework of literary humanitarianism, Rickel argues, the narrator is required to perform a particular subjectivity in order to "access the right to have rights" (89), thus excluding the subaltern from the rights framework and empowering instead those who speak for the subaltern. My reading of the ways in which Sinha brings together photography, posthumanism, and new materialism extends Rickel's arguments by helping further a relational approach to humanitarianism rather than a spectacularizing one.

7

# A "fresh way of looking at the photograph": Citizenship and Photographic Spectatorship in Siddhartha Deb's *Surface*

> Why does the person in the photograph direct her gaze at me? Who am I for her? What allows her to assume the existence of a civil spectator? What is the relation between her gaze at the photographer and the manner in which she looks at me? Am I the effect of her having been photographed? What does she expect from me?
>
> Ariella Azoulay, *Civil Imagination*, 47

After considering various events of photography in the preceding chapters, I return in this final chapter to the question of photographic spectatorship as theorized by Ariella Azoulay. Azoulay suggests that we should not see photography as being only about the photographer and the camera but also about those being photographed and the future spectators of the photograph. In opposition to the commonly held assumption that a photograph is a final product of a photographic event, Azoulay argues that the photograph is simply one of many possible outcomes of the event of photography. In many ways, the photograph continues to be produced and reproduced by the spectator. In Azoulay's ontology of photography, the sovereignty of the photographer is illegitimate. Instead, Azoulay endows the often-overlooked spectator of photographs with greater importance. Consequently, the event of photography does not require the presence of an actual, physical photograph. By denying images an actual presence, we are able to prioritize the spectator over the photographer. Azoulay asserts that the event of photography (unlike the photographed event) can never be over because a photograph can always be picked up by a spectator as it travels through circuits of being looked at, blurring the rigid boundary between the inside and outside of a photograph.

Ostensibly Siddhartha Deb's novel *Surface*,[1] seems to be about the powerful role of photography's indexicality as evidence, but one of the novel's epigraphs – from Conrad's *Heart of Darkness*, "Do you see the story? Do you see anything?" – hints at how much the novel is also about seeing. The inclusion of an absent image at the heart of the novel foregrounds the question of spectatorship by including several scenes where the protagonist looks at this photograph. *Surface* tells the story of Amrit Singh, a young journalist with the *Sentinel*, who discovers a six-month-old photograph in the basement of his office in Calcutta. The photograph in question captures a dramatic moment. It shows three people, an unidentified woman flanked by two masked, gun-toting men, standing in front of a faded blue wall. A note scrawled on the back claims that the woman is a porn actress who was "exhibited" (71) and then shot by the MORLS[2] leadership "to impress upon the people the importance of desisting from all corrupt activities encouraged by Indian imperialism" (71). A German magazine tasks Amrit with excavating the story behind this photograph. With all the weight of overinterpretation that so commonly accompanies photographs, the Germans describe the photograph as "A portrait of the mystery and sorrow of India through the story of the woman in the photograph" (5). Amrit, in a dangerous attempt at appropriation, wonders how he might "find the small, expressionless woman in the photograph," and "make her story my story, perhaps my best story yet" (6). The entire novel then becomes a quest to identify the woman in this photograph, who is always already burdened by being made to speak not only for Amrit but also for the entire nation. While, on the surface, the photograph seems crucially important in establishing the identity of the woman and the veracity of the claim made in the caption, reading Deb's novel as a manifestation of Azoulay's event of photography and the engagement of the civil imagination allows us to undermine the importance of the (absent) photograph and instead consider Amrit's role as the spectator of the photograph who continues the event of photography. Furthermore, my reading of the absent presence of photography in the novel suggests that Amrit's spectatorship of the photograph becomes an act of civic duty that acknowledges the citizenship of the photograph's subject through what Azoulay has termed the "civil contract of photography." Writing in the

[1] Deb's novel has two editions: it was published with the title *Surface* by Picador for the non-US market and with the title *An Outline of the Republic* by Ecco for the US market. Both editions were published in 2006. I have used the former edition in this chapter.

[2] The fictional insurgency group in the novel.

context of the prolonged Israeli occupation of Palestine, Azoulay argues for a contractual framework of photographic viewership that relinquishes terms like "empathy," "compassion," "shame," or "pity," thereby creating an equitable plane of spectatorship. Set in the "troubled periphery" (Bhaumik 2009) of India's Northeast, I suggest that Deb's novel employs a similar form of spectatorship to draw attention to the compromised citizenship of the people of the region.

## Citizenship and the Gendered Subaltern in the "troubled periphery"

Coming into being as an "accident of geography" (Bhaumik 2009: 1) rather than the commonalities of history and culture that normally bind people of a nation, India's Northeast has always been a troubled and, many would say, a much-neglected region. The historian David Ludden has argued that a region like Northeast India challenges the separation of the colonial from the national (qtd. in Bhaumik 2009: xiv). Other scholars working on the region (e.g. Akoijam 2005; Vajpeyi 2009) have used the Agambenian framework to think of the Northeastern border regions as a "zone of exception." Papori Bora has pointed out the simultaneous existence of democratic institutions alongside multiple extra-constitutional and emergency laws in the region. The prime example of this is the Armed Forces Special Power Act (AFSPA), which gives the armed forces wide-ranging special powers in counterinsurgency operations, which in turn override the provisions of civil laws (Bora 2010: 342). Vajpeyi reads the AFSPA as a spatialization of the exception to the rule of law, which then suggests that the Northeast should be thought of as an Agambenian camp where the inhabitants are reduced to bare life (2009: 39–40). A hotbed of secessionist activity and guerrilla warfare for much of its history, the last decade has seen the gradual neutralizing of insurgent groups in the Northeast through military deployment by the central government. Since its sweeping victory in the national polls in 2014, the Hindu right-wing Bharatiya Janata Party (BJP) turned its attention to this marginalized territory and began a very deliberate and strategic campaign of saffronization by forming a number of alliances in the region. Their efforts bore ample fruit, resulting in the party's stunning victory in the region in the 2019 elections. However, in 2019 the Northeast also erupted in protest against the Citizenship Amendment Bill (CAB), which was widely seen as an attempt to alter the demographics of the region, forcing the government to withdraw the bill in parliament. In the assembly elections of 2021, the incumbent BJP-led National Democratic Alliance (NDA) won a second term in Assam, the largest state in the region. The NDA became the first non-Congress alliance to win consecutive terms in the state.

Published in 2005, Siddhartha Deb's novel attempts to capture the fractured, peripheral region that he characterized as "in reality the invisible centre of the republic" (Deb, qtd. in Baishya 2010: 202). The novel can then be read as an attempt to make visible the invisible and restore relevance to the marginalized region and its people. The phenotypical differences between people from the Northeast and mainland India lend a problematic racial dimension to the region. In the past, people of the region were described as belonging to the Mongoloid race (Baruah 2005: 165) and many who have left the Northeast in search of jobs have encountered vicious racism in metropolitan cities like Delhi, Mumbai, and Bangalore. Young Northeast Indian women have become particularly mobile as their "Oriental" appearance and English language skills make them desirable employees in the service industry. The woman in the photograph in Deb's novel, with her "high cheekbones, narrow eyes [...] wearing a traditional looking long skirt" (128), is clearly from the region. In this chapter, by returning to Azoulay's notion of the civil imagination and the civil contract of photography, I argue that the absent visual signifier of the Northeastern woman, so central to Deb's novel, demands civil spectatorship primarily from Deb's narrator Amrit but, through him, from us as well. The absent presence of photography in Deb's novel functions to recenter the marginalized through a process of prolonged spectatorship in the event of photography. It becomes an act of acknowledging the citizenship of the marginalized.

Citizenship has long been a fraught issue in Northeast India. Ironically, the region was far more integrated with the rest of India under colonial rule than in the post-Independence period. Once the contours of the independent Indian nation-state were drawn, the Northeast found itself on the periphery of the nation, some of the region's small princely states still as they were under colonialism, but now surrounded by much larger nations like India and China. Through the 1960s to the '80s, several smaller states (namely Nagaland, Mizoram, Arunachal Pradesh, and Meghalaya) were carved out of the larger territory of Assam while the princely states of Tripura and Manipur remained Union Territories from 1956 until they achieved full statehood in 1972. Sikkim was granted statehood only as recently as 2002, becoming the eighth state to join the Seven Sisters.[3] This somewhat forced tethering of polyglot peoples to the periphery of the Indian nation resulting

[3] A term used to refer to India's Northeastern states – Arunachal Pradesh, Assam, Manipur, Meghalaya, Mizoram, Nagaland, and Tripura.

in the formation of a landmass ninety-nine percent of whose borders are international did not happen in a straightforward manner. Nor did the ethnically diverse populations of this region buy into the idea of one nation bolstered by Indian nationalism. Udayon Misra (2005) traces the challenges posed to the concept of nationalism by the Nagas, the Mizos, the Meitis, and finally the Assamese. The second half of the twentieth century saw the rise of both secessionist and independence movements in the region; the former came from those like the Assamese, who felt a shared kinship with the rest of India but felt neglected by the centre, and the latter from those like the Nagas, who had never been part of India and felt an urgent need to preserve their way of life. Although the nation-state has preserved its Northeastern territories and fended off the armed insurgencies that rocked the region for many decades, writing in 2006, Misra opined that in India's Northeast "a federal structure in the true sense of the term where each nationality would have some degree of autonomy [...] may sound a bit utopian, it must remain a stated goal of the Indian Republic" (2005: 272).

Instead of moving toward a utopian federalism, politics in the Northeast has lurched to the right with the BJP government's push to saffronize the region.[4] In May 2016, the BJP formed a political coalition, the North East Democratic Alliance (NEDA), bringing together the non-Congress political parties in the region, thereby defanging the Congress Party. From May 2016 until May 2019, the Alliance made significant gains culminating in the 2019 assembly elections, where it won eighteen of the twenty-four seats in the seven Northeastern states. In 2019, the parliament passed the Citizenship Amendment Act (CAA), which for the first time brought religion into determinations of citizenship. According to the CAA, non-Muslim refugees from the Muslim-majority nations of Pakistan, Bangladesh, and Afghanistan who had arrived in India before 2014 would be granted Indian citizenship. The Act does not grant eligibility to persecuted Muslims from these countries, nor does it include other neighboring countries like Sri Lanka, China, and Myanmar. Mahmood Mamdani (2019: n.pag.) finds the answers to questions raised by these inexplicable criteria in two claims – that "the legislation intends to present the perpetrator as Muslim, and only Muslim" and that the legislation "recognizes no Muslim victim" (such as the Uighurs and Rohingyas). This Amendment Act stands in stark contrast to the earlier Citizenship Act of 1955, which does not define citizenship according to one's

4 Arkotong Longkumer's book *The Greater India Experiment: Hindutva and the Northeast* (2020) provides a timely ethnographic study of the operations of right-wing Hindu organizations in Northeast India, particularly their engagement with the indigenous people in the region.

religion. In yoking together religion and citizenship rights in such a bald attempt to privilege Hindus, the government set a dangerous precedent and undermined India's secularism, which is enshrined in the nation's Constitution. The CAA led to several months of violent protests around the country; yet it was passed in both houses of parliament. By virtue of new rules notified by the Ministry of Home Affairs, the CAA was operationalized on March 11, 2024, three months before the federal elections in which the BJP won a third term in office.[5]

During the CAA protests that rocked the country in 2019, some of the bloodiest were seen in the Northeast. Prior to enacting the CAA in 2019, the government implemented the National Register of Citizens (NRC, mandated by the 2003 Amendment of the Citizenship Amendment Act 1955) in 2013–2014, with plans for a nationwide implementation in 2021. This is an official record of all legal citizens of India and requires people to provide official documents to prove their citizenship. The BJP rejected the final NRC published on August 31, 2019 because it excluded a large number of Bengali Hindus who comprise the bulk of the party's vote bank in Assam. A sizable number of tribal communities were also excluded. The migrant tribal populations of the region had been resettled by the British and again in postcolonial India. Underscoring the strong indigenous/tribal identity of the protests, Roluahpuia argues that the NRC and CAA "strengthen old memories of resettlement that much fear will result in further undermining tribal community rights and their marginalization" (2020: n.pag.).

The anxiety felt by the tribal populations of the Northeast regarding their citizenship rights is not without basis. Papori Bora has argued that the Northeastern tribes are characterized as "incomplete Indian citizens" and the region as "anti-state" (2010: 347) because both colonial historiography and postcolonial, nationalist historiography have portrayed the people of the Northeast as Orientalist outsiders. While colonial discourse represented the Northeastern tribes as the "Mongolian Other of Aryan India" (346), in post-independence India the tribes continued to be considered outsiders, dissimilar to Indic civilization, and therefore came to be characterized as immigrants in need of integration into the Indian mainstream. There is no place for these tribes in the normative ideal of post-independence Indian citizenship. Bora elucidates the manner in which the nationalist discourse's attempts to dismantle the colonial Orientalist narrative by

[5] Manipur was again rocked by ethnic and religious violence in 2023, when the majority-Hindu Meitis clashed with the Christian Kukis in the wake of protests against the Meiti-controlled state government for pursuing policies that were seen as discriminatory against the minority Kukis.

granting autonomy to the tribes of the region to govern themselves through tribal laws, which only served to portray them as "ethnic subjects inhabiting ethnic homelands" (347). This in turn fostered the various sovereignty movements in the region that claimed a different nationality based on their racial and cultural differences from the rest of India. Wouters and Subba have identified the misrecognition (as foreigner) and nonrecognition (as Indian) of Northeasterners as due to their Mongoloid phenotypical features, which find no place in what Wouters and Subba call the "Indian face" (2013: 127).

Given this complex history of disenfranchisement and marginalization, citizenship in the Northeast can hardly be taken for granted. It is constantly under threat and almost never equal. Plagued by secessionist violence, the threat of detention centers, the burden of proving citizenship through documents, the possibility of statelessness is a constant reality for the people of the region. The Northeastern woman captured in the absent photograph in Deb's novel already carries with her the burden of her compromised citizenship. We learn that she is Leela, a young woman who came to work for a project called the Prosperity Project in Imphal. How she got from there to becoming a cautionary tale for other women in a photo used by an insurgent group is gradually revealed in the second half of the novel. When he asks for some context for the photograph, it is suggested to Amrit early in the novel that this is simply an instance of moral policing of the gendered subaltern by radical groups who wish to instill fear and compliance in the general populace as they impose strict moral codes. Robiul, one of Amrit's informants, sums it up by resorting to a list of precedents: "Did the Khalistanis in Punjab not go around telling women how to dress? You were in Punjab [...] reporting the end of Bhindranwale's men. Did you miss everything that happened? Are there not groups in Kashmir that flung acid on women without the veil?" (46) This reminds us that in addition to the limits of citizenship in the Northeast, women of the region are further marginalized by being made the repositories and upholders of stringent moral codes. As Robiul's comment suggests, there are repeated instances of this sort of moral policing in different times and places in postcolonial India. However, this takes on a slightly different valence when it comes to the women of the Northeast. As insider-outsiders (in Bora's terms), women of the Northeast often face the brunt of what Wouters and Subba have called "the conflation between 'Mongoloid hill-dwellers' and 'sexual liberty'" (2013: 135). This dual racialization and sexualization results in a problematic stereotype of the Northeastern woman when she travels in the rest of India. As a woman quoted by Wouters and Subba puts it, "They think we are cheap because we look different and inferior because we don't follow their culture" (135). The Northeastern woman then becomes the Orientalized female Other of India, simultaneously lusted after and resented (see Deb 2011: 229).

About halfway through Deb's novel we find out that the photograph central to its plot is not what it seems; MORLS agents did not stage it to send a message about moral codes. Neither is Leela a porn star but instead "a smart girl who went to a great college in Delhi on a scholarship" (149). The Prosperity Project, the impressive developmental project that Leela worked for, was a front for a counterfeiting project run by its director, Malik. Photography played a significant role in perpetuating the lie of the Prosperity Project. Photographs of the project's initiatives accompanied reports sent to funding agencies in the nation's capital and in foreign countries. A filmmaker employed by Malik used ordinary items to build basic sets as backdrops for the photos: "They looked real enough in the photographs he took, with MORLS insurgents playing the parts of addicts and project workers" (240). Leela grew suspicious and began asking questions. The insurgents and Malik then used her as a pawn for their own purposes. At a staged press conference, she was charged with immoral activities and given a "minor punishment" (243); this served the dual purpose of showing that the MORLS "meant business" and completely discrediting Leela. Malik had played the role of a member of the public at the press conference and pleaded with the insurgents to spare Leela from execution; this garnered him credit as a kind and generous man "and his stock as a peace negotiator rose dramatically" (244).

The two Leelas in the novel – the one attached to a false narrative in the photograph and the real Leela whose story is unearthed by Maria, a local journalist helping Amrit – cover the gamut of stereotypical representations of the Northeast Indian woman. These include the Orientalized, hypersexualized, immoral woman (as in the photo) and the educated, ambitious, mobile, and highly employable woman – the subject in Leela's success story as "Malik's right hand" (149). Although the photograph purportedly tells a far sadder story than the reality, Leela's identity as a Northeast Indian woman is always already fixed by stereotype and marginalization. Consequently, the photograph of her as an abducted victim is exactly the kind of photograph that requires a civic gaze. The revelation of the real story behind Leela's photograph highlights the failure of photographs to tell the truth despite appearances of verisimilitude. As a filmmaker suggests to Amrit, echoing the novel's title, it is all about "surfaces." Robiul develops a complete narrative of Leela's story from the photograph early in the novel, thereby underscoring photography's power to tell stories while also concealing or even distorting the truth. He claims she was a young local woman who had turned to working in porn films to provide for her family, and was probably being blackmailed into doing so by someone she trusted (48). Like the Germans, he too makes Leela's story representative of the entire Northeast, "A sad story. Like the story of my people, my region" (48–49). This easy appropriation of Leela's (false) story to tell the story of the people of Northeast India silences her yet again. Throughout the novel, she is equated with the Northeast, remote and forgotten, and her plight with that of her people: "Too far. It was a phrase I heard echoing from many mouths during my journey along that troubled highway, as if the woman I was looking for was not a person but a place, the very embodiment of an edge over which I could plummet if I didn't maintain the proper distance and disinterest" (71–72). Amrit himself goes through a gradual process of acknowledging the real Leela. He is quick to sexualize her from the photograph and even after learning that the photograph is not what it seems; he struggles to see her in nonsexualized terms. I contend that the absent image of the "porn star" Leela requires active and sustained spectatorship by Amrit in order to be recognized for more than its apparent, indexical meaning. The process of spectatorship proves to be necessary for Amrit as well, in order for him to recognize his own privileged citizenship within the nation and to acknowledge Leela's compromised citizenship as a Northeast Indian woman.

In a curious doubling of Leela's photo, another photo emerges, this time of Malik, whose fortunes have turned; Amrit finds out that the MORLS has abducted Malik. The photograph accompanying the news item reporting the abduction is almost identical to Leela's photograph – "only the objects – and targets – in the set-up had changed: Leela absent, Malik in her place, and, instead of rifles, pistols in the hands of the two men" (179–180). The differences between these two doubled photographs lie far deeper than the superficial dissimilarities in "set-up" – while Leela's photograph constructs a false narrative that sets Amrit on a long journey to discover the truth, Malik's photo tells the truth about his abduction and his (presumed) execution at a later point. The captain points out the irony to Amrit: "Poor Malik. He was so interested in photographs and the power of images. Now he has become a picture himself, but an image without any power" (180). Malik had been instrumental behind the staging of Leela's photograph, using it strategically for his own purposes, but had come to occupy her place in the photograph, reversing the real and the apparent. Through these doubled images, Deb suggests the double-edged capacity and power of photography to both tell and distort the truth. By pursuing the truth of Leela's photograph, Amrit continues the event of photography and in the process acknowledges and draws much-needed attention to Leela's citizenship through his protracted spectatorship of her image.

## Photographic Citizenship: From Sovereign Spectator to Equal Citizen

In *The Civil Contract of Photography*, Ariella Azoulay argues that citizenship should be indifferent to ties that connect some while excluding others. This kind of equal citizenship that is devoid of essentialism, she argues, resembles photographic relations. She claims that photographs carry traces of political relations and the act of watching can enable the transformation of what is viewed into claims for action. Watching photographs then becomes a political action, which carries with it the power to demand citizenship for the disenfranchised in the photograph. Azoulay sees the civil contract of photography as akin to Rousseau's social contract – something that had never been formally acknowledged or recognized but was always already present. Azoulay's theory is premised on the understanding that a photograph is not a representation. This, of course, is not a new or startling claim. As I have discussed in parts of this book, photography lost its claim to indexicality several decades ago, or at least this claim is far more contentious than was believed in the early years of photographic practice. John Berger and Jean Mohr have concluded that photographs can only tell a "limited" (1989: 97) truth. However, through her articulation of the event of photography, Azoulay extends this premise to open up the possibility of photographic meaning to a constant process of interaction and interpretation. By disempowering the photographer and stripping authorship of the photograph from him/her, Azoulay creates what she calls the "citizenry of photography" which initially develops from the encounter between the photographer and the photographed, but also incorporates spectators of the photograph across time. This alters our understanding of photography as a fixed moment in time, a slice of life, a closed event. Instead, Azoulay enables us to see the ways in which images bear "traces of the encounter that it represents" (2012a: 78). Her introduction of the spectator into the circuit of encounters and relationships empowers the spectator and allows for new kinds of meaning-making through the spectator's encounters with the photograph.

Azoulay proposes a political theory of citizenship based on the encounters between the citizenry of photography, which give multiple and ever-evolving meanings to photographs. She incorporates a dimension of civility into practices of viewing photography. She distinguishes between the practical gaze (2012a: 66), the gaze of leisure or entertainment (2012a: 71), and the civil gaze. The civil gaze has the power to make present those who have been excluded and to call out the excluding sovereign power. Azoulay draws attention to the "additional participants who play a role in the act of photography" (2012a: 71) and are always present though they may not be easily visible by the spectator. Their absence is often so naturalized in photographic discourse as to go unnoticed. However, to Azoulay this absence suggests a violent act of expulsion. Drawing attention to the valences between photography and citizenship, Azoulay cites meaning-making through mutual (mis)recognition and the preservation of plurality. The activation of the civil gaze allows for this plurality of participants to be recognized and acknowledged by diminishing the power of the visible (2012a: 72).

Drawing on parallels between Conrad's *Heart of Darkness* and Deb's novel, Amit Baishya reads Malik as a Kurtz-like figure and the novel primarily as a quest narrative that takes Amrit deeper into India's "heart of darkness." As suggested by the title of his article "The Act of Watching with One's Own Eyes," the visible and the ocular play an important role in Baishya's reading. He identifies a gradual change in Amrit and his attitude toward Leela as the novel progresses. Baishya notes Amrit's initial projection of fantasies onto Leela's photos and his desire to somehow appropriate her story, which is replaced by a more nuanced and sympathetic understanding of her suffering. He argues that Amrit "slowly begins to recognize alternative modalities of being and seeing as he travels through India's Northeastern borderlands" (2015: 2). Baishya also notes a concurrent change in Amrit's sense of self that occurs as the novel progresses (9); Amrit moves toward a less individualistic sense of self as things that were invisible to him when he began his journey now become visible. He concludes that Amrit moves from "narcissistic identification" (9) with Leela to becoming more receptive to her suffering. Building on Baishya's reading, I argue that the absent photograph of the mute subaltern in the novel and the event of photography that gives this image an afterlife lies at the heart of Amrit's understanding of Leela and her troubled citizenship within the peripheries of the postcolonial nation-state. I extend Baishya's reading to suggest that Amrit's spectatorship of Leela's photo throughout the novel allows for this change in Amrit's perception of Leela and himself. I further suggest that his photographic spectatorship not only gives him a renewed understanding of what Baishya calls "alternative modalities of being and seeing," but also enables him to consider Leela's compromised citizenship, which is in sharp contrast to his own citizenship. Azoulay writes: "A photograph is an *enonce* within the pragmatics of obligation" (2008: 143). Leela's photograph obliges Amrit to redress the wrongs done to her.

Leela does not appear in person in the novel, her character is conveyed to the reader mainly through the image of her as a hostage, and through other photographs Amrit sees when he visits Leela's aunt. We also hear her voice through some letters that her aunt shares with Amrit. Notably, since all of Leela's photographs are absent presences in the novel, they are always mediated to us through Amrit's vision as he studies them. I argue that he eventually comes to engage his civil imagination in these scenes and is thus able to recognize her as more than the gendered, mute pawn of the photograph. I read the repeated scenes throughout the novel of Amrit gazing at Leela's photograph as instances of him gradually activating his civil imagination, continuing the event of photography that happened elsewhere, and entering a civil contract with Leela through which her violated citizenship is restored. Through this process, Amrit is able to arrive at what Baishya reads as him "giving an account of himself" (2015: 9). Unlike Baishya, though, I analyze this process of providing an account of the Self and the Other through Azoulay's rich vocabulary of gazes, arguing that Amrit recognizes Leela as a fellow citizen, though a severely marginalized one, only when he engages the event of photography and uses his civil gaze to read Leela's (absent) photograph. Although he is deeply interested in the photograph from the very beginning, he does not deploy the civil gaze upon his first viewing of the image. He comes to it heavily burdened by representation and stereotype along with the pressure to please the Germans, who are looking for "something exemplary" (13) in the photograph. Amrit must school himself to shed the sovereign gaze and look at the woman in the photograph with civility (in Azoulay's sense). From this vantage point, he is then able to understand her marginalization and objectification as well as her compromised citizenship in contrast to his own privileged one.

Amrit's initial sovereign spectatorship comes from his subject position as an investigative journalist who is advised to remain detached. Early in the novel, his informant Robiul says to him, "Proceed to Imphal for story, but proceed with caution. Avoid extreme reactions, avoid involvement, and concentrate on practicing the journalist's objectivity. Detachment [...] You are coming from the outside, you say? Good. Detached observer" (45). When Amrit first discovers the photograph in the office basement – called "the morgue" because it was where the "anticipatory obituaries of public figures" (50) were kept – he quickly makes it representative of the place of its origin, Manipur, offering him "a glimpse into that faraway corner of the country" although the place "simply did not exist" (53) in his mind. In essentializing the photo immediately upon its discovery, with the full burden of stereotypical representation, Amrit fixes the photograph's apparent though misleading, self-evident truth. Despite the chasm that divides Amrit and Leela in every way possible, he is keen to bridge the gap and the discovery of the photograph itself, though not providing any clues to Leela's identity, bolsters his confidence that he "had already closed the gap" (72). At this point in the novel, his eagerness to close the gap is not about learning more about Leela; instead, he wants to appropriate her story and speak for her. His sovereign spectatorship of the photograph lies at the root of this troubling impulse.

Amrit's gaze at this time may be characterized as what Azoulay has called the practical gaze, in particular the professional gaze,[6] which is a controlling gaze allowing the viewer to "organize the visible world and to control it by means of knowledge that is accumulated in an evolving and continuing fashion" (2012a: 68). It is very different from the civil gaze, which belongs to the contemplative rather than active realism in Azoulay's schema. The latter is a far more democratic gaze that does not privilege the viewer, or the gaze. It exists in plurality with other gazes and can change in accordance with the reactions from other gazes. Pressured to find "something exemplary" in the photograph, Amrit at first uses his professional, disciplining gaze to fix Leela as representative of the stereotypical Northeast Indian woman. As the novel progresses, he must learn to shed his sovereign gaze and activate his civil gaze, which will allow him to recognize Leela as an equal citizen, but one who has been deprived of her citizenship by the twin burdens of racialization and objectification. Azoulay suggests that photographed persons are reduced to "having certain attributes or exemplifying certain categories" (2012a: 225) when photographs are stripped of their heterogeneity of information and the photographed person becomes the "stable signified of a political category" (225). Leela's photograph exemplifies her (false) fixity as an immoral Northeastern woman. Amrit's protracted spectatorship of the photograph attends to the event of photography and gradually disrupts its fixedness. Once the apparent truth of the photograph is revealed as a staged lie, this fixity is further disrupted and Amrit begins to see her for who she is and not simply as a woman from the Northeast being used as a warning to others like her.

Along with the photo, Amrit discovers a book called *Eastern Eyes* written by Euan Sutherland, the editor of the *Sentinel*'s colonial precursor

6 Azoulay's practical gaze has three forms: the orienting gaze, the professional (or deliberate) gaze, and the observing or astonished gaze that becomes the civil gaze with the advent of photography. See Azoulay 2012a (64–76) for a discussion of the various gazes that Azoulay maps on to Hannah Arendt's three categories of the *vita activa*.

the *Imperial* and published in 1946. It is Sutherland's memoir and parts of it are conveyed to us as Amrit reads Sutherland's encounters with Jim, a British soldier fighting in the Kohima war against the Japanese invasion of the eastern part of the British Empire from 1942 to 1944. The title of the memoir suggests an appropriation of an Orientalist gaze by Sutherland as he narrates his experiences in the east. The chapter that catches Amrit's attention is on Manipur, and remains etched in his memory, and he recalls the "sonorous place names" as he travels through the region along Highway 39. Sutherland's memoir becomes for Amrit a guidebook, opening "the door to a time long past, to people very different from me" (86). A curious visuality emerges where the mainland Indian traveling into the farthest eastern reaches of the country comes to see the region through the White colonizer's appropriated Orientalist gaze. The alignment of Amrit's gaze with that of Sutherland reinforces the narrator's imperial gaze, which he must learn to relinquish.

As Amrit gazes at Leela's photo, her face is "inscrutable" (84) to him. She seems to be returning his gaze but then he notices her eyes appear to be trained on something behind him:

> I was seeing her the way the camera lens had, the way the photographer had seen her through the viewfinder – that photographer who would also have been aware of other things: the voices of people from the local press, the presence of the insurgent leaders, perhaps the murmur of guards posted as lookouts. (84)

Although Amrit is aware of all the other gazes that must have been in operation at the time Leela's photograph was taken, it is important to note that he aligns his own gaze with that of the camera lens and the photographer. This sovereign gaze seeks to fix the meaning of the photograph. It gives the privileged position of power as well as authorship to the photographer alone, sealing the event of photography once and for all. However, while appropriating the photographer's sovereign gaze, Amrit also invokes the camera, the photographer, and the others present on the scene along with himself as the viewer and Leela as the subject of the photographer. In doing so, he evokes Azoulay's "citizenry of photography" while connecting the various temporalities of the photo. The citizenry in this case transcends time and even mortality. Amrit wonders who the photographer might be and then realizes it is the now-dead Thoiba: "the reason the woman did not meet my gaze was because she was really looking at the invisible spectre of Thoiba hovering somewhere, occasionally behind my shoulder, at other times slightly in front of me" (84). Amrit's act of viewing the photograph shows his contradictory spectatorship of the photograph at this time. On the one hand, he claims the photographer's sovereign gaze for himself while also, on the other, attempting to engage the civil gaze, which requires civil intention. In doing so, he prolongs the event of photography, recognizing the traces left in the image of the interaction between the members of the citizenry. Instead of reading the photograph as simply an indexical event, which is now complete, Amrit begins to resist the violent fixing of Leela as a powerless woman, immoral prostitute, or hostage. Instead, by triggering the event of photography, he demands Leela's citizenship simultaneously refuting the indexical veracity of the photograph itself. Unlike Baishya, who reads Amrit's initial engagement with the photograph as resulting in "narcissistic identification" (2015: 9), I read this scene and others from early in the novel as Amrit's attempts to invoke Leela's citizenship or at the very least draw attention to its compromised state by initiating the event of photography.

The Captain raises the possibility that Leela's photograph may be a fake quite early when he enigmatically proclaims, "if the photograph is fake, people will not want it to be known as fake. This is the nature of the counterfeit and the untrue – it's true nature can never be revealed. Otherwise, it ceases to be what it is" (96). Amrit is of course after the "true nature" of the photograph and wishes to discover Leela's real identity, if she is "not victim of circumstance, but rather agent in creating specific circumstance" (96), yet he looks "skeptical about all this," wanting to believe what the photograph seems to suggest. Here Deb suggests photography's power to conceal the "true nature" of things while Amrit's essentializing and fixing gaze seems oblivious to that power. Photography's power to dissemble is in evidence again when Amrit learns that Leela's photograph does in fact portray a false reality; again, when Amrit's passport photo is taken in order to create a fake identity card, identifying him as a special correspondent for the *Nagaland Post*; and finally in all the fake photographs used by the Prosperity Project to raise huge sums of money for a counterfeiting business.

Deb repeatedly acknowledges the role of the spectator in photography through the scenes of Amrit looking at the photograph and studying it closely. The photograph is meant to serve as a warning to others like Leela and so is itself aware of the ways in which it might be viewed. In the first of these scenes, Amrit recognizes that the "men with the guns were in the picture not for her but for those who might see the photograph [...] It could be you, they were saying without speaking a single word [...] this image will be all the world will have to remember your final moments" (70). For Amrit, however, Leela is not a stand-in for any immoral woman. He is interested in her identity and consequently his role as a spectator changes from that envisioned as the intended purpose of the photograph. Once Amrit discovers the real identity of the woman in the photograph – that she is Leela, who worked closely with Malik on the Prosperity Project and is unlikely to be a porn actress – he feels that his "relationship to the photograph ha[s] changed" (153). This is when he begins to connect his understanding and knowledge of the photograph with himself, his newfound awareness of his "own predilections" (153) that now alters his thinking about the photograph. Amrit sees his "fresh way of looking at the photograph" as part of his own transformation. He realizes that he has been spinning a web around the photograph based on false assumptions. He acknowledges that he has trouble understanding women and this makes him indisposed to fully understanding the nuances of Leela's story: "Could I ever feel anything other than contempt, lust or pity for a porn actress?" (154). Despite this realization, Amrit continues to view Leela in sensationalized and sexualized ways, desperate to provide the German newspaper with an "exemplary story." Now that the violence of the abduction photo has proven to be a setup, Amrit turns to the familiar narrative of a small-town girl from the Northeast who has run into trouble because of poor decisions. He quickly becomes convinced that Malik had been her lover although he has no evidence of this. Looking at the abduction photo as well as other photographs of Leela, he sexualizes her: "I scrutinized her face and her eyes and her body, examining her slim ankles and small breasts, wondering how long it had taken Malik before he had put his hands on her" (155). Giving her no agency whatsoever, he spins another tale of victimhood, "a familiar old triangle, a Bollywood family drama" in which Leela entices the lascivious man from the city, putting on a more "open and welcoming expression" (155) for him. This misadventure leaves her recuperating from gunshot wounds in hiding. Amrit ends his imagined tale asking, "what would Leela do with the rest of her life?" (155). Soon afterward he acknowledges he is probably being "too quick to put her into a readymade slot" (156) but he also welcomes the reality she has now taken on for him.

Having solved the mystery of Leela's identity, though never actually setting eyes on her, Amrit prepares to return to Calcutta. He stops for a few days in Imphal, where he joins a demonstration organized by the Manipuris demanding they be included in the peace negotiations between the Indian government and the Manipuri rebels. It quickly becomes evident that Amrit has undergone a transformation during his time in the Northeast. He sees the region with a renewed vision and it "never looked so beautiful to me as it did then" (253). He is able to see things with increased clarity and to discern in the homogeneous masses "distinct, individual faces [...] faces that were here not just to defend some boundary or other but to show the uncaring, unheeding world that they existed and could not be forgotten" (253). He credits this new way of looking at the region and its long-neglected people to "a touch of grace, of wisdom" (253) conferred upon him by Leela and the others he had encountered during his travels through the Northeast. Amrit's prolonged spectatorship of Leela's photograph gradually allows him to come to see her as a non-racialized, nonsexualized fellow citizen. Instead of her "slim ankles and small breasts," he comes to appreciate her "yearning for something better" (197) and she seems as familiar as a sister.

Ariella Azoulay's theorization of photography has undoubtedly taken it in a new direction and achieved much in ameliorating misgivings about the hegemony of the gaze, the fixity of the photographed moment, and the sovereignty of the photograph, which have long plagued the form. However, despite her attempts at expanding the citizenry of photography not only to the photographer, the photographed subject, and onlookers, but also to any and all subsequent spectators of the photograph, questions of sovereignty remain. Critiquing the liberal, humanist origins of Azoulay's theories, Patricia Hayes questions the true plurality of Azoulay's civil imagination (2015: 184). She argues that the Palestinian subject of Azoulay's discourse often gets fixed "(yet again) in a single posture, that of overwhelming abjection and annihilation" (187). Writing in the context of South Africa, Hayes suggests that many such violated subjects of photography often respond to their visual abjection with "outright rejection" (187). Consequently, she asserts that the political space shared by participants at either end of the photographic process is "uneven and unequal" (190). Summoning Solomon-Godeau's (1991) much earlier phrase, Hayes finds photography "back at the dock" reproducing the noncitizenship Azoulay attempts so hard to redress.

Amrit's gaze through much of Deb's novel may be characterized as the kind of problematic humanitarian gaze that Hayes objects to in her critique of Azoulay. He fixes her as the silenced subaltern in the photograph and even attempts to appropriate her identity, notwithstanding his vast differences with her:

> The account of Leela's past was many times removed from me just as her life itself had been, but still I saw it all as clearly as if the memories and experiences were my own, as if I had become Leela for that brief span of time, making my way through the uncertain bewildering world where fulfillment and failure often appeared in the same guise. (204)

This is Amrit's Kurtz-like, imperial gaze that Baishya condemns. However, I would argue that Deb's novel creates the event of photography, and not simply the (absent) photograph, to include us, the readers, in the citizenry of photography. We "see" the photograph through Amrit's gaze and recognize it as simply a moment in the event of photography. Amrit's gaze changes as the novel progresses. He gradually turns inwards in order to assess his own citizenship and its privileges as he moves away from the proverbial center to the margins of the postcolonial nation. In addition to the photo that lies at the heart of the novel, there are other photographs of Leela that her aunt shows Amrit. These are accompanied by her aunt's narrative comprising of facts garnered from Leela's letters to her aunt, that informs both Amrit and the reader about Leela's childhood in Imphal, her family life, her sister Radha's illness and subsequent death, Leela's departure for the nation's capital, and her eventual return to Imphal to work for the Prosperity Project. Amrit's response to this narrative is to see "far more than those words and images" (207) as he imagines "the two of us circling each other without ever quite meeting" (207). His attempts at sympathy for her, albeit still somewhat Orientalizing as he imagines how difficult it must have been for her because "she looked so different with her yellowish complexion and almond eyes" (207), signals a shift in his perception from seeing her as a racialized, gendered stereotype, to a wronged fellow citizen. The mute woman fixed in Amrit's hegemonic gaze at the beginning of the novel is gradually transformed for us into a character. This transformation takes place through the event of photography in which we are made to participate. Although we never meet Leela, her personhood is communicated to us first through the photograph, which tells a false narrative but also heightens our awareness of Leela's noncitizenship as a Manipuri woman.

## Conclusion

Ariella Azoulay has argued passionately that the civil contract of photography disallows any hierarchies or relationships of subjugation. According to this contract, "all are in principle equal before photography" (2008: 389). She acknowledges that the end addressee of the photograph who is able to see unencumbered by considerations of time, place, self, or other is "an ideal concept, a necessary logical postulate," and actual addressees can only be "imperfect copies" of this. However, the task of ethical spectatorship is urgent and to be such a spectator is aspirational. My reading of Deb's novel suggests that Amrit's journey through India's troubled Northeast schools him in becoming an ethical spectator, Azoulay's ideal addressee. At first, he misrecognizes Leela due to the central photograph's false narrative, attempting to appropriate her identity and speak for her as he acknowledges her troubled citizenship. However, he gradually turns his gaze inward toward his own privileged citizenship, which enables him to see Leela as an equal. Through Amrit, we the readers assume the position of the universal spectator continuing the event of photography while also activating the civil contract of photography.

Sovereign regimes have long used photography for representation. Leela's absent image in Deb's novel is no different. She is the mute subaltern in the image when Amrit first finds the photograph. We may question why he so easily believes the story the photograph purportedly tells. The answer of course lies in the burden of representation of the Northeastern woman. Leela's photograph, coupled with the accompanying caption, is immediately fixed in its indexicality, burdened by the excess of representation. What it lacks at this time is an alternative narrative. Amrit's investigative journalism gradually reveals this lack in the photo – the true story behind Leela's identity. However, Amrit must alter his own gaze in order to be able to see Leela as an equal and a citizen. He initially indulges in what Azoulay has called "sovereign spectatorship" (2012a: 225), which entails reading the photograph as a closed, fixed event and thereby ascribing meaning to it which is always already inscribed within the photograph. Azoulay calls for a rebellion "against the paradigm of sovereign spectatorship, and to undermine that which constituent violence renders self-evident" (225). Although the violence encapsulated in the image of Leela as hostage is a false violence, incipient within the image is the violence of Leela's exclusion from the national citizenry.

Mainland India's representation of the Northeast, particularly the women of the region, is a hegemonic one and is reinstated regularly via stereotypical representations in popular film and media. Sanjib Baruah has argued that the Indian image of the troubled region has been "mediated by a visual regime" (2005: 166) created by Bollywood films, television, and images in newspapers and magazines. He concludes that the "battle for the future of Northeast India is also a battle over images" (175). My reading of Leela's absent photograph in Deb's novel as laid out in this chapter functions in a number of ways to offer alternative ways of viewing the people of India's Northeast. Firstly, an analysis of Amrit's sovereign gaze allows me to highlight the problematic scopic regime that dominates the visual representation of the gendered subaltern in the Northeast. Having established the limitations of this regime, I then use Azoulay's framework of the civil contract of photography to offer an alternative visual paradigm that acknowledges and attempts to recognize Leela's marginalized citizenship. In examining the relationships between subalternity, representation, and photography, it may be said that photography plays a dual role in both producing and subverting visual hegemonies in issues related to subaltern representation. In this chapter, I extend this by arguing that the absent image, read as a continuation of the event of photography, can provide the affordances of looking differently and even recognizing and restoring the citizenship of the marginalized. During the scenes of Amrit's prolonged viewing of the absent image in the novel, I imagine him saying in Azoulay's words: "*Over there, within the photo, someone addresses me; she claims my civil gaze, struggles for her citizenship in the world of photography, and puts my own citizenship in the state into question*" (Azoulay, 2008: 143, emphasis original). Amrit's protracted viewership of Leela's photograph heightens his understanding and awareness of his own citizenship in India, which he had taken for granted until his journey to the nation's farthest corners. My reading of Deb's novel contends that the event of photography which began at the press conference where Leela's staged hostage photo was taken continues via Amrit's protracted spectatorship of the absent photograph, and ultimately results in Amrit's recognition of his own privileged citizenship as well as his powerful acknowledgment of the citizenship of the forgotten masses at the edge of the republic.

# Coda

On March 10, 2020, Shafiqul Islam Kajol, a Dhaka-based photojournalist and editor of the daily newspaper *The Daily Pokkhokal*, disappeared after leaving his office to return home in the evening. Fifty-three days later he was found bound and blindfolded in a field in Jessore, a fair distance from where he had gone missing. The night before Kajol went missing; a politician had filed a case against him and thirty-one other journalists under Bangladesh's draconian Digital Securities Act. After he was found near the India Bangladesh border on May 3, Kajol was detained and later arrested and denied bail. He was finally released from the Dhaka Central Jail in December 2020. Kajol's 21-year-old son, Monorom Polok, started an online campaign to raise awareness of Kajol's disappearance and subsequent detention under a law considered by many human rights activists to be far too stringent and stifling dissent and free speech in Bangladesh. The "Where is Kajol" campaign was a photographic project. Monorom took several photographs from the family album and digitally edited out images of his father. Consequently, Kajol appears as a white silhouette in each photograph. Speaking about the project, Monorom said, "What I did was that I scanned them digitally and I cut out my father, basically taking my father out of memories too. Because, as he was not physically present, he is only present in memories" (Utkarsh 2020: n.pag.).

"Where is Kajol" then results in a double erasure. Monorom erases his father from the photographs in order to heighten his absence from their lives. Since he is erasing him from photographs in a family album, the repository of memories, he is also erasing him from the family's memories. Given the avowed intention of the project is to draw attention to Kajol's case, the project acts in a paradoxical way to perform a curious kind of absent presence of Kajol through the altered photographs. The viewers' eyes are immediately drawn to the white silhouette in each image. The lack in each photograph is its most striking feature. Although the white outline signals Kajol's absence from the photograph, it in fact heightens his (absent) presence by drawing disproportionate attention and focus to it. Monorom's accompanying commentary on the images seems to ignore his father's absence from them. The captions read: "Here he is with [...]" or "My father smoking a cigarette in Surja Sen Hall [...]" and "My father giving (me) a massage with mustard oil." Instead of erasure, what we get in these images is a heightened absent presence. The white silhouette seems to jump out of the image demanding to be seen, to be recognized and acknowledged, and ultimately to be returned in full color and detail to the page. It is as though Kajol had momentarily left the photo somewhat abruptly, leaving in the space he occupied a temporary outline that functions as a placeholder so that he might reoccupy it upon his return. The answer to a son's anguished question "Where is Kajol?" seems to be "He was here a minute ago [...] surely he will be right back."

Monorom's assertion that he has cut his father out of memories by cutting him out of the pages of the family album also works in paradoxical ways, not to erase, but to sharpen the memory of his father. He speaks of two particular images from the album that are his favorites. One shows Kajol massaging the infant Monorom with mustard oil (see Figure 8) and the other shows him bathing his son.

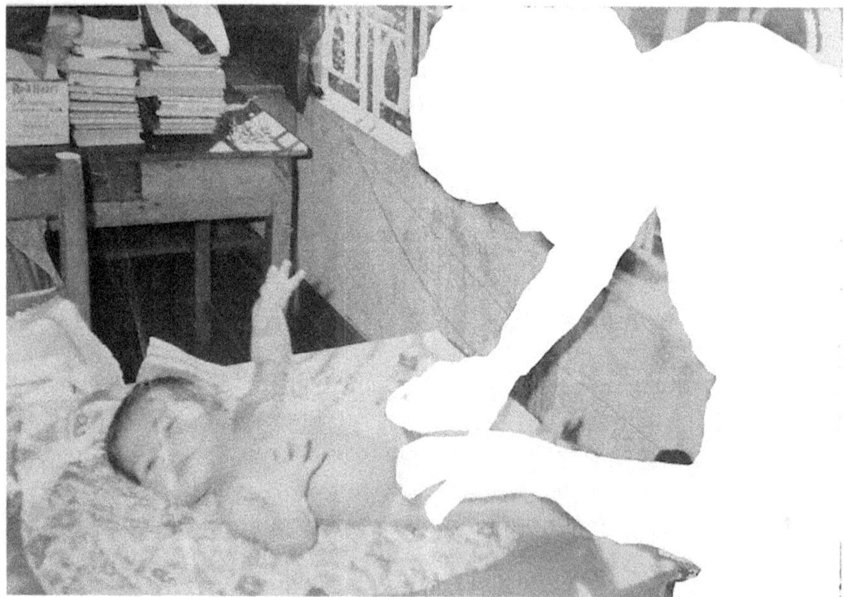

Figure 8. Reproduced with permission from Monorom Polok

In both images, Monorom is a child and he admits to having no real memory of the time captured in the photographs. However, he says, "I see from the pictures and it connects with me that that's the kind of father he was at home." Therefore, it is not in fact a memory that the photograph recalls which is now erased by the erasure of Kajol; instead, the photograph becomes a stand-in for and proof of "the kind of father he (Kajol) was."

The ability of photographs to bestow upon people a particular identity as well as a strong sense of who they are works in paradoxically absent-present ways. As moments plucked from the flow of time, they are simply replicas of a particular scene and nothing more. However, photographs are often read as being much more than that. They are seen as offering testimonials of a person's existence as well as their character, but because it is also a relic of a past that no longer exists, the photograph constantly undermines its own ability to bestow an identity to the person.

"Where is Kajol" highlights the potency of the absent photograph. *Traces of the Real* suggests that the absent image works in a similarly potent manner in literary texts, particularly postcolonial literary texts. Given photography's complicitous role in the colonial enterprise, the erasure or performative absence of the indexical photograph in the pages of postcolonial texts draws heightened attention to a host of issues: the absence of the actual photograph invites us to look in different ways, read the absent image metaphorically, or to recognize in the traces left by the photographs a different kind of assemblage. Above all, *Traces of the Real* posits that considering the absent presence of photographs in literary texts more closely rewards us the rich affordances of Azoulay's event of photography. It sets this event in motion and invites our civil spectatorship as we engage our civil imagination in looking at the Other. This makes it a potent tool for the postcolonial moment.

# Appendix

This appendix includes three pages from the now defunct website www.khaufpur.com. The pages have been provided by Indra Sinha. I am deeply grateful to him for reconstructing the pages for me.

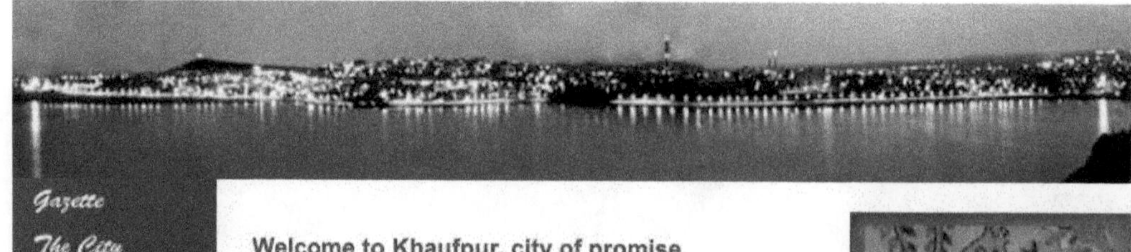

Gazette
The City
History
Culture
Government
Business
Tourism
What's on?
Horoscopes
Matrimonials
Classifieds
Advertisers
Links

## Welcome to Khaufpur, city of promise

Khaufpur is a city of approaching a million souls situated at the absolute centre of India. The lakes around which our city is built were made a thousand years ago. Since that time the city was lost in jungles, rediscovered and rebuilt. Again in the lifetime of those living, a terrible calamity came upon this city, but again it has risen and continues toward a future filled with promise. Khaufpur is many things to many people, and sometimes, when we recall particular pages in its history, we lose sight of all the things that our city is: the capital of an ancient kingdom, a place of romantic beauty, fine architecture and splendid scenery, a historic city surrounded by the deepest forests in India, a centre of music and arts, where the ghazal and the khayal flourished, where as great a voice as our own Aawaaz-e-Khaufpur made those amazing flights of fancy and fantasy by the shores of this very lake pictured below; our city has been touched by great tragedy, but it is also a city of science, of engineering, of scholarship and of hope. Welcome again, to our city of lakes, the famous, the beautiful city of Khaufpur.
--*S Allaudin*

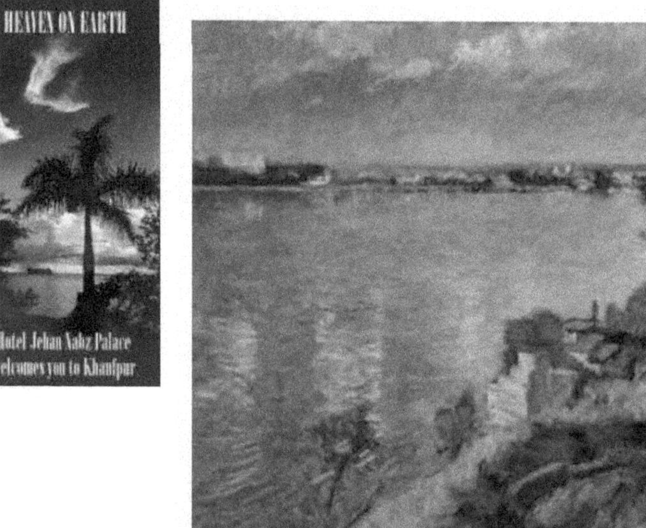


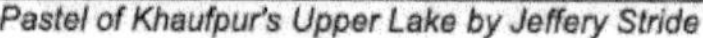
*Pastel of Khaufpur's Upper Lake by Jeffery Stride*

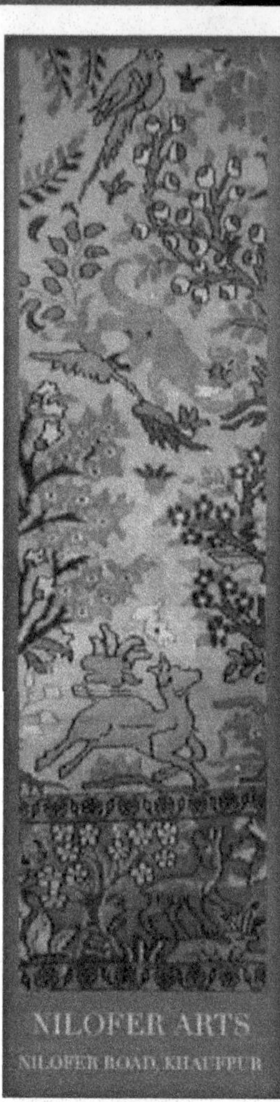


Website maintained by The Khaufpur Gazette in partnership with Khaufpur Municipal Corporation and Khaufpur Chamber of Commerce, Khaufpur CP

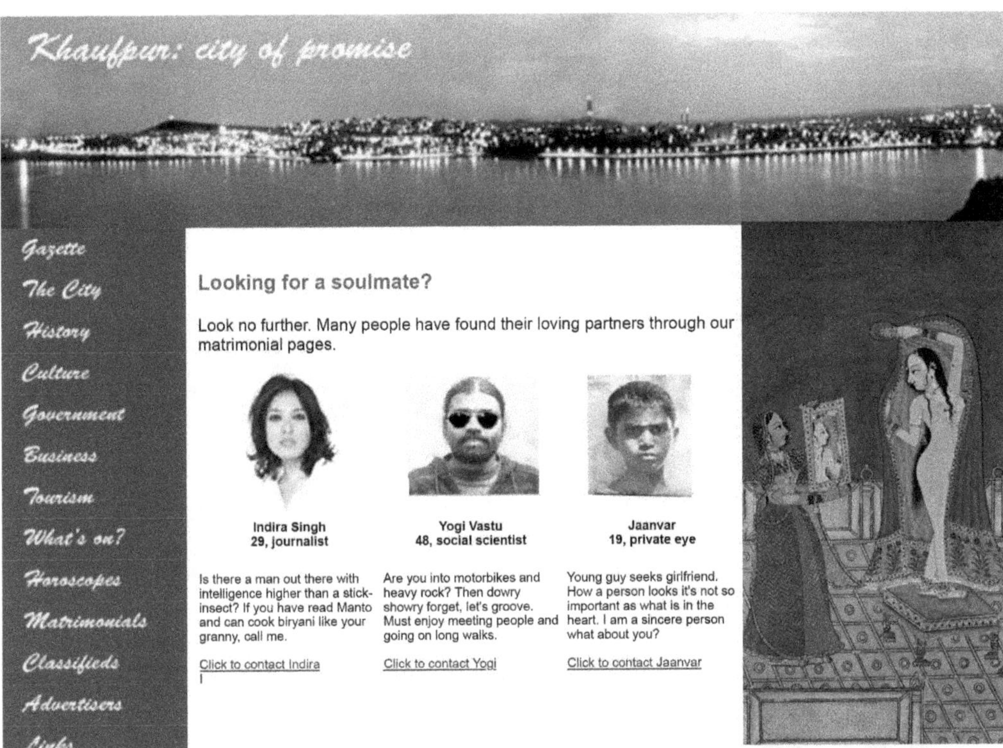


Website maintained by The Khaufpur Gazette in partnership with Khaufpur Municipal Corporation and Khaufpur Chamber of Commerce, Khaufpur CP

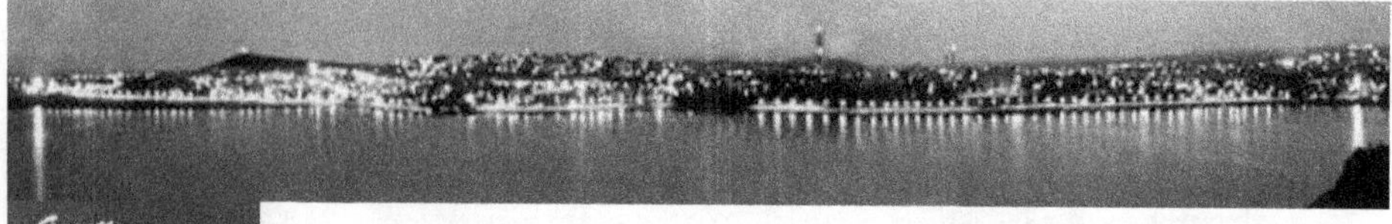

Gazette
The City
History
Culture
Government
Business
Tourism
What's on?
Horoscopes
Matrimonials
Classifieds
Advertisers
Links

**Brewing a royal heritage in Khaufpur**

*Khaufpur, known for its lakes legendary heroes and festivals has another attraction now. Heritage liquor is making a comeback with its centuries-old recipes making a splash, reports Sarvadarshi Gupta*

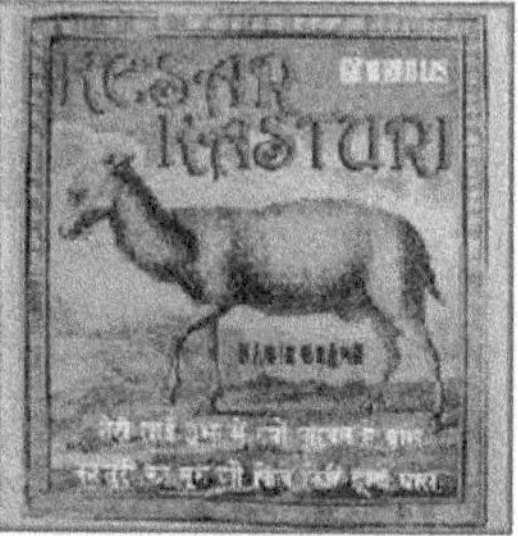


Website maintained by The Khaufpur Gazette in partnership with Khaufpur Municipal Corporation and Khaufpur Chamber of Commerce, Khaufpur CP

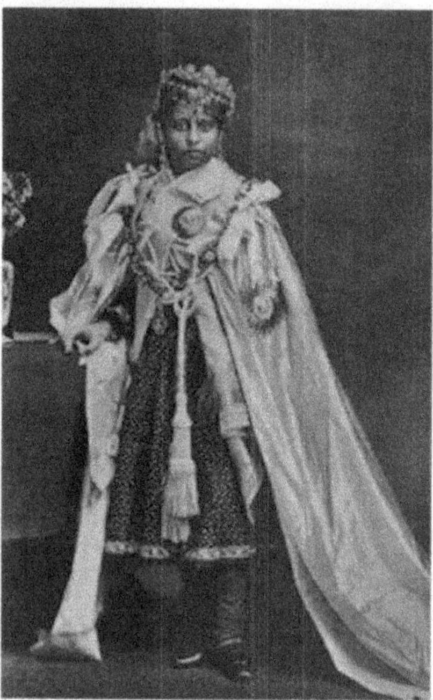

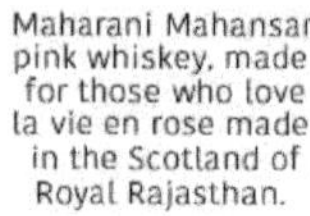

Maharani Mahansar, pink whiskey, made for those who love la vie en rose made in the Scotland of Royal Rajasthan.

Kesar Kasturi, a liqueur imbued with saffron and musk, is not the name of a perfume of yore but a heritage liqueur launched by the Khaufpur Sugar Mills (KSM) in an attempt to keep our city's unique traditions alive. Royal families concocted such inimitable liquors, but after Independence production of these liquors was banned plus the apparatuses in which these were prepared were also seized. Only the recipes were penned down painstakingly by the rulers, which were preserved by their descendants. Says O P Agarwal, general manager, KSM: "By launching this heritage liqueur concocted from saffron and genuine musk obtained from the musk deer, we are trying to encash on the heritage and royal quotient so palpable in our state."

# Bibliography

Abel, Elizabeth. 2010. *Signs of the Times: The Visual Politics of Jim Crow.* Berkeley and Los Angeles: University of California Press.

Adams, Timothy Dow. 2000. *Light Writing and Life Writing: Photography in Autobiography.* Chapel Hill: University of North Carolina Press.

——. 2008. "Photographs on the Walls of the House of Fiction." *Poetics Today*, 29.1, 175–195.

Agee, James, and Walker Evans. 1941. *Let Us Now Praise Famous Men: Three Tenant Families.* Boston: Houghton Mifflin.

Aguiar, Marian. 2008. "Making Modernity: Inside the Technological Space of the Railway." *Cultural Critique*, 68, 66–85.

Ahmed, Sara. 2000. *Strange Encounters: Embodied Others in Postcoloniality.* Routledge: London and New York.

Akoijam, Angomcha Bimol. 2005. "Another 9/11, Another Act of Terror: The 'Embedded Disorder' of the AFSPA." In *Sarai Reader 2005: Bare Acts.* New Delhi: Center for the Study of Developing Societies, 481–491.

——. 2020. "If 'Ma Bharati's Children' Are Linked By Blood, Modi Believes Muslims Aren't Real Indians." *The Wire*, Jan. 4. thewire.in/communalism/caa-muslims-citizens-india.

Allana, Rahaab, ed. 2022. *Unframed: Discovering Image Practices in South Asia.* New Delhi: Harper Design.

Anker, Suzanne, and Dorothy Nelkin. 2004. *The Molecular Gaze: Art in the Genetic Age.* Cold Spring Harbor: Cold Spring Harbor Laboratory Press.

Armstrong, Nancy. 1999. *Fiction in the Age of Photography: The Legacy of British Realism.* Cambridge, MA: Harvard University Press.

Ashcroft, Bill, Gareth Griffiths, and Helen Tiffin. 1989. *The Empire Writes Back.* New York: Routledge.

Azoulay, Ariella. 2001. *Death's Showcase: The Power of Image in Contemporary Democracy.* Translated by Ruvik Danieli. Cambridge, MA: MIT Press.

——. 2008. *The Civil Contract of Photography.* Translated by Rela Mazali and Ruvik Danieli. New York: Zone Books.

——. 2012a. *Civil Imagination: A Political Ontology of Photography.* Translated by Louise Bethlehem. London and New York: Verso.

——. 2012b. *Potential History: Unlearning Imperialism.* London and New York: Verso Books.

——. 2018. "Imperial Rights and the Origins of Photography." The 8th Adrian Gerbrands Lecture, Nov. 22. https://www.materialculture.nl/en/events/imperial-rights-and-origins-photography.

Bahri, Deepika, and Mary Vasudevan. 1996. "Pedagogical Alternatives: Issues in Postcolonial Studies. Interview with Gauri Vishwanathan." In *Between the Lines: South Asians and Postcoloniality.* Philadelphia: Temple University Press, 54–63.

Baishya, Amit. 2015. "The Act of Watching with One's Own Eyes." *Interventions: International Journal of Postcolonial Studies*, 17.4, 603–620.

Bajorek, Jennifer. 2020. *Unfixed: Photography and Decolonial Imagination in West Africa.* Durham, NC: Duke University Press.

Bal, Mieke. 2006 [1991]. *Reading Rembrandt: Beyond the Word Image Opposition.* Amsterdam: Amsterdam University Press – Amsterdam Academic Archive.

Bal, Mieke, and Norman Bryson. 1991. "Semiotics and Art History: A Discussion of Context and Senders." *The Art Bulletin*, 73.2, 174–298.

Balaev, Michelle. 2012. *The Nature of Trauma in American Novels.* Evanston: Northwestern University Press.

Banerjee, Bidisha. 2009. "Revisions, Rerouting and Return: Reversing the Teleology of Diaspora in Sunetra Gupta's *Memories of Rain.*" *Postcolonial Text*, 5.2. https://www.postcolonial.org/index.php/pct/article/view/1025/955.

——. 2010. "Diaspora's Dark Room: Photography and the Vision of Loss in Jhumpa Lahiri's Story 'Hema and Kaushik.'" *The Journal of Commonwealth Literature*, 45.3, 443–456.

Banerji, Debashish, and Makarand R. Paranjape, eds. 2016. *Critical Posthumanism and Planetary Futures.* New Delhi: Springer.

Barad, Karen. 2007. *Meeting the Universe Halfway: Quantum Physics and the Entanglement of Matter and Meaning.* Durham, NC: Duke University Press.

——. 2014. "Diffracting Diffraction: Cutting Together-Apart." *Parallax*, 20.3, 168–187.

Barthes, Roland. 1981. *Camera Lucida: Reflections on Photography.* Translated by Richard Howard. New York: Hill and Wang.

Baruah, Sanjib. 2005. "A New Politics of Race: India and Its North-east." *IIC Quarterly*, 32.2–3, 165–176.

——. 2020. "CAA-Led Narrative on Religious Persecution Ignores Political Specificity, Nuance in Neighbourhood." *The Indian Express*, Jan. 22. https://indianexpress.com/article/opinion/columns/bangladesh-minorities-caa-nrc-citizenship-act-india-6228629/.

Batchen, Geoffrey. 1994. "Ghost Stories: The Beginnings and Ends of Photography." *Art Monthly Australia*, 76, 4–8.

Baxter, Katherine Isobel. 2011. "Memory and Photography: Rethinking Postcolonial Trauma Studies." *Journal of Postcolonial Writing*, 47.1, 18–29.

Behdad, Ali, and Luke Gartlan, eds. 2013. *Photography's Orientalism: New Essays on Colonial Representation.* Los Angeles: Getty Research Institute.

Belting, Hans. 1994. *Likeness and Presence: A History of the Image Before the Era of Art.* Translated by Edmund Jephcott. Chicago: University of Chicago Press.

——. 2011. *An Anthropology of Images: Picture, Medium, Body.* Translated by Thomas Dunlap. Princeton: Princeton University Press.

Benjamin, Walter. 1968. "The Work of Art in the Age of Mechanical Reproduction." In *Illuminations: Essays and Reflections.* Edited by Hannah Arendt. New York: Schocken, 217–251.

——. 1985. "A Short History of Photography." In *One Way Street.* Edited by Susan Sontag. London: Verso, 240–257.

Bennett, Jane. 2010. *Vibrant Matter: A Political Ecology of Things.* Durham, NC: Duke University Press.

Berger, John, and Jean Mohr. 1989. *Another Way of Telling.* Cambridge: Granta.

Bergson, Henri. 2005. *Matter and Memory.* Translated by Nancy Margaret Paul and Scott Palmer. New York: Zone Books.

Bezboruah, Jiten. 2019. "Do We Return to the Nineties?" Translated by Biswajit K. Bora. *RAIOT,* Dec. 14. https://raiot.in/do-we-return-to-the-nineties/.

Bhabha, Homi K. 1990. *Nation and Narration.* New York: Routledge.

——. 1994. *The Location of Culture.* New York: Routledge.

Bhaumik, Subir. 2009. *Troubled Periphery.* New Delhi: Sage.

Bhullar, Dilpreet. 2013. "'Tryst with Destiny': Remapping the Promised Land(s)." *E-International Relations,* Jan. 14. https://www.e-ir.info/2013/01/14/tryst-with-destiny-remapping-the-promised-lands-with-the-study-of-margaret-bourke-whites-photographic-essay/.

Bolton, Richard. 1989. "Introduction. The Contest of Meaning: Critial Histories of Photography." In *The Contest of Meaning: Critial Histories of Photography.* Cambridge, MA: MIT Press, ix–xix.

Bora, Papori. 2010. "Between the Human, the Citizen and the Tribal." *International Feminist Journal of Politics,* 12.3–4, 341–360.

Bourke-White, Margaret. 1949. *Halfway to Freedom: A Report on the New India in the Words and Photographs of Margaret Bourke-White.* New York: Simon & Schuster.

Brah, Avtar. 1996. *Cartographies of Diaspora: Contesting Identities.* London: Routledge.

Braidotti, Rosi. 2013. *The Posthuman.* Cambridge: Polity Press.

Brown, Elspeth H., and Thy Phu, eds. 2014. *Feeling Photography.* Durham, NC: Duke University Press.

Brown, Juanita. 2024. *Mortevivum: Photography and the Politics of the Visual (On Seeing).* Cambridge, MA: MIT Press.

Brunet, Francois. 2009. *Photography and Literature.* London: Reaktion Books.

Bryant, Marsha, ed. 1996. *Photo-Textualities: Reading Photographs and Literature*. Newark: University of Delaware Press.

Buelens, Gert, Sam Durrant, and Robert Eaglestone. 2013. *The Future of Trauma Theory: Contemporary Literary and Cultural Criticism*. London: Routledge.

Burgin, Victor, ed. 1982. *Thinking Photography*. London: Macmillan.

Burrows, Victoria. 2008. "The Heterotopic Spaces of Postcolonial Trauma in Michael Ondaatje's *Anil's Ghost*." *Studies in the Novel*, 40.1–2, 161–177.

Butalia, Urvashi. 2017. "The Body as Weapon." *New Internationalist*, Jul. 5. https://newint.org/columns/viewfrom/2004/09/01/body-as-weapon.

Butler, Judith. 2006. *Precarious Life: The Powers of Mourning and Violence*. London: Verso.

——. 2009. *Frames of War: When Is Life Grievable?* London: Verso.

Cadava, Eduardo. 1998. *Words of Light: Theses on the Photography of History*. Princeton: Princeton University Press.

Caldwell, Erskine, and Margaret Bourke-White (photographs). 1937. *You Have Seen Their Faces*. New York: Viking Press.

Campt, Tina. 2017. *Listening to Images*. Durham, NC: Duke University Press.

Cappelli, Mary Louisa. 2016. "Sites of Commodification and Exploitation in Mahasweta Devi's *Breast Stories*." *Bharatiya Pragna: An Interdisciplinary Journal of Indian Studies*, 1.3, 47–52.

Cartwright, Lisa. 1995. *Screening the Body: Tracing Medicine's Visual Culture*. Minneapolis: University of Minnesota Press.

Cartwright, Lisa, and Elizabeth Wolfson. 2018. "Introduction: Affect at the Limits of Photography." *Journal of Visual Culture*, 17.2, 141–151.

Caruth, Cathy. 1996. *Unclaimed Experience: Trauma, Narrative and History*. Baltimore: The Johns Hopkins University Press.

Cavell, Stanley. 1971. *The World Viewed: Reflections on the Ontology of Film*. New York: Viking Press.

Chakraborty, Mridula Nath. 2011. "Leaving No Remains: Death among the Bengalis in Jhumpa Lahiri's Fiction." *The South Atlantic Quarterly*, 110.4, 813–829.

Chakravorty, Mrinalini. 2014. "The Dead That Haunt *Anil's Ghost*: Subaltern Stereotype and Postcolonial Melancholia." In *In Stereotype: South Asia in the Global Literary Imaginary*. New York: Columbia University Press, 119–150.

Chattopadhyay, Sagarika, and Amarjeet Nayak. 2014. "Performing the Stare in Indra Sinha's *Animal's People*." *Disability and the Global South*, 1.1, 29–43.

Chaudhary, Zahid R. 2012. *Afterimage of Empire: Photography in Nineteenth-Century India*. Minneapolis: University of Minnesota Press.

Chen, Mel Y. 2012. *Animacies: Biopolitics, Racial Mattering, and Queer Affect*. Durham, NC: Duke University Press.

Christen, Matthias. 2007. "Symbolic Bodies, Real Pain: Post-Soviet History, Boris Mikhailov and the Impasse of Documentary Photography." In *The Image and the Witness: Trauma, Memory and Visual Culture*. Edited by Frances Guerin and Roger Hallas. New York: Wallflower Press, 52–66.

Clifford, James. 1994. "Diasporas." *Cultural Anthropology*, 9.3, 302–338.

Clough, Patricia T., and Jean Halley, eds. 2007. *The Affective Turn: Theorizing the Social*. Durham, NC: Duke University Press.

Clüver, Claus. 2017. "A New Look at an Old Topic: Ekphrasis Revisited." *Todas as Letras Revista de Língua e Literatura*, 19.1, 30–44.

Cohen, Robin. 2008. *Global Diasporas: An Introduction*. 2nd ed. London: Routledge.

Coleman, Kevin, and Daniel James. 2021. *Capitalism and the Camera: Essays on Photography and Extraction*. London and New York: Verso.

Connor, Walker. 1986. "The Impact of Homelands upon Diasporas." In *Modern Diasporas in International Politics*. Edited by Gabriel Sheffer. London: Croom Helm, 16–46.

Craps, Steph. 2013. *Postcolonial Witnessing: Trauma out of Bounds*. New York: Palgrave Macmillan.

Craps, Steph, and Gert Buelens. 2008. "Introduction: Postcolonial Trauma Novels." *Studies in the Novel*, 40.1–2, special issue: "The Postcolonial Trauma Novel," 1–12.

Crary, Jonathan. 1990. *Techniques of the Observer: On Vision and Modernity in the Nineteenth Century*. Cambridge, MA: MIT Press.

Creekmur, Corey. 1996. "Lost Objects: Photography, Fiction and Mourning." In *Photo-Textualities: Reading Photographs and Literature*. Edited by Marsha Bryant. Newark: University of Delaware Press, 730–782.

Cunningham, David, Andrew Fisher, and Sas Mays, eds. 2008. *Photography and Literature in the Twentieth Century*. Newcastle upon Tyne: Cambridge Scholars.

De Alwis, Malathi. 2009. "'Disappearance' and 'Displacement' in Sri Lanka." *Journal of Refugee Studies*, 22.3, 378–391.

Deb, Siddhartha. 2005. *Surface: A Novel*. London: Picador.

——. 2006. *An Outline of the Republic: A Novel*. New York: Harper Perennial.

——. 2011. "The Girl from F&B: A Portrait of the New India." *The Nation*. Jul. 12. https://www.thenation.com/article/archive/girl-fb-portrait-new-india/.

Deleuze, Gilles. 2004. *Difference and Repetition*. Translated by Paul Patton. London: Continuum.

Deleuze, Gilles, and Felix Guattari. 1987. *A Thousand Plateaus: Capitalism and Schizophrenia*. Translated by Brian Massumi. Minneapolis: University of Minnesota Press.

——. 2003. *A Thousand Plateaus*. Translated by Brian Massumi. London: Continuum.

Derrida, Jacques. 2010. *Copy, Archive, Signature: A Conversation on Photography*. Stanford University Press.

Derrickson, Teresa. 2004. "Will the 'Un-Truth' Set You Free? A Critical Look at Global Human Rights Discourse in Michael Ondaatje's *Anil's Ghost*." *Literature, Interpretation, Theory*, 15.2, 131–152.

Dery, Mark. 1999. *The Pyrotechnic Insanitarium: American Culture on the Brink*. New York: Grove Atlantic.

Devi, Mahasweta. 1995. *Imaginary Maps.* Translated by Gayatri Chakravorty Spivak. New York: Routledge.
——. 1997. "Behind the Bodice: Choli ke Pichhe." In *Breast Stories.* Translated by Gayatri Chakravorty Spivak. Calcutta: Seagull Books, 138–160.
Dewdney, Andrew. 2021. *Forget Photography.* Cambridge, MA: MIT Press.
Dhingra, Lavina, and Floyd Cheung, eds. 2012. *Naming Jhumpa Lahiri: Canons and Controversies.* Plymouth: Lexington Books.
Dutt-Ballerstadt, Reshmi. 2012. "Gendered (Be)Longing: First and Second Generation Migrants in the Works of Jhumpa Lahiri." In *Naming Jhumpa Lahiri: Canons and Controversies.* Edited by Lavina Dhingra and Floyd Cheung. Plymouth: Lexington Books, 157–180.
Dwivedi, Divya, and Shaj Mohan. 2020. "From Protesting the CAA to Embracing the Dalit-Bahujan Position on Citizenship." *The Wire,* Jan. 13. thewire.in/caste/caa-protest-dalit-bahujan-position-citizenship.
Edwards, Elizabeth. [n.d.]. "Photographs as Relational Objects." *Photography and Orality: Dialogues in Bamako, Dakar and Elsewhere.* http://dakar-bamako-photo.eu.
——. 2012. "Objects of Affect: Photography beyond the Image." *Annual Review of Anthropology,* 41, 221–234. https://www.jstor.org/stable/23270708.
Eggers, Dave. 2003. *You Shall Know our Velocity.* London: Hamish Hamilton.
Eliot. T.S. 2010. "The Waste Land." In *The Waste Land and Other Poems.* Edited by Joseph Black et al. Peterborough, Ontario: Broadview Press.
Elkins, James. 1998. *On Pictures and the Words That Fail Them.* Cambridge: Cambridge University Press.
——. 2011. *What Photography Is.* New York: Routledge.
Eng, David L., and David Kazanjian, eds. 2003. *Loss: The Politics of Mourning.* Berkeley: University of California Press.
Falconi, Jose Luis. 2008. "Two Double Negatives." In *The Meaning of Photography.* Edited by Robin Kelsey and Blake Stimson. New Haven and London: Yale University Press, 130–147.
Felman, Shoshana, and Dori Laub. 1992. *Testimony: Crises of Witnessing in Literature, Psychoanalysis, and History.* London: Routledge.
Field, Robin E. 2004. "Writing the Second Generation: Negotiating Cultural Borderlands in Jhumpa Lahiri's *Interpreter of Maladies* and *The Namesake.*" *South Asia Review,* 25.2, 165–177.
Foer, Jonathan Safran. 2006. *Extremely Loud and Incredibly Close: A Novel.* Boston: Mariner.
Foote, Timothy. 1986. "She Was Above Self-Reproach." *New York Times,* Jul. 20, https://www.nytimes.com/1986/07/20/books/she-was-above-self-reproach.html.
Freed, Joanne Lipson. 2012. "Invisible Victims, Visible Absences: Imagining Disappearance for an International Audience." *Ariel* 43.2, 25. https://journalhosting.ucalgary.ca/index.php/ariel/article/view/35245.
Freeland, Cynthia. 2008. "Photographs and Icons." in *Photography and Philosophy: Essays on the Pencil of Nature.* Edited by Scott Walden. Chichester: Wiley-Blackwell.

Freitag, Sandria B., ed. 2015. *The Visual Turn: South Asia across the Disciplines*. London: Routledge.

French, Patrick. 2016. "A New Way of Seeing Indian Independence and the Brutal 'Great Migration'." *Time Magazine*, Aug. 14. https://time.com/4421746/margaret-bourke-white-great-migration/.

Garrett-Petts, William F., and Donald Lawrence. 2000. *PhotoGraphic Encounters: The Edges and Edginess of Reading Prose Pictures*. Edmonton: University of Alberta Press.

Gasiorowski, Dominika. 2018. *Photographing the Unseen Mexico: Maya Goded's Socially Engaged Documentaries*. Oxford: Legenda.

Giffney, Noreen, and Myra J. Hird, eds. 2008. *Queering the Non/Human*. Aldershot: Ashgate.

Gillespie, Diane. 1993. "'Her Kodak Pointed at His Head': Virginia Woolf and Photography." In *Multiple Muses of Virginia Woolf*. Edited. D. Gillespie. Columbia: University of Missouri Press, 113–147.

Gilroy, Paul. 1987. *There Ain't No Black in the Union Jack*. Chicago: University of Chicago Press.

——. 1993. *The Black Atlantic: Modernity and Double Consciousness*. Cambridge, MA: Harvard University Press.

Giri, Bed Prasad. 2009. "Diasporic Postcolonialism and its Antinomies." *Diaspora*, 14.2–3, 215–235.

Goldberg, Susan. 2018. "For Decades, Our Coverage Was Racist. To Rise Above Our Past, We Must Acknowledge It." *National Geographic*, Mar. 12. https://www.nationalgeographic.com/magazine/2018/04/from-the-editor-race-racism-history/.

Gopinath, Gayatri. 2018. *Unruly Visions: The Aesthetic Practices of Queer Diaspora*. Durham, NC and London: Duke University Press.

Green-Lewis, Jennifer. 1997. *Framing the Victorians: Photography and the Culture of Realism*. Ithaca: Cornell University Press.

Guerin, Frances, and Roger Hallas. 2007. "Introduction." In *The Image and the Witness: Trauma, Memory and Visual Culture*. New York: Wallflower Press, 1–20.

Guha, Ranajit. 1983. *Elementary Aspects of Peasant Insurgency in Colonial India*. Delhi, India:Oxford University Press.

Gunne, Sorcha, and Zoe Brigley Thompson. 2009. *Feminism, Literature and Rape Narratives: Violence and Violation*. New York: Routledge.

Hai, Ambreen. 2012. "Re-Rooting Families: The Alter/Natal as the Central Dynamic of Jhumpa Lahiri's *Unaccustomed Earth*." On *Naming Jhumpa Lahiri: Canons and Controversies*. Edited by Lavina Dhingra and Floyd Cheung. Lanham: Lexington Books, 181–209.

Hannavy, John, ed. 2008. *Encyclopedia of Nineteenth-Century Photography*, Vol. 1: A–I Index. New York and London: Routledge.

Haraway, Donna J. 2003. *The Companion Species Manifesto: Dogs, People and Significant Otherness*. Cambridge: Prickly Paradigm Press.

——. 2007. *When Species Meet*. Minneapolis: University of Minnesota Press.

Hargreaves, Roger, and Peter Hamilton. 2001. *Beautiful and the Damned: The Creation of Identity in Nineteenth Century Photography*. London: Lund Humphries Publishers Ltd.

Hargreaves, Alec G., and David Murphy, eds. 2008. "Introduction: New Directions in Postcolonial Studies." *Journal of Postcolonial Writing*, 44.3, special issue: "New Directions in Postcolonial Studies," 221–225.

Hartman, Saidiya. 1997. *Scenes of Subjection: Terror, Slavery, and Self-Making in Nineteenth-Century America*. Oxford: Oxford University Press.

Hartmann, W., J. Sylvester, and P. Hayes, eds. 1998. *The Colonizing Camera: Photographs in the Making of Namibian History*. Cape Town: University of Cape Town Press.

Hayes, Patricia. 2015. "The Uneven Citizenry of Photography: Reading the 'Political Ontology' of Photography from Southern Africa." *Cultural Critique*, 89, 173–193.

Heffernan, James A. W. 1993. *Museum of Words: The Poetics of Ekphrasis from Homer to Ashbery*. Chicago, IL: The University of Chicago Press.

Hesford, Wendy. 2011. *Spectacular Rhetorics: Human Rights Visions, Recognitions, Feminisms*. Durham, NC: Duke University Press.

Hight, Eleanor M., and Gary D. Sampson, eds. 2004. *Colonialist Photography: Imag(in)ing Race and Place*. London: Routledge.

Hirsch, Marianne. 1989. *The Mother Daughter Plot: Narrative, Psychoanalysis, Feminism*. Bloomington and Indianapolis: Indiana University Press.

——. 2012a. *Family Frames: Photography, Narrative and Postmemory*. Cambridge, MA: Harvard University Press.

——. 2012b. *The Generation of Postmemory: Writing and Visual Culture after the Holocaust*. New York: Columbia University Press.

Hirsch, Marianne, and Nancy K. Miller, eds. 2011. *Rites of Return: Diaspora Poetics and the Politics of Return*. New York: Columbia University Press.

Hortskotte, Silke. 2008. "Photo-Text Topographies: Photography and the Representation of Space in W.G. Sebald and Monika Maron." *Poetics Today*, 29.1, 49–78.

——. 2006. "Visual Memory and Ekphrasis in W.G. Sebald's *The Rings of Saturn*." *English Language Notes*, 44.2, 117–129.

Horstkotte, Silke, and Nancy Pedri. 2008. "Introduction: Photographic Interventions." *Poetics Today*, 29.1, 1–29.

Huggan, Graham. 2008. *Interdisciplinary Measures: Literature and the Future of Postcolonial Studies*. Liverpool: Liverpool University Press.

Hughes, Alex, and Andrea Noble, eds. 2003. *Phototextualities: Intersections of Photography and Narrative*. Albuquerque: University of New Mexico Press.

Humm, Maggie. 2003. *Modernist Women and Visual Culture*. New Brunswick: Rutgers University Press.

Hunter, Jefferson. 1987. *Image and Word: The Interaction of Twentieth Century Photographs and Texts*. Cambridge, MA: Harvard University Press.

Iversen, Margaret. 2017. *Photography, Trace and Trauma*. Chicago: University of Chicago Press.

Jacobs, Karen. 2006. "Visual Developments and Narrative Exposures." *English Language Notes*, 44.2, 1–7.

Jaggi, Maya. 2004. "Michael Ondaatje with Maya Jaggi (2000)." In *Writing across Worlds: Contemporary Writers Talk*. Edited by Susheila Nasta. London: Routledge, 250–265.

Jaikumar, Priya. 2019. *Where Histories Reside: India as Filmed Space*. Durham, NC and London: Duke University Press.

Johnston, Justin Omar. 2019. *Posthuman Capital and Biotechnology in Contemporary Novels*. Cham: Palgrave Macmillan.

Joshi, Devina. 2006. "Leo Burnet Scores a Bronze for Dinodia Photo Library at the Andy Awards." *Afaqs!* https://www.afaqs.com/news/advertising/14982_leo-burnett-scores-a-bronze-for-dinodia-photo-library-at-the-andy-awards.

Joshua, A. 2006. "United by Partition." *The Hindu*, Aug. 6. www. thehindu.com/todays-paper/tp-features/tp-literaryreview/united-by-partition/article3219128.ece.

Kabir, Ananya Jahanara. 2013. "Affect, Body, Place: Trauma Theory in the World." In *The Future of Trauma Theory: Contemporary Literary and Cultural Criticism*. Edited by Gert Buelens, Sam Durrant, and Robert Eaglestone. London: Routledge, 63–75.

Kakutani, Michiko. 2013. "A Brother, Long Gone, Is Painfully Present: Jhumpa Lahiri's New Novel, 'The Lowland.'" *New York Times*, Sept. 20. https://www.nytimes.com/2013/09/20/books/jhumpa-lahiris-new-novel-the-lowland.html.

Kelsey, Robin, and Blake Stimson, eds. 2008. *The Meaning of Photography*. New Haven and London: Yale University Press.

Kenaan, Hagi. 2013. *The Ethics of Visuality: Levinas and the Contemporary Gaze*. Translated by Batya Stein. New York: I.B. Tauris.

——. 2020. *Photography and Its Shadow*. Stanford: Stanford University Press.

Kincaid, Jamaica. 1997. *Annie John*. repr. London: Farrar, Straus and Giroux.

——. 2002. *Lucy*. London: Farrar, Straus and Giroux.

Knoll, Robert E., ed. 1977. *Conversations with Wright Morris: Critical Views and Responses*. Lincoln, NE and London: University of Nebraska Press.

Koshy, Susan. 2013. "Neoliberal Family Matters." *American Literary History*, 25.2, 344–380.

Kozloff, Max. 1987. *The Privileged Eye: Essays on Photography*. Alberquerque: University of New Mexico Press.

Kozol, Wendy. 1994. *Life's America: Family and Nation in Postwar Photojournalism*. Philadelphia: Temple University Press.

Kracauer, Siegfried. 1997. *Theory of Film: The Redemption of Physical Reality*. Princeton: Princeton University Press.

Kramp, Michael. 2012. "Unburdening Life, or the Deleuzian Potential of Photography." *Rhizomes*, no. 23. http://rhizomes.net/issue23/kramp/.

Krauss, Rosalind. 1978. "Tracing Nadar." *October*, 5, 29–47.

Krieger, Murray. 1992. *Ekphrasis: The Illusion of the Natural Sign*. Baltimore and London: Johns Hopkins University Press.

Krishnan, Satya. 2014. "Bhopal Gas Tragedy: There Was Death All Around, as if a War Had Just Ended Says Photojournalist Raghu Rai." *The Economic Times*, Dec. 7. https://economictimes.indiatimes.com/opinion/interviews/bhopal-gas-tragedy-there-was-death-all-around-as-if-a-war-had-just-ended-says-photojournalist-raghu-rai/articleshow/45398478.cms.

LaCapra, Dominic. 2013. *Writing History, Writing Trauma*. Baltimore: Johns Hopkins University Press.

Lahiri, Jhumpa. 1999. *Interpreter of Maladies*. Boston and New York: Mariner.

——. 2004. *The Namesake*. Boston and New York: Mariner.

——. 2008. "Hema and Kaushik." In *Unaccustomed Earth*. Delhi: Random House, 3–59.

——. 2014. *The Lowland*. New York: Vintage.

Lasdun, James. 2013. "*The Lowland* by Jhumpa Lahiri – Review." *Guardian*, Sept. 12. https://www.theguardian.com/books/2013/sep/12/lowland-jhumpa-lahiri-review.

Latour, Bruno. 2007. *Reassembling the Social: An Introduction to Actor-Network-Theory*. Oxford: Oxford University Press.

Laub, Dori. 1992. "Bearing Witness, or the Vicissitudes of Listening." In *Testimony: Crises of Witnessing in Literature, Psychoanalysis, and History*. Edited by Shoshana Felman and Dori Laub. London: Routledge, 57–74.

Lee, Anthony W., ed. 2014. *Trans Asia Photography Review*, 5.1, special issue: "Photography and Diaspora."

Lien, Sigrid. 2018. *Pictures of Longing: Photography and the Norwegian-American Migration*. Translated by Barbara Sjoholm. Minneapolis: University of Minneapolis Press.

Livingston, Julie, and Jasbir K. Puar, eds. 2011. *Social Text*, 29.1, special issue: "Interspecies."

Lloyd, David. 2000. "Colonial Trauma/Postcolonial Recovery?" *Interventions: International Journal of Postcolonial Studies*, 2.2, 212–228.

Lockhurst, Roger. 2008. *The Trauma Question*. London: Routledge.

Longkumer, Arkotong. 2020. "Anti-Indigenous Sentiment in the Citizenship Amendment Act." *Berkley Center For Religion, Peace and World Affairs*, Mar. 9. berkleycenter.georgetown.edu/responses/anti-indigenous-sentiment-in-the-citizenship-amendment-act.

——. 2020. *The Greater India Experiment: Hindutva and the Northeast*. Palo Alto: Stanford University Press.

Lorenz-Meyer, Dagmar. 2018. "Snapshot." *New Materialism: How Matter Comes to Matter*, May 15. https://newmaterialism.eu/almanac/s/snapshot.html.

Louvel, Liliane. 2018. *The Pictorial Third: An Essay into Intermedial Criticism*. Edited and translated by Angeliki Tseti. New York: Routledge.

McCabe, Hugh. 2013. "Photography and the Nonhuman." MA dissertation, Technological University, Dublin.

Mackinnon, Lee. 2016. "Toward a Materialist Photography: The Body of Work." *Third Text*, 30.3–4, 149–158.

Mahadevan-Dasgupta, Uma. 2007. "A Human Story: Review of *Animal's People*." *Frontline*, 24.19. https://www.bhopal.net/review-of-animals-people-in-frontline/.

Mahlstedt, Andrew. 2013. "Animal's Eyes: Spectacular Invisibility and the Terms of Recognition in Indra Sinha's *Animal's People*." *Mosaic: An Interdisciplinary Critical Journal*, 46.3, 59–74.

Malone, Noreen. 2013. "Jhumpa Lahiri's Book for Unhappy Mothers." *The New Republic*, Oct 10. https://newrepublic.com/article/115074/jhumpa-lahiris-lowland-reviewed-noreen-malone.

Mamdani, Mahmood. 2019. "Uncovering the CAA's Larger Stratagem." *The Hindu*, Dec. 30. www.thehindu.com/opinion/op-ed/uncovering-the-caas-larger-stratagem/article30436029.ece.

Manheimer, Joan. 1979. "Murderous Mothers: The Problem of Parenting in the Victorian Novel." *Feminist Studies*, 5.3, 530–546.

Mani, Bakirathi. 2020. *Unseeing Empire: Photography, Representation, South Asian America*. Durham, NC and London: Duke University Press.

Marquardt, Jennifer A. 2014. "Jhumpa Lahiri *The Lowland*." *Transnational Literature*, 6.2. https://www.academia.edu/103170534/Review_of_The_Lowlands_by_Jhumpa_Lahiri.

Mason, John Edwin. 2012. "Picturing the Beloved Country: Margaret Bourke-White, 'Life' Magazine, and South Africa, 1949–1950." *Kronos*, 38, 154–176.

Mathew, Mary. 2007. "Globalization and Diasporic Family Dynamics: Reconciling the Old and the New." In *The Indian Family in Transition: Reading Literary and Cultural Texts*. Edited by Sanjukta Dasgupta and Malashri Lal. New Delhi: Sage, 213–220.

Maxwell, Ann. 2000. *Colonial Photography and Exhibitions: Representations of the Native and the Making of European Identities*. Leicester: Leicester University Press.

Mbembe, Achille. 2019. *Necropolitics*. Translated by Steven Corcoran. Durham, NC: Duke University Press.

Mehta, Monika. 2001. "What Is Behind Film Censorship: The Khalnayak Debates." *Jouvert*, 5.3, 1–12.

Mirzoeff, Nicholas. 2002. "Multiple Viewpoint: Diaspora and Visual Culture." In *The Visual Culture Reader*. Edited by Nicholas Mirzoeff. London and New York: Routledge, 204–214.

——. 2011. *The Right to Look: A Counterhistory of Visuality*. Durham, NC: Duke University Press.

Mishra, Vijay. 2007. *The Literature of the Indian Diaspora: Theorizing the Diasporic Imaginary*. London: Routledge.

Misra, Udayon. 2005. "The Margins Strike Back: Echoes of Sovereignty and the Indian State." *India International Centre Quarterly*, 32.2–3, 265–274.

Mitchell, W.J.T., ed. 1980. *The Language of Images*. Chicago: University of Chicago Press.

——. 1986. *Iconology*. Chicago: University of Chicago Press.

——. 1992. *The Reconfigured Eye: Visual Truth in the Post-Photographic Era*. Cambridge, MA: MIT Press.

——. 1995. *Picture Theory: Essays on Verbal and Visual Representation.* Chicago: University of Chicago Press.

Moore, Alexandra Schultheis S. 2015. *Vulnerability and Security in Human Rights Literature and Visual Culture.* New York: Taylor and Francis.

Morgan, Lynn M., and Meredith W. Michaels, eds. 1999. *Fetal Subjects, Feminist Positions.* Philadelphia: University of Pennsylvania Press.

Morris, Wright. 1948. *The Home Place.* New York: Scribner's.

Mukherjee, Upamanyu Pablo. 2010. *Postcolonial Environments: Nature, Culture and the Contemporary Indian Novel in English.* Basingstoke: Palgrave Macmillan/Arts & Humanities Research Council.

Munos, Delphine. 2010. "Diasporic Hereafters in Jhumpa Lahiri's 'Once in a Lifetime.'" In *A Fluid Sense of Self: The Politics of Transnational Identity.* Edited by Silvia Schultermandl and Sebnem Toplu. Berlin, Germany: LIT Verlag, 139–157.

——. 2013. *After Melancholia: A Reappraisal of Second-Generation Diasporic Subjectivity in the Work of Jhumpa Lahiri.* Leiden: Brill.

Natrajan, Balmurli. 2020. "'Howdy, People?' Tackling the Question of Who India's Citizen-Subjects Are." *The Wire,* Jan. 9. thewire.in/politics/partha-chatterjee-i-am-the-people-caa-nrc.

Neumann, Birgit, and Gabriele Rippl. 2020. *Verbal-Visual Configurations in Postcolonial Literature: Intermedial Aesthetics: Intermedial Aesthetics.* New York: Routledge.

Newns, Lucinda. 2020. *Domestic Intersections in Contemporary Migration Fiction: Homing the Metropole.* New York: Routledge.

Nilsson, Lennart. 1965. "Drama of Life Before Birth." *Life,* Apr. 30.

Nilsson, Lennart, and Lars Hamberger. 1990. *A Child Is Born.* New York: Doubleday.

Nixon, Rob. 2011. *Slow Violence and the Environmentalism of the Poor.* Cambridge, MA: Harvard University Press.

Novak, Daniel A. 2008. *Realism, Photography and Nineteenth-Century Fiction.* Cambridge: Cambridge University Press.

Ondaatje, Michael. 1993. *The English Patient.* New York: Vintage.

——. 1993. *Running in the Family.* New York: Vintage.

——. 1996. *The Collected Works of Billy the Kid.* New York: Vintage.

——. 2000. *Anil's Ghost.* New York: Alfred A. Knopf.

——. 2008. *Divisadero.* New York: Vintage.

Parikka, Jussi. 2012. "New Materialism as Media Theory: Medianatures and Dirty Matter." *Communication and Critical/Cultural Studies,* 9.1, 95–100.

Parthiban, R., and Amutha Dhanaraj. 2019. "Historical Elements in *Train to Pakistan.*" *Journal of Emerging Technologies and Innovative Research,* 6.3, 369–371.

Pears, Tim. 2011. *Landed: A Novel.* Berkeley: Counterpoint.

Pedri, Nancy. 2005. "Critical Encounters with Gender: Photography in Virginia Woolf's *Orlando.*" *Inbetween: Essays and Studies in Literary Criticism,* 14.2, 167–176.

Pedri, Nancy, and Laurence Petit. 2013. *Picturing the Language of Images*. Newcastle upon Tyne: Cambridge Scholars.
Perera, Suvendrini. 2015. "Visibility, Atrocity and the Subject of Postcolonial Justice." *Borderlands: E-Journal*, 14.1, 1–27.
Petit, Laurence. 2006. "Alchemy of the Word and Image: Towards a New 'Iconographics' of Postmodern Culture." *English Language Notes*, 44.2, 313–321.
Pettersson, Mikael. 2011. "Depictive Traces: On the Phenomenology of Photography." *The Journal of Aesthetics and Art Criticism*, 69.2, 185–196.
Pinney, Christopher. 1997. *Camera Indica: The Social Life of Indian Photographs*. Chicago: University of Chicago Press.
——. 2003. "Introduction: 'How the Other Half ...'." In *Photography's Other Histories*. Edited by Christopher Pinney and Nicolas Peterson. Durham, NC: Duke University Press, 1–14.
——. 2012. "Seven Theses on Photography." *Thesis Eleven*, 113.1, 141–156.
Pinney, Christopher, and Nicolas Peterson, eds. 2003. *Photography's Other Histories*. Durham, NC: Duke University Press.
Pinney, Christopher, and Suresh Punjabi. 2014. "What Remains," *BioScope*, 5.1, 63–79.
Plummer, Sandra, Harriet Riches, and Duncan Wooldridge. 2016. "Photography's New Materiality." *Photoworks*. https://photoworks.org.uk/photographys-new-materiality/.
Price, Mary. 1994. *The Photograph: A Strange, Confined Space*. Stanford: Stanford University Press.
Prosser, Jay. 2005. *Light in the Dark Room: Photography and Loss*. Minneapolis: University of Minnesota Press.
——. 2012. "Introduction." In *Picturing Atrocity: Photography in Crisis*. Edited by Geoffrey Batchen, Mick Gidley, Nancy K. Miller, and Jay Prosser Chicago: University of Chicago Press, 7–13.
"Punjab 1947: The Great Migration." *Scraps from the Loft*. Jun. 17, 2020. https://scrapsfromtheloft.com/photography/punjab-1947-great-migration-margaret-bourke-white/. Source: *LIFE* magazine, Nov. 3, 1947.
Rabb, Jane. 1998. *Literature and Photography: Interactions 1840–1990*. Albuquerque: University of New Mexico Press.
Rai, Raghu. [n.d.] "Exposure: Portrait of a Corporate Crime." Magnum Photos. https://www.magnumphotos.com/newsroom/exposure-portrait-corporate-crime-raghu-rai/.
RAIOT Collective. "Do the Tribals of Assam Have an Opinion on NRC?" *RAIOT*, Aug. 8, 2018. raiot.in/do-the-tribals-of-assam-have-an-opinion-on-nrc/#:~:text=No%2C%20it%20is%20not.,not%20figure%20in%20the%20NRC.
Rajagopal, Arvind. 2011. "Notes on Postcolonial Visual Culture." *BioScope*, 2.1, 11–22.
——. 2015. "Postcolonial Visual Culture: Arguments from India." In *Internationalizing "International Communication."* Edited by Chin-Chuan Lee. Ann Arbor: University of Michigan Press, 302–318.

Rancière, Jacques. 2009. *The Future of the Image*. Translated by Gregory Elliott. New York: Verso.

Rapport, Nigel, and Andrew Dawson, eds. 1998. *Migrants of Identity: Perceptions of Home in a World of Movement*. Oxford: Oxford University Press.

Rath, Brigitte. 2013. "'His Words Only?' Indra Sinha's Pseudotranslation *Animal's People* as Hallucinations of a Subaltern Voice." *AAA: Arbeiten aus Anglistik und Amerikanistik*, 38.2, 161–183.

Rickel, Jennifer. 2012. "The Poor Remain a Posthumanist Rethinking of Literary Humanitarianism in Indra Sinha's *Animal's People*." *Ariel-A Review of International English Literature*, 43.1, 87–108.

Roberts, John. 2014. *Photography and its Violations*. New York, NY: Columbia University Press.

Roluahpuia. 2020. "Peripheral Protests: CAA, NRC and Tribal Politics in Northeast India." Feb. 20. www.law.ox.ac.uk/research-subject-groups/centre-criminology/centreborder-criminologies/blog/2020/02/peripheral.

Rosen, Zachary. 2020. "Confronting the Weapon of Photography: An Interview with Maaza Mengiste." *Africa Is a Country*, May 22. africasacountry.com/2020/05/confronting-the-weapon-of-photography.

Rosler, Martha. 1981. *In, Around, and Afterthoughts (on Documentary Photography)*. Nova Scotia: The Press of the Nova Scotia College of Art and Design.

Rothberg, Michael. 2008. "Decolonizing Trauma Studies: A Response." *Studies in the Novel* Special Issue: "The Postcolonial Trauma Novel." 40.1/2, 224–234.

Rubinstein, Daniel. 2018. "Posthuman Photography." In *The Evolution of the Image: Political Action and the Digital Self*. Edited by Marco Bohr and Basia Silwinska. New York: Routledge, 97–109.

Rushdie, Salman. 1991. *Imaginary Homelands*. London: Granta Books.

Ryan, J.R. 1997. *Picturing Empire: Photography and the Visualization of the British Empire*. London: Reaktion Books.

Safran, William. 1991. "Diasporas in Modern Societies: Myths of Homeland and Return." *Diaspora: A Journal of Transnational Studies*, 1.1, 83–99.

Salgado, Minoli. 2013. "Vanishing Points/Visible Fictions: The Textual Politics of Terror." *Textual Practice*, 27.2, 207–223.

Saltzman, Lisa, and Eric Rosenberg, eds. 2006. *Trauma and Visuality in Modernity*. Lebanon, NH: Dartmouth College Press.

Sarma, Ira. 2015. "Khushwant Singh's *Train to Pakistan* and Margaret Bourke-White's Partition Photographs: Clash of Narratives or Postmemory Project". *Cracow Indological Studies*, 17 (December), 269–292. https://doi.org/10.12797/CIS.17.2015.17.14.

Scanlan, Margaret. 2004. "'Anil's Ghost' and Terrorism's Time." *Studies in the Novel*, 36.3, 302–317.

Schwab, Gabriele. 2014. "Unofficial Wars: The Politics of Disappearance." *European Review*, 22.4, 642–651.

Scott, Clive. 1999. *The Spoken Image: Photography and Language*. London: Reaktion Books.
Sekula, A. 1982. "On the Invention of Photographic Meaning." In *Thinking Photography*. Edited by Victor Burgin. Palgrave, London. 84–109.
——. 1984. *Photography Against the Grain: Essays and Photo Works, 1973–83*. Nova Scotia: The Press of the Nova Scotia College of Art and Design.
Sen, Geeti, ed. 2006. *Where the Sun Rises When the Shadow Falls: The North-East*. New Delhi: Oxford University Press.
Sen, Shoma. 2013. "Some Lows, Many Highs." *Economic and Political Weekly*, 48.50, Dec. 14, 140–141.
Seppanen, Janne. 2017. "Unruly Representation: Materiality, Indexicality and Agency of the Photographic Trace." *Photographies*, 10.1, 110–128.
Sestanovich, Claire. 2013. "The Bleakest Story Jhumpa Lahiri Has Ever Told." *The Atlantic*, Oct. 1. https://www.theatlantic.com/entertainment/archive/2013/09/the-bleakest-story-jhumpa-lahiri-has-ever-told/280122/.
Shah, Esha. 2014. "The Self and the Political: A Reading of Jhumpa Lahiri's *The Lowland*." *Economic and Political Weekly*, 49.4, Jan. 25, 30–32.
Sheehan, Tanya. 2018. "Photography and Migration: Keywords." In *Photography and Migration*. London and New York: Routledge, 23–26.
Siddique, Nazimuddin, and Roshni Sengupta. 2020. "Assam: Anti-CAA Protests and the Silence of the Media." *The Polis Project*, Jan. 15. https://www.thepolisproject.com/read/assam-anti-caa-protests-and-the-silence-of-the-media/.
Singh, Julietta. 2015. "Post-humanitarian Fictions." *Symplokē*, 23.1–2, 137–152.
Singh, Khushwant. 1956 [2006]. *Train to Pakistan*. Edited by Pramod Kapoor. New Delhi: Roli Books.
Sinha, Indra. 2007a. *Animal's People*. London: Simon & Schuster.
——. 2007b. "Bhopal: A Novel Quest for Justice." *Guardian*. Oct. 10. https://www.theguardian.com/world/2007/oct/10/india-bhopal.
Smith, Shawn Michelle. 2013. *At the Edge of Sight: Photography and the Unseen*. Durham, NC: Duke University Press.
Smith, Shawn Michelle, and Sharon Sliwinski, eds. 2017. *Photography and the Optical Unconscious*. Durham, NC: Duke University Press.
Snell, Heather. 2008. "Assessing the Limitations of Laughter in Indra Sinha's *Animal's People*." *Postcolonial Text*, 4.4, 1–15.
Solomon-Godeau, Abigail. 1991. *Photography at the Dock: Essays on Photographic History, Institutions and Practices*. Minneapolis: University of Minnesota Press.
Sontag, Susan. 1977. *On Photography*. London: Penguin.
——. 2004. *Regarding the Pain of Others*. London: Picador.
Spivak, Gayatri Chakravorty. 1997. "Introduction." In Mahasweta Devi, *Breast Stories*. Translated by Gayatri Chakravorty Spivak. Calcutta: Seagull Books, vii–xvi.
Stapleton, Rachel F., and Antonio Viselli, eds. 2019. *Iconoclasm: The Breaking and Making of Images*. Montreal: McGill University Press.

Suleri, Sara. 1992. *The Rhetoric of English India*. Chicago: University of Chicago Press.

Sunder Rajan, Rajeshwari 1994. "Life after Rape: Narrative, Theory and Feminism." In *Borderwork: Feminist Engagements with Comparative Literature*. Edited by R.H. Margaret. Ithaca: Cornell University Press, 61–78.

Tagg, John. 1988. *The Burden of Representation: Essays on Photography and Histories*. London: Macmillan.

——. 1992. *Grounds of Dispute: Art History, Cultural Politics and the Discursive Field*. Minneapolis: University of Minnesota Press.

——. 2009. *The Disciplinary Frame: Photographic Truths and the Capture of Meaning*. Minneapolis: University of Minnesota Press.

Trachtenburg, Alan. 1990. *Reading American Photographs: Images as History, Matthew Brady to Walker Evans*. New York: Hill and Wang.

Utkarsh. 2020. "'Didn't have the option to be scared': Jailed Bangladeshi Journalist Shafiqul Kajol's Son on His Disappearance and Arrest." *Caravan*, Jul. 26. https://caravanmagazine.in/media/son-of-jailed-bangladeshi-journalist-on-photo-campaign.

Vajpeyi, Ananya. 2009. "Resenting the Indian State: For a New Political Practice in the Northeast." In *Beyond Counter-Insurgency: Breaking the Impasse in Northeast India*. Edited by Sanjib Baruah. New Delhi: Oxford University Press, 25–48.

Vials, Chris. 2006. "The Popular Front in the American Century: 'Life' Magazine, Margaret Bourke-White, and Consumer Realism, 1936–1941." *American Periodicals*, 16.1, 74–102.

Visser, Irene. 2011. "Trauma Theory and Postcolonial Literary Studies." *Journal of Postcolonial Writing*, 47.3, 270–282.

Wagner, Peter, ed. 1996. *Icons – Texts – Iconotexts: Essays on Ekphrasis and Intermediality*. Berlin: Walter de Gruyter.

Ward, Abigail. 2015. *Postcolonial Traumas: Memory, Narrative, Resistance*. Basingstoke: Palgrave Macmillan.

Wiggins, Marianne. 2008. *The Shadow Catcher*. New York: Simon & Schuster.

Wilhite, Keith. 2016. "Blank Spaces: Outdated Maps and Unsettled Subjects in Jhumpa Lahiri's 'Interpreter of Maladies'." *MELUS*, 41.2, 76–96.

Williams, Délice. 2018. "Spectacular Subjects: Abjection, Agency, and Embodiment in Indra Sinha's *Animal's People*." *Interventions*, 20.4, 586–603.

Wouters, Jelle J.P., and Tanka B. Subba. 2013. "The 'Indian Face,' India's Northeast, and 'The Idea of India'." *Asian Anthropology*, 12.2, 126–140.

York, Lorraine. 1988. *Other Side of Dailiness: Photography in the Works of Alice Munro, Timothy Findley, Michael Ondaatje and Margaret Laurence*. Toronto: ECW Press.

Zitzewitz, Karin. 2008. "The Secular Icon: Secularist Practice and Indian Visual Culture." *Visual Anthropology Review*, 24.1, 12–28.

Zylinska, Joanna. 2017. *Nonhuman Photography*. Boston: MIT Press.

# Index

References to illustrations are given in *italics*

www.ingramcontent.com/pod-product-compliance
Lightning Source LLC
Chambersburg PA
CBHW071137170125
20481CB00004BA/145

* 9 7 8 1 8 3 5 5 3 7 2 9 9 *